JAPANESE KANJI MNEMONICS JLPT

N2

JAPANESE KANJI

MNEMONICS

JLPT

N2

Lindsay Jimenez

Dioxelis Lopez

2024

ACKNOWLEDGEMENTS

For this last book, I would like this dedication to be to my dream of going to Japan and become fluent in the language. It has not been an easy path, but it has been worth it. I met great people and it is always a fun topic to talk about. I hope you have had as much fun as I had with this journey.

Thank you for your support!

Book designed and written by Lindsay Jimenez

Cover design by Harold Jimenez

Formatting by Dioxelis Lopez

English editing by Lindsay Jimenez

Kanji stroke diagrams are based on data from KanjiVG

Contents

HOW TO USE THIS BOOK

The main goal of this book is to help those who are studying Japanese as a second language. For this reason, the book is centered on a specific Japanese Language Proficiency Test (JLPT) level. This third book, of the Japanese Kanji Mnemonics Series, focuses on the next 415 Japanese characters (kanji) found on the N2 level test and it assumes the reader has knowledge of the two Japanese alphabets (Hiragana and Katakana) as well as the kanji required for the JLPT N5, JLPT N4 and JLPT N3. In order to start using this book, please follow the following steps:

1. THE FRONT PAGE:
a. <u>Flashcard Style</u>: The book is recommended to be used as flashcards. Therefore, the student will find the kanji mnemonic on the front page and the kanji information on the other side. Each front page contains a total of 3 kanji, which are related based on similarities such as radicals, same meanings, synonyms or antonyms.
b. <u>Mnemonic</u>: Whenever possible, the drawings have been made to match the characters' radicals, elements and history as much as possible. In the cases where this was not possible, this book tries to make it easy to remember. Some notes on etymology have also been included for clarification.

2. THE REVERSE PAGE:
a. <u>Common Meaning(s)</u>: The student will find the meanings that are most appropriate for the N3 level.
b. <u>Sentence</u>: a sentence to help remember the kanji better and that also creates a story that can be used as a mnemonic device. Each sentence was formed by breaking down the kanji into different elements for easy memorization. The elements can be radicals, components, kanji or hanzi.
c. <u>Stroke Order</u>: The order in which the kanji must be written.
d. <u>Writing Exercise</u>: The student will have the opportunity to write the kanji in this section of the book for extra practice.
e. <u>ON and Kun readings</u>: These serve as a guide for the student to only focus on learning and practicing the readings that will be required in the exam. Note: When a particular reading does not fall in either category, it will be noted as *ODD*
f. <u>Examples</u>: In this section of the book, you will find the following:
   • Vocabulary: The words chosen for each kanji in this book are words relevant to the JLPT N3. This is to give the student the opportunity to practice vocabulary found in the exam.
   • Furigana: All words contain their corresponding furigana on top of each kanji.
g. <u>Similar Kanji</u>: In this box the student will find kanji that is similar to the one they are learning and that the student can get easily confused with.

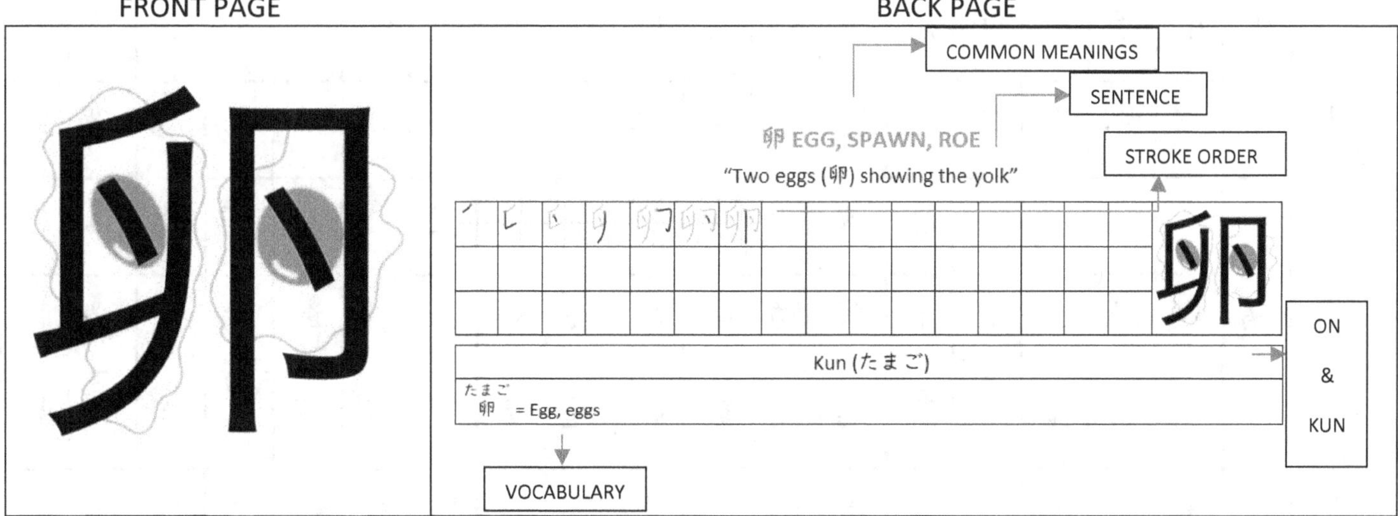

3. This book is not meant to be used on its own. It is highly recommended that the student also uses reading comprehension materials, such a fairy tales or books, as after seeing the different kanji in actual sentences it will reinforce what was learned in this book.

JLPT N5 KANJI

山	川	土	日	月	雨	水	木	天	火	本	魚	気	花	国	金	空	電	人	子
女	友	父	母	男	口	耳	目	足	手	社	車	店	校	道	駅	名	円	大	小
少	白	古	多	安	長	高	新	上	下	中	外	先	後	前	右	左	北	西	東
南	分	今	半	年	毎	何	時	週	間	午	一	二	三	四	五	六	七	八	九
十	百	千	万	入	出	生	立	会	行	休	見	言	来	学	食	買	飲	語	聞
読	書	話																	

JLPT N4 KANJI

力	工	夕	方	不	区	心	文	元	引	止	切	太	牛	犬	民	市	代	田	主
用	以	世	正	台	広	仕	去	写	冬	兄	同	自	地	合	回	考	死	有	早
好	字	光	色	池	肉	体	作	近	売	別	私	村	住	町	究	声	低	医	図
赤	走	弟	事	者	明	京	画	知	物	使	所	始	英	味	門	夜	注	歩	青
林	服	妹	姉	発	首	度	持	思	県	界	重	海	品	計	建	急	送	研	乗
待	映	音	室	風	春	屋	秋	便	洋	昼	茶	洗	員	通	家	院	特	真	料
起	病	帰	紙	夏	旅	借	弱	勉	問	動	理	強	野	都	進	産	教	終	転
族	悪	黒	習	堂	鳥	菜	場	開	集	朝	運	着	答	森	短	軽	貸	飯	暑
寒	業	意	楽	試	働	遠	暗	漢	説	銀	歌	質	親	頭	館	薬	題	顔	曜
験																			

虫	貝	羊	馬	象	牧	羽	巣	皮	酒	油	氷	麦	梅	果	豆	塩	米	孫	児
童	王	士	夫	司	福	臣	卒	記	博	客	君	老	軍	兵	隊	係	治	官	胃
腸	脈	鼻	歯	身	指	毛	血	星	景	原	波	湖	汽	流	湯	陽	芽	葉	草
石	岩	島	岸	炭	畑	熱	陸	毒	農	根	松	粉	種	季	候	節	竹	雲	雪
鉄	玉	球	柱	機	械	材	札	標	票	帯	席	帳	糸	絵	束	船	器	荷	賞
貨	管	筆	箱	笛	矢	弓	刀	具	旗	輪	型	板	印	灯	皿	衣	鏡	面	角
庫	庭	府	園	坂	街	戸	局	橋	倉	宮	宿	公	谷	路	郡	部	階	港	州
科	丁	寺	里	神	福	礼	貯	相	観	組	給	級	利	列	残	戦	式	差	由
位	氏	役	徒	欠	順	類	共	令	命	的	協	芸	形	量	予	祭	実	害	関
愛	恋	想	念	感	信	功	勇	希	幸	栄	和	敗	丸	才	良	悲	必	変	最
昭	温	浅	深	満	清	静	令	速	苦	完	単	平	美	細	緑	黄	等	努	全
健	康	直	央	仲	側	内	周	表	末	横	秒	反	歴	史	次	辺	対	昔	昨
期	囲	底	紀	未	様	極	課	議	詩	調	訓	談	各	願	章	例	他	典	無
然	録	案	法	約	号	第	番	数	算	点	両	倍	径	兆	億	積	決	落	消
浴	泳	漁	泣	活	拾	当	争	挙	折	打	投	固	登	喜	航	商	停	化	伝
付	整	散	救	放	改	包	遊	追	選	連	返	達	辞	曲	覚	労	加	助	失
求	笑	察	守	定	飛	要	養	息	刷	初	成	配	照	晴	唱	得	委	交	申
鳴	向	告	競	祝	焼	殺	取	受	省	植	置	育	望	勝	負	費	参	練	続
結																			

ELEMENTS & RADICALS

STROKE	ELEMENT	MEANING	STROKE	ELEMENT	MEANING	STROKE	ELEMENT	MEANING
1	乚	Bent	3	巾	Cloth, scroll	4	灬	Fire
2	冫	Ice, two	3	口	Mouth, opening	4	止	To stop
2	又	Hand	3	囗	Enclosure	4	月	Moon
2	ナ	Hand	3	己	Straighten up	4	戈	Halberd
2	亻	Person	3	彳	Road	4	月	Flesh, body
2	人	Person	3	尸	Awning, corpse	4	火	Fire
2	厶	I, myself	3	也	To be	4	木	Tree
2	十	Ten	3	廾	Hands	4	卝	Flood, plant
2	儿	Legs	3	川	River	4	牛	Cow
2	冂	Enclosure	3	山	Mountain	4	牜	Cow
2	力	Strength	3	干	To dry	4	心	Heart
2	𠂊	Bent person	3	ヨ	Hand	4	水	Water
2	冖	Cover	3	彐	Hand	4	龶	Plants
2	刀	Sword, knife	3	扌	Hands	4	斤	Axe
2	刂	Sword, knife	3	𠆢	Roof	4	气	Air
2	匕	Spoon, ladle	3	勺	Spoon	4	礻	Altar
2	厂	Cliff	4	耂	Old	5	且	Ancestor
2	卩	Kneel down	4	宀	Cave	5	合	Along
2	八	Divide	4	中	Middle	5	申	Lighting, to say
3	大	Big	4	毛	Hair	5	田	Rice field
3	寸	Measurement	4	井	Well	5	生	Life
3	艹	Plant, grass	4	犬	Dog	5	甲	Shield
3	辶	Road	4	斗	Dipper, ladle	5	乍	Create
3	彡	Hair, bright	4	歹	Death	5	癶	Footsteps
3	广	Tent	4	开	Two poles	5	皿	Net
3	夂	Feet	4	云	Cloud	5	弗	Dollar
3	氵	Water, liquid	4	攵	Hit, whip	5	皿	Chalice, dish
3	土	Soil, ground	4	欠	To lack	5	白	White
3	士	Man, samurai	4	爫	Hand	5	王	King
3	小	Small	4	氏	Family, clan	5	矢	Arrow
3	弋	Spike	4	方	Direction	5	立	To stand
3	几	Table	4	尹	Govern	5	石	Stone
3	女	Woman	4	文	Literature, letters	5	由	Gourd
3	弓	Bow	4	夭	Young man	5	目	Eye
3	宀	Roof, house	4	厶	Child	5	衣	Clothing
3	子	Child	4	亢	High	5	禾	Grain
3	阝	Hill	4	殳	Tool	5	甘	Sweet

3	阝	City	4	日	Day, sun	5	示	Altar
3	工	Work, craft	4	爻	Cross	5	戈	Halberd
6	羊	Sheep	6	襾	Covering	8	隹	Small bird
6	扒	Flag pole	7	呂	Rooms	8	尚	High status
6	糸	Yarn, Thread	7	走	To run	8	雨	Rain
6	虫	Insect	7	車	Car, cart	8	長	Long
6	自	Stacks	7	豆	Bean	8	音	Split
6	舟	Boat	7	豕	Pig	8	其	Basket
6	米	Rice	7	辛	Bitter, tattooing needle	8	录	Green
6	囟	Brain	7	貝	Shell, money	8	門	Gate
6	聿	Brush	7	酉	Drinking vessel	9	畐	Container
6	羽	Feather	7	豆	Beans	9	昜	Sun rays
6	舌	Tongue	7	里	Village	9	食	Food
6	⺮	Bamboo	7	系	Lineage	9	頁	Head
6	艮	Good	7	言	Speech, word	10	馬	Horse
6	自	Self	7	辰	Garden fork	11	魚	Fish
6	丝	Yarn	8	金	Gold, metal	11	鳥	Bird
6	羊	Sheep	8	食	Food			

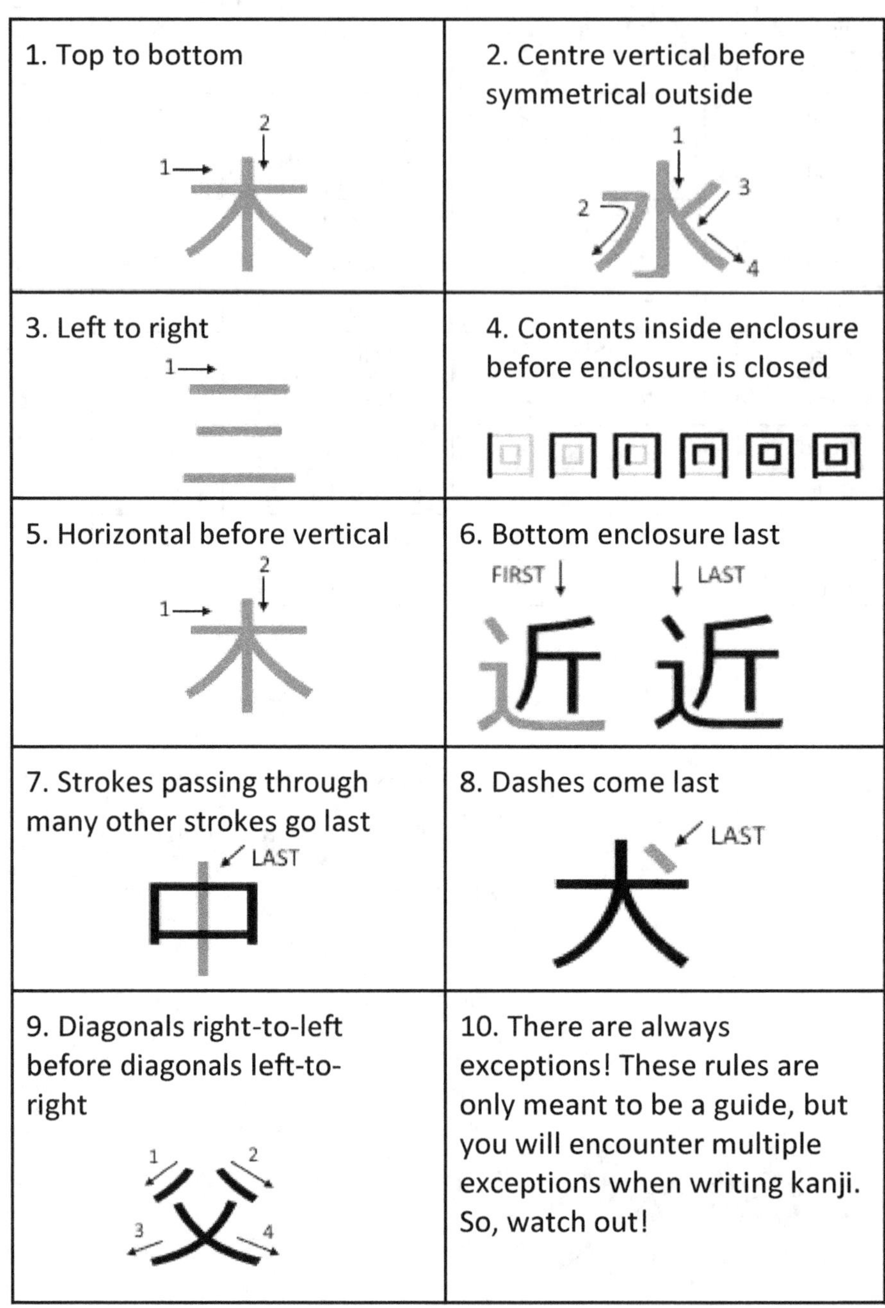

<table>
<tr><td>1. Top to bottom</td><td>2. Centre vertical before symmetrical outside</td></tr>
<tr><td>3. Left to right</td><td>4. Contents inside enclosure before enclosure is closed</td></tr>
<tr><td>5. Horizontal before vertical</td><td>6. Bottom enclosure last</td></tr>
<tr><td>7. Strokes passing through many other strokes go last</td><td>8. Dashes come last</td></tr>
<tr><td>9. Diagonals right-to-left before diagonals left-to-right</td><td>10. There are always exceptions! These rules are only meant to be a guide, but you will encounter multiple exceptions when writing kanji. So, watch out!</td></tr>
</table>

CHAPTER 1: BODY PARTS

腹	腕	脳	肌	腰	脂
1	2	3	4	5	6
臓	胸	背	骨	膚	肩
7	8	9	10	11	12
髪	額	性	汗	涙	
13	14	15	16	17	

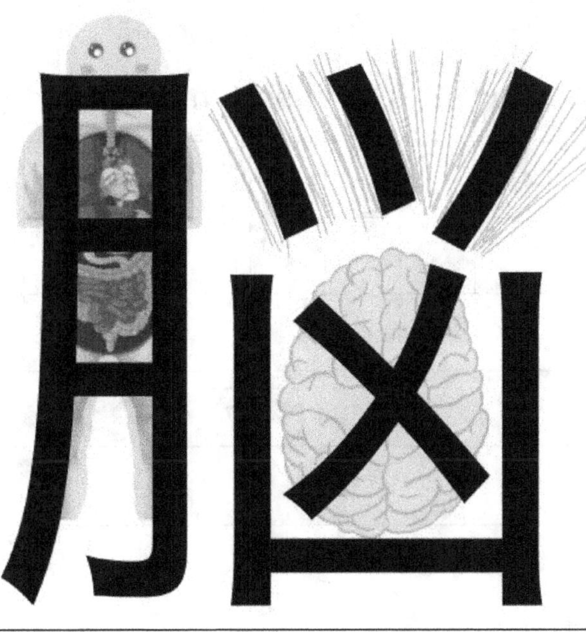

腹 STOMACH

"The stomach (腹) is a body part (月) that is repeatedly (复) acidic"

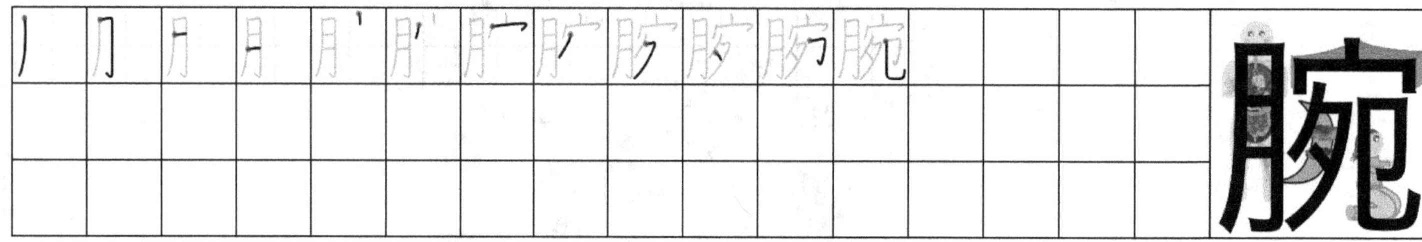

Kun (はら)	ODD (なか)
はら 腹 = Belly, stomach	なか お 腹 = Stomach, belly

腕 ARM

"The person kneels down (卩) on the roof (宀) to worship the moon (夕) with his arms (腕)"

Kun (うで)
うで 腕 = Arm

脳 BRAIN

"The brain (脳) is an important body part (月)"

ON (ノ ウ)
ずのう 頭 脳 = Head, brains

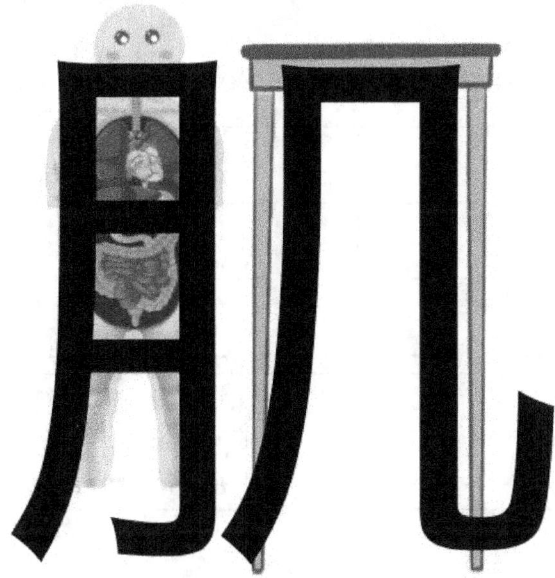

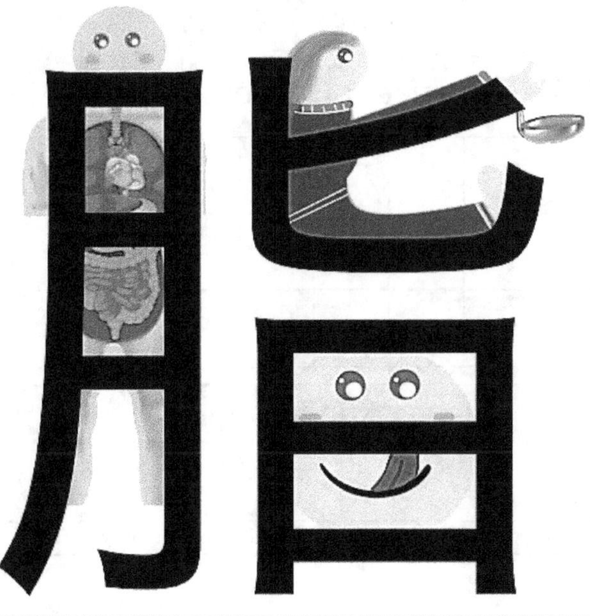

肌 SKIN, TEXTURE

"Feel the surface of the table (几) with your skin (肌)"

Kun (はだ)

はだ 肌 = Skin	はだぎ 肌 着 = Underwear

腰 HIPS, WAIST

"The waist (腰) is a body part (月) that needs (要) to grow during pregnancy"

Kun (こし)

こし 腰 = Hip	こしか 腰 掛け = Seat, bench	こしか 腰 掛ける = To sit (down)

Note: This kanji was originally a woman with two hands pointing to her midsection.

脂 FAT, GREASE

"I love grabbing a spoon (匕) with sweet (甘) food, but that's just fat (脂) for my flesh (月)"

Kun (あぶら)

あぶら 脂 = Fat, lard

Note: Even though this kanji seems to have the element for sun (日), it is actually the element for sweet (甘)

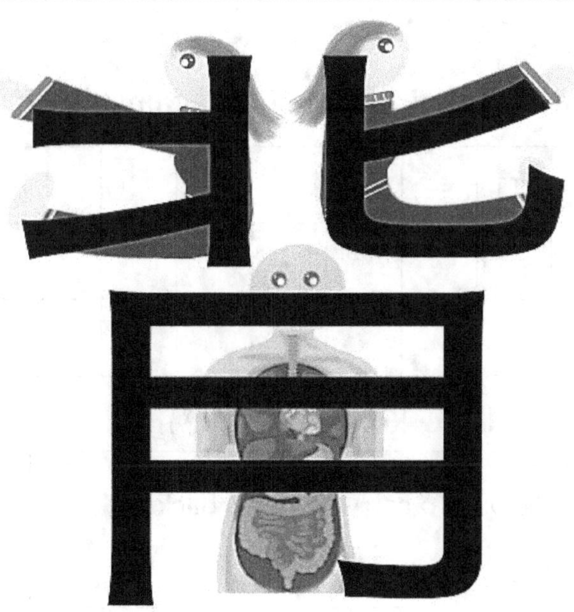

臓 BOWELS, VISCERA, ENTRAILS

"The bowels (臓) are a part of the body (月) that act as a vault (蔵)"

ON (ゾウ)

しんぞう
心 臓 = Heart (organ)

胸 CHEST, BREAST

"The chest (胸) is a part of the body (月) wrapped (勹) by the ribcage"

Kun (むね)

むね
胸　= Chest, breast

背 STATURE, HEIGHT, BACK

"Two people are resting their bodies (月) against each other's back(背)"

Kun (せ、せい)

せ
背 = Back, spine, reverse
せい
背 = Height, stature

せお
背 負う = To carry on one's back
せなか
背 中 = Back (of body)

せびろ
背 広 = Business suit

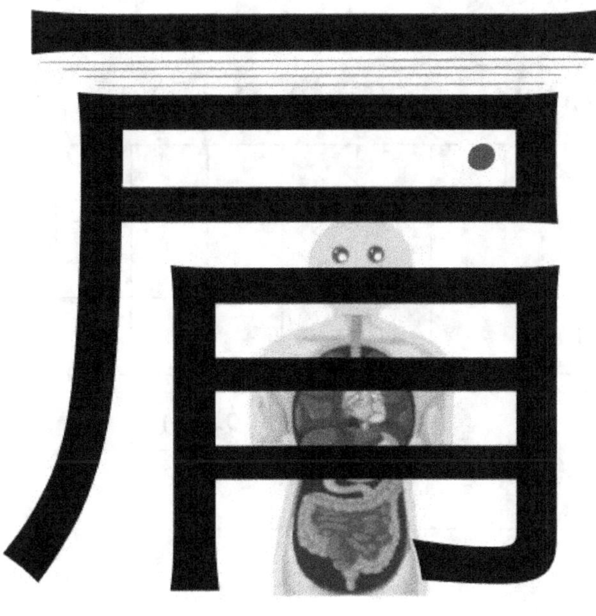

骨 BONE, SKELETON

"The skull (冎) is a part of the body (月) made out of bone (骨)"

ON (コツ)		Kun (ほね)	
こっせつ 骨 折 = Bone fracture		ほね 骨 = Bone	

膚 SKIN

"The skin (膚) of a tiger's (虍) stomach (胃) is saggy"

ON (フ)
ひふ 皮膚= Skin

肩 SHOULDER

"The shoulder (肩) is a part of the body (月) that acts as a door (戸) hinge"

Kun (かた)
かた 肩 = Shoulder

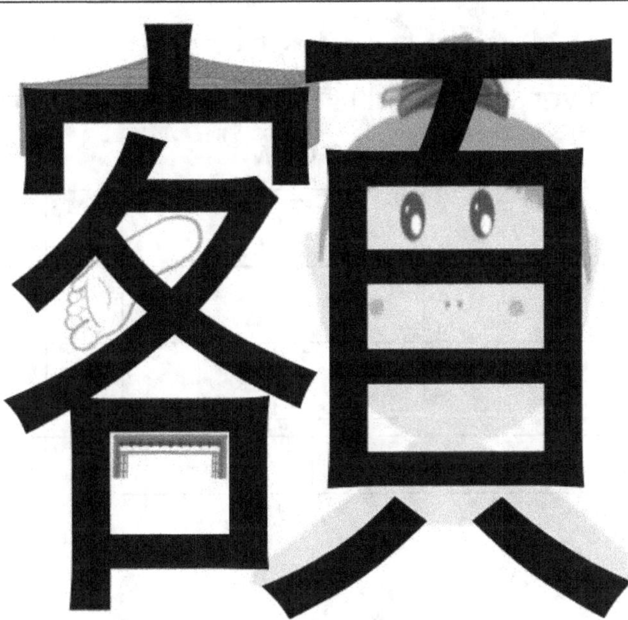

髪 HAIR

"My friend (友) has long (長) hair (髪)"

Kun (かみ)	ODD (が)
かみ 髪 = Hair (on the head) かみ　け 髪 の毛 = Hair (head)	しらが 白 髪 = White / gray hair

Note: Originally it had the element of dog (犬), not of friend.

額 FOREHEAD, FRAMED PICTURE, AMOUNT

"In some customer, you lower your head (頁) at a guest (客), while your forehead (額) is facing down"

ON (ガク)	Kun (ひたい)
がく 額 = Picture (framed) きんがく 金 額 = Amount of money	ひたい 額 　= Forehead

性 SEX, GENDER, NATURE

"Your heart (忄) and gender (性) are part of your life (生)"

ON (セイ)

じょせい 女 性 = Woman	せいかく 性 格 = Personality	せいのう 性 能 = Ability	だんせい 男 性 = Male
せい 性 = Sex, gender	せいしつ 性 質 = Disposition	せいべつ 性 別 = Gender	ちゅうせい 中 性 = Neutrality

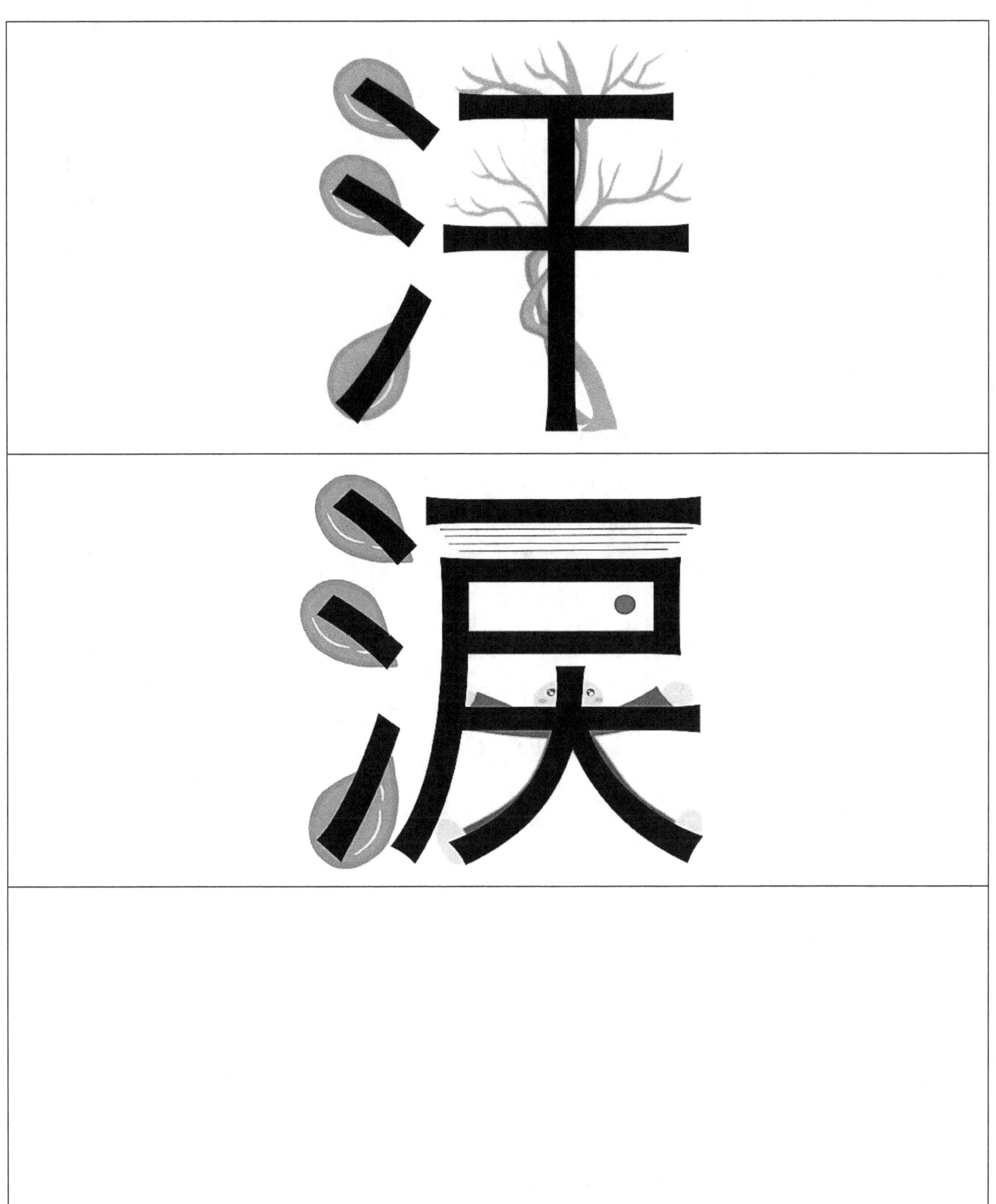

汗 SWEAT

"Today is so hot and dry (干) that you can see my sweat (汗)"

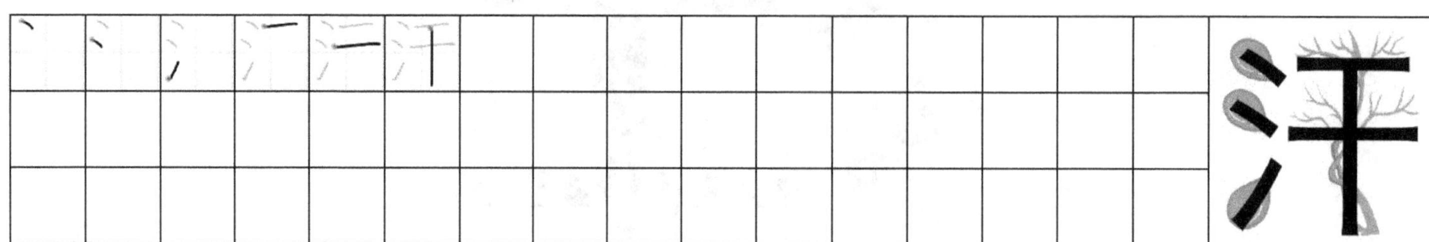

Kun (あせ)

あせ
汗　= Sweat, perspiration

涙 TEARS, SYMPATHY

"Tears (涙) are a liquid (氵) that comes out of little doors (戸) in my big (大) eyes"

Kun (なみだ)

なみだ
涙　= Tear

CHAPTER 2: PEOPLE

仏	供	優	妻	娘	婦
18	19	20	21	22	23
将	団	師	武	祖	皆
24	25	26	27	28	29
坊	殿	彼			
30	31	32			

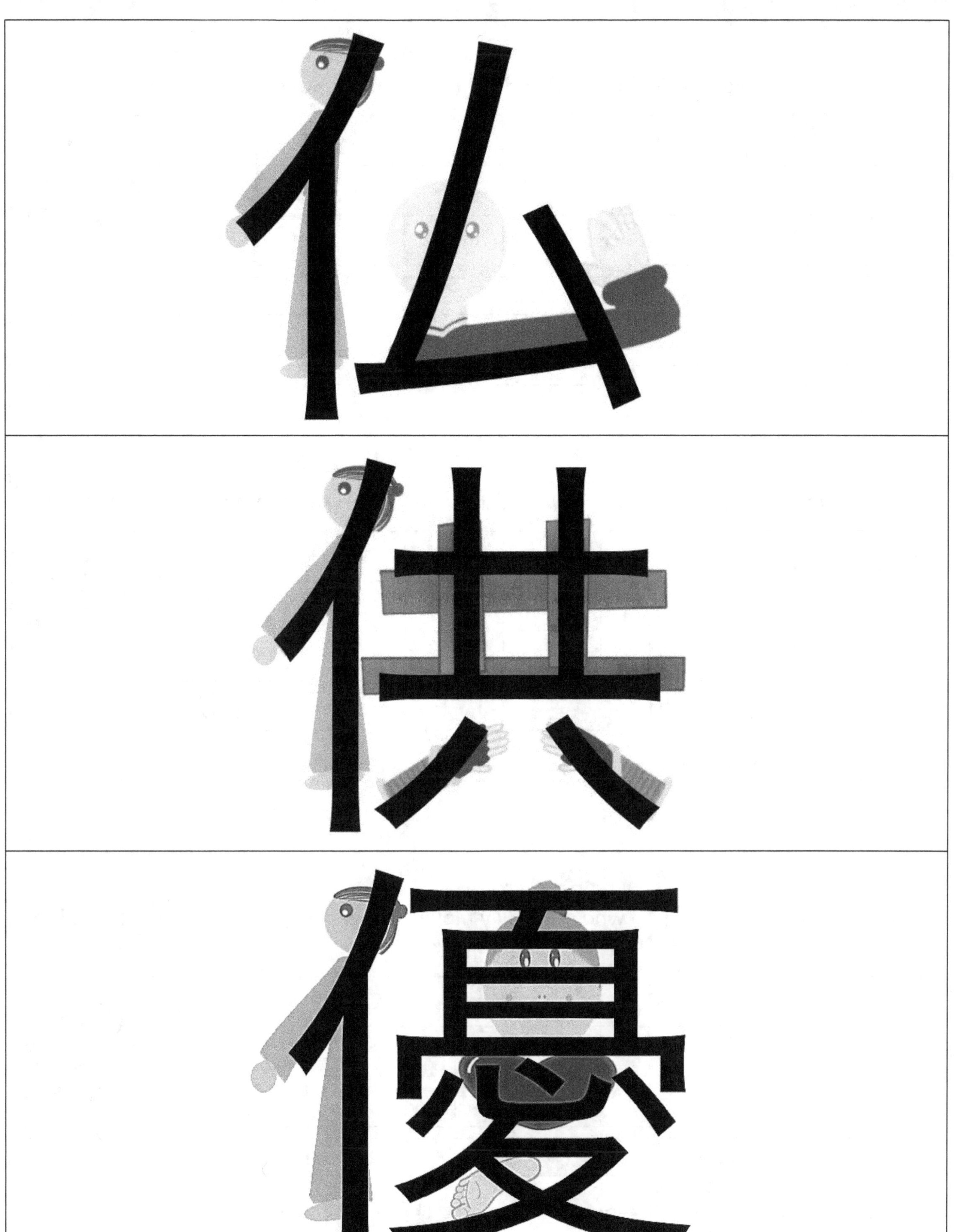

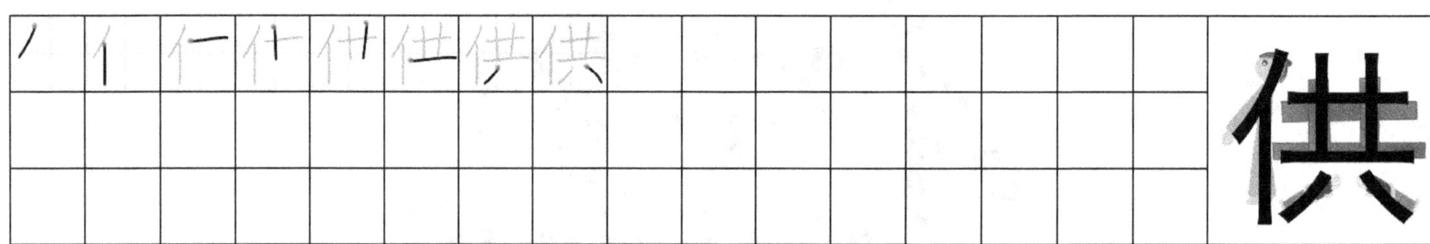

Kun (ほとけ)

ほとけ
仏 = Buddha

* Originally the word Buddha was written phonetically as 佛陀 Budda. The right side of the kanji 佛 was replaced by ム

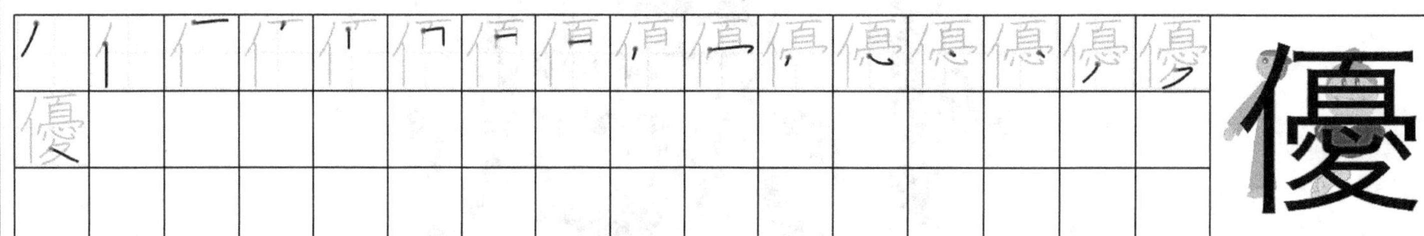

ON (キョウ)	Kun (ども)
きょうきゅう 供 給 = Supply, provision	こども 子 供 = Child, children

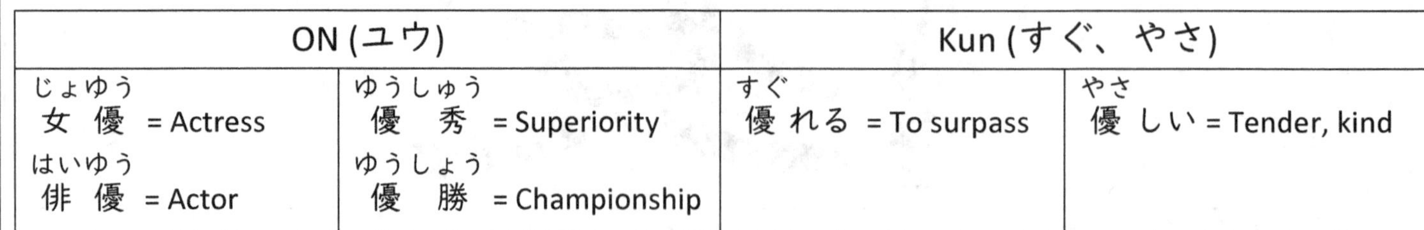

ON (ユウ)		Kun (すぐ、やさ)	
じょゆう 女 優 = Actress	ゆうしゅう 優 秀 = Superiority	すぐ 優 れる = To surpass	やさ 優 しい = Tender, kind
はいゆう 俳 優 = Actor	ゆうしょう 優 勝 = Championship		

妻

娘

婦

妻 WIFE, SPOUSE

"The woman (女) uses her hand (ヨ) to put on her wedding accessories, before becoming a beautiful wife (妻)"

ON (サイ)		Kun (つま)	
ふさい 夫 妻　= Married couple		つま 妻　= Wife	

娘 DAUGHTER, GIRL

"Her daughter (娘) is a good (良) woman (女)"

Kun (むすめ)
むすめ 娘　= (hum) daughter

婦 WOMAN, LADY, WIFE

"The woman (女) cleans the wife's (婦) room with a broom (帚)"

ON (フ)	
かんごふ 看 護 婦　= (Female) nurse	ふうふ 夫 婦 = Married couple
しゅふ 主 婦 = Housewife	ふじん 婦 人 = Woman, adult female

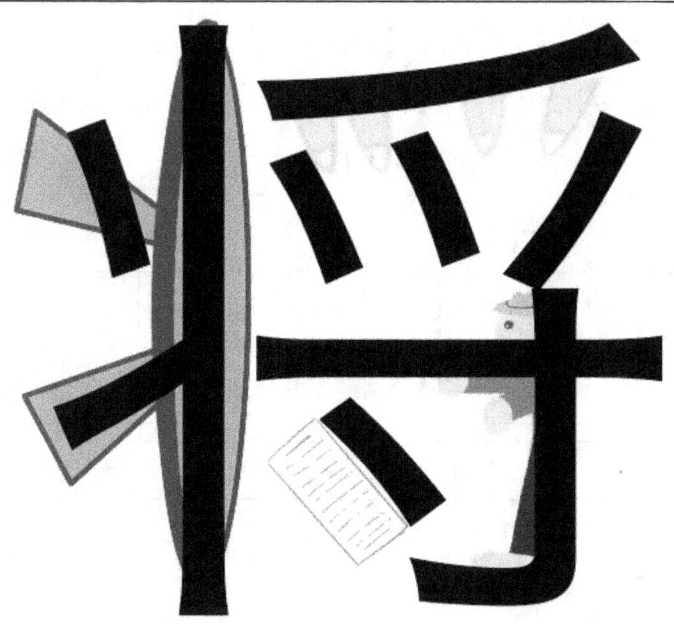

将 LEADER, COMMANDER

"The commander (将) extends his hand (⺶) to measure (寸) the size of the offerings on the table (爿)"

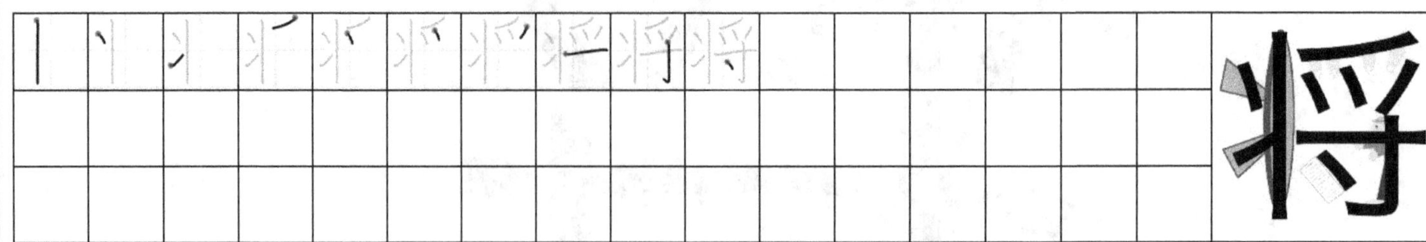

ON (ショウ)

しょうらい 将 来 = Future, prospects	しょうぎ 将 棋 = Japanese chess, shogi

団 GROUP, ASSOCIATION

"The enclosure (囗) was measured (寸) and built by the group (団)"

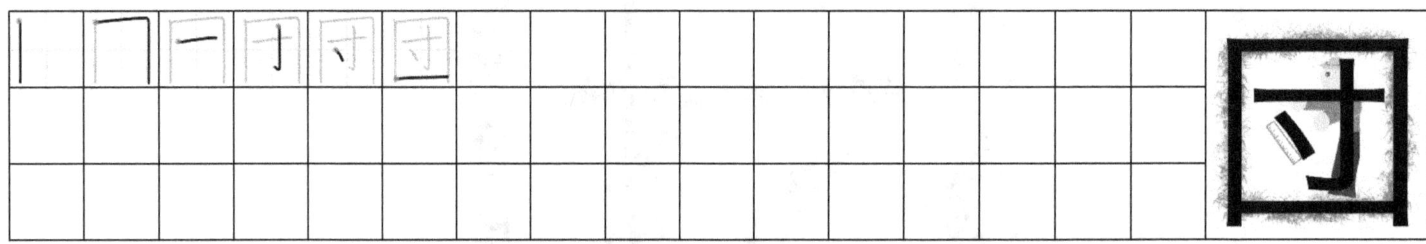

ON (トン、ダン)

ざぶとん 座布団 = Cushion (Jap.) ふとん 布団 = Futon (Jap. Bedding)	しゅうだん 集 団 = Group, mass だんたい 団 体 = Organization	だんち 団 地 = Multi-unit apts.

師 EXPERT, TEACHER, MASTER

"The master (師) in warrior clothes (巾) helped us hide behind the stack (𠂤)"

ON (シ)

いし 医師 = Doctor ぎし 技師 = Engineer, technician	きょうし 教 師 = Teacher (classroom) こうし 講 師 = Lecturer	りょうし 漁 師 = Fisherman

武

祖

皆

武 MILITARY, WARRIOR

"The warrior (武) holding the halberd (弋) stops (止) to verify his surroundings"

ON (ブ)	
ぶき 武器 = Weapons, arms	ぶし 武士 = Warrior, samurai

祖 ANCESTOR, FOUNDER

"Go to the altar (ネ) and pray to the ancestors (祖)"

ON (ソ)	
せんぞ 先祖 = Ancestor そせん 祖先 = Ancestor	そふ 祖父 = Grandfather そぼ 祖母 = Grandmother

皆 EVERYBODY

"Everyone (皆) is comparing (比) the twins to white (白) angels"

Kun (みんな、 みな)	
みんな 皆 = All, everybody	みな 皆 = All, everbody

Note: The kanji originally had 曰 (To say) on the bottom, instead of white.

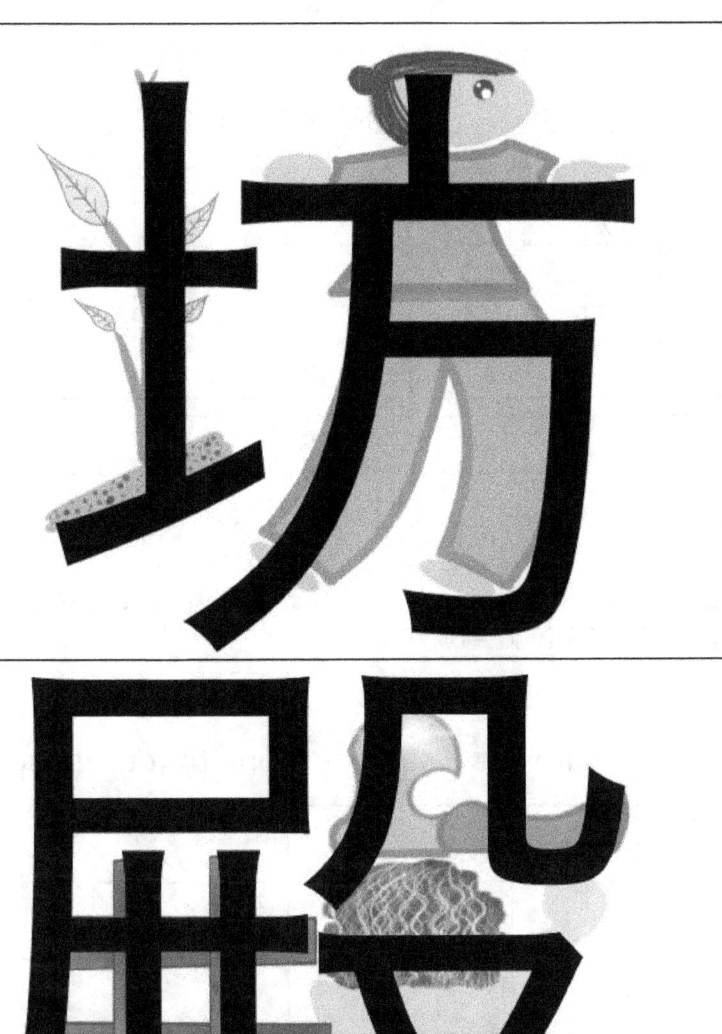

坊

殿

彼

坊 BOY, PRIEST

"The priest (坊) always goes in direction (方) of the ground (土) before praying"

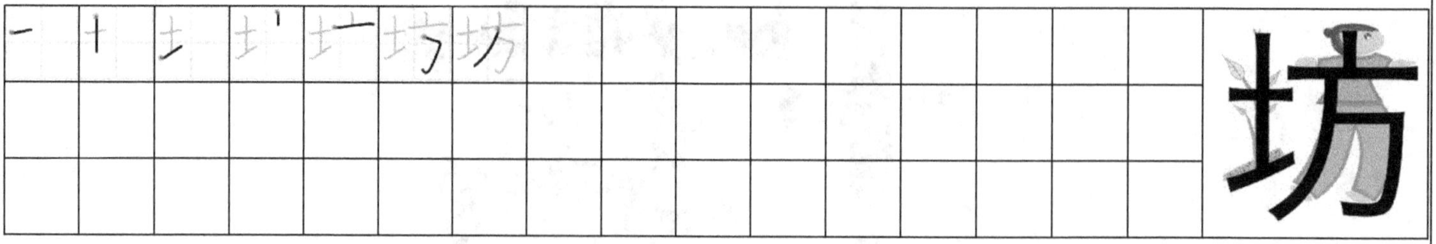

ON (ボウ)

ねぼう 寝坊 = Sleeping in late	ぼう 坊 や = Boy
ぼう 坊 さん = Buddhist priest, monk	ぼ 坊っちゃん = Son (others)

Note: The kanji was originally to mean a section of a temple that was on the ground.

殿 MR., HALL, MANSION

"The mansion's Mr. (殿) is the only one that uses the tools (殳)"

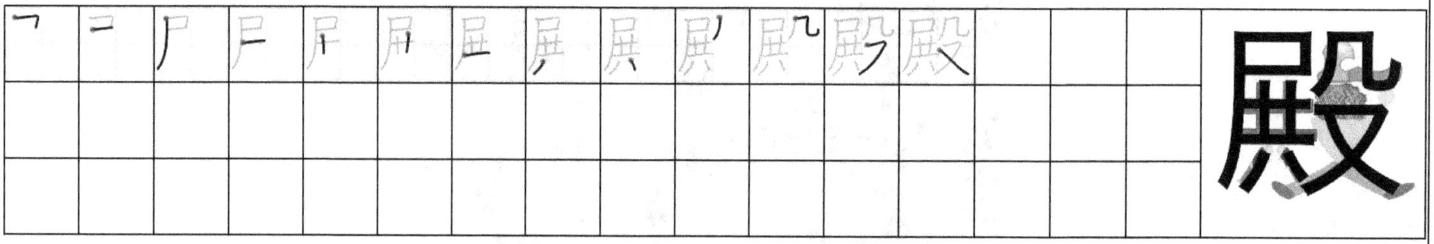

Kun (との)

との
殿 = Mr., Mrs.

Note: The original meaning of this kanji was buttock, which came from bridegroom being slapped on the buttock on his wedding day.

彼 HE, THAT, BOYFRIEND

"The person on the road (彳) wearing the fur (皮) is my boyfriend (彼)"

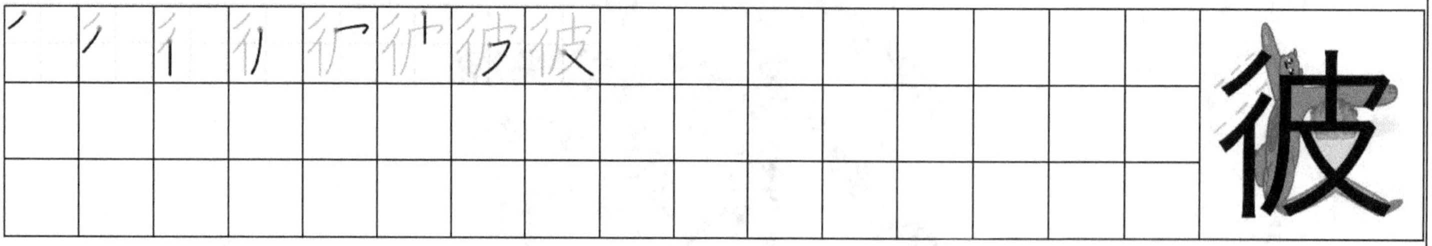

Kun (かれ、かの)

かれ 彼 = He, boyfriend	かのじょ 彼 女 = She, girlfriend	かれ 彼 ら = They (usually male)

CHAPTER 3: NATURE & FOOD

蒸	煙	灰	湾	泥	液
33	34	35	36	37	38
宙	綿	革	猫	畜	砂
39	40	41	42	43	44
銅	鉱	曇	枝	粒	卵
45	46	47	48	49	50
乳	菓	群			
51	52	53			

蒸 STEAM, HEAT, FOMENT

"We hold hands together (丞) while getting heat (蒸) from the fire (灬) burning grass (艹)"

ON (ジョウ)		Kun (む)
じょうき 蒸 気 = Steam, vapor	すいじょうき 水 蒸 気 = Water vapor	む　あつ 蒸し 暑 い = Humid
じょうはつ 蒸 発 = Evaporation		む 蒸す = To steam

煙 SMOKE

"Add a covering (覀) of soil (土) to the fire (火) before the smoke (煙) grows bigger"

ON (エン)	Kun (けむ、 けむり)
えんとつ 煙 突 = Chimney	けむ 煙 い = Smoky
きんえん 禁 煙 = No smoking	けむり 煙 = Smoke, fumes

灰 ASHES, CREMATE

"The fire (火) that burnt under the cliff (厂) left ashes (灰) behind"

Kun (はい)	
はい 灰 = Ash	はいざら 灰 皿 = Ashtray
はいいろ 灰 色 = Grey	

Note: This kanji originally had a hand instead of a cliff. It signified what a hand collected after the fire was gone.

湾
泥
液

湾 BAY, GULF, INLET

"The water (氵) marks in this bay (湾) form the shape of a bow (弓)"

ON (ワン)

わん
湾　= Bay, gulf, inlet

Note: The original kanji 灣 was simplified to this current form. Losing some of the meaning.

泥 MUD

"The nun (尼) found a corpse (尸) in the watery (氵) mud (泥)"

Kun (どろ)

どろ	どろぼう
泥　= Mud	泥 棒　= Thief

液 FLUID, LIQUID, JUICE

"It is easy to hear a liquid (液), such as water (氵), dripping at night (夜)"

ON (エキ)

えきたい	けつえき
液 体　= Liquid, fluid	血 液　= Blood

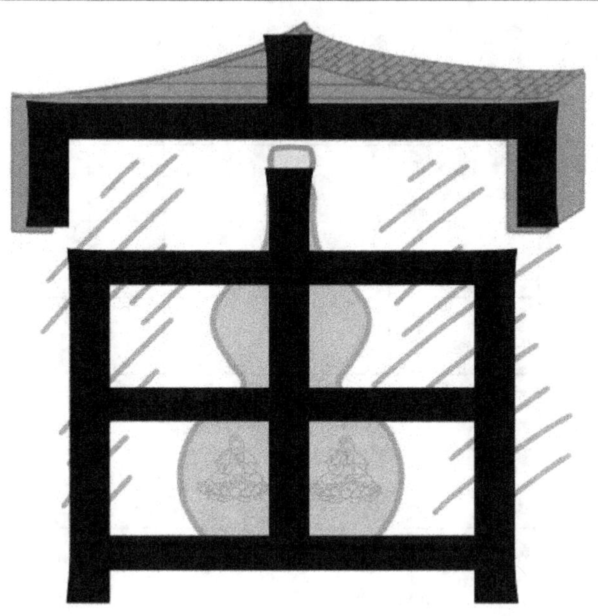

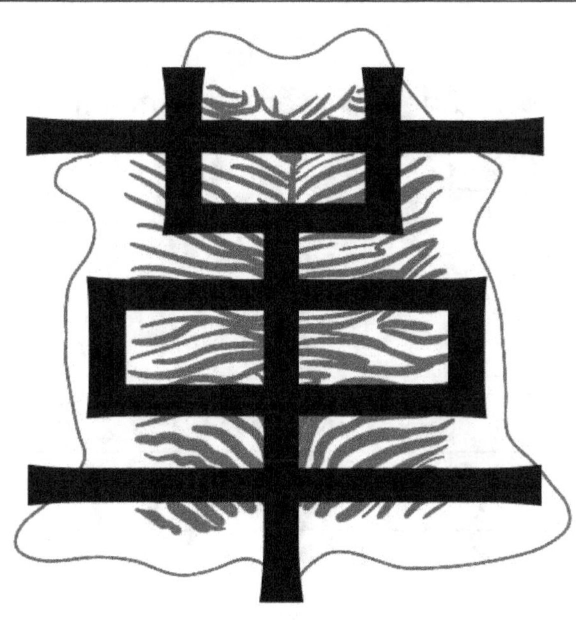

宙 SPACE, SKY, AIR

"The empty gourd (由) has enough space (宙) to store the oil leaking under the roof (宀)"

ON (チュウ)

うちゅう
宇宙 = Space

綿 COTTON

"These clothes (巾) have white (白) cotton (綿) threads (糸)"

ON (メン)	Kun (わた)
めん 綿 = Cotton もめん 木綿 = Cotton	わた 綿 = Cotton plant, padding

革 LEATHER, SKIN

"Leather (革) comes from animals"

Kun (かわ)

かわ
革 = Leather

猫 CAT

"A wild cat (猫) is a beast (犭) that can destroy plants (艹) and fields (田)"

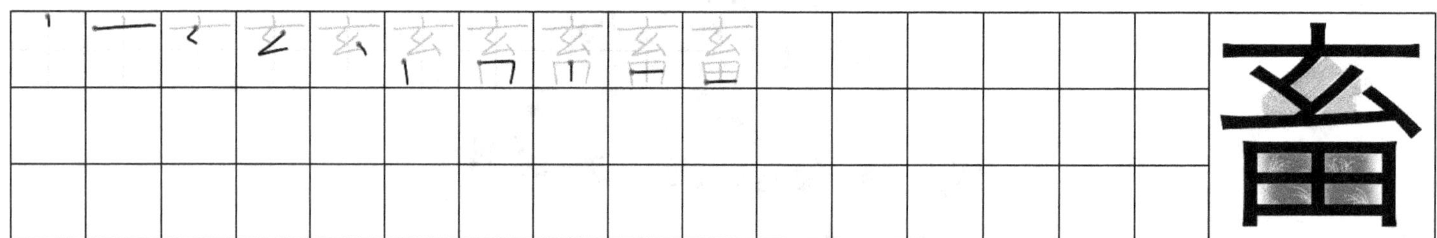

Kun (ねこ)

ねこ
猫　= Cat

畜 LIVESTOCK

"The fences protecting the fields (田) for livestock (畜) are sealed with threads (玄)"

ON (チク)

ぼくちく
牧　畜　= Stock-farming

砂 SAND

"Sand (砂) is technically just little (少) rocks (石)"

ON (サ)	Kun (すな)
さとう 砂 糖　= Sugar さばく 砂 漠　= Desert	すな 砂　= Sand

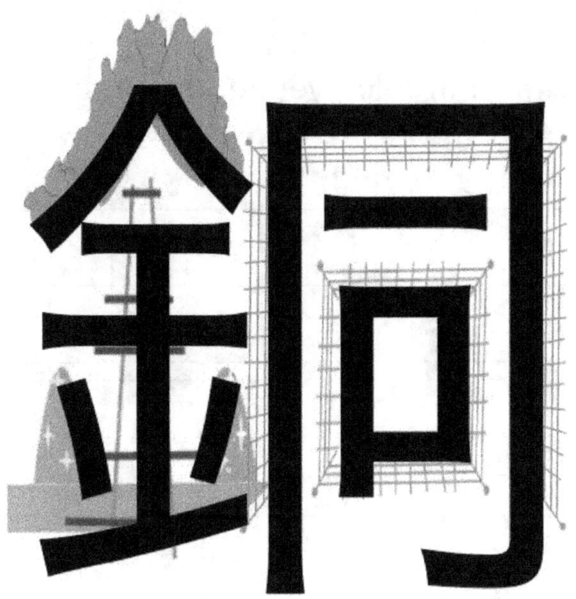

銅 COPPER

"Copper (銅) is similar in color, yet not the same (同) as gold (金)"

ノ 人 ト 仁 牟 争 余 金 釘 釘 銅 銅 銅 銅

ON (ドウ)

どう
銅 = Copper

鉱 ORE, MINERAL

"Metals (金) can be extracted from wide (広) rocks known as ores (鉱)"

ノ 人 ト 仁 牟 争 余 金 金' 釘 釘 鉱 鉱

ON (コウ)

こうぶつ	たんこう
鉱 物 = Mineral	炭 鉱 = Coal mine

曇 CLOUDY WEATHER

"When we have a cloudy weather (曇), the clouds (雲) cover the sun (日)"

亅 冂 冎 日 目 昌 昌 昌 昇 昇 昇 昇 曇 曇 曇

Kun (くも)

くもり	くも
曇 = Cloudiness, cloudy weather	曇 る = To become cloudy

枝

粒

卵

枝 BRANCH, TWIG

"A twig (枝) is a small branch (支) from a tree (木)"

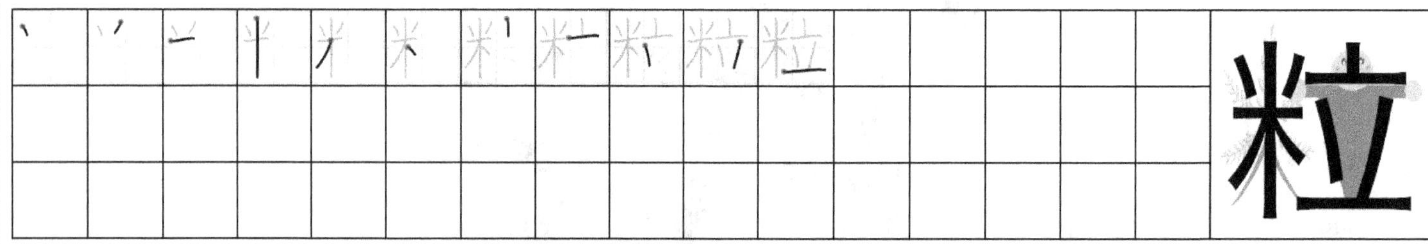

Kun (え だ)

えだ
枝　= Branch, twig

粒 GRAINS, DROP

"The workers stand up (立) to pick up the rice (米) grains (粒)"

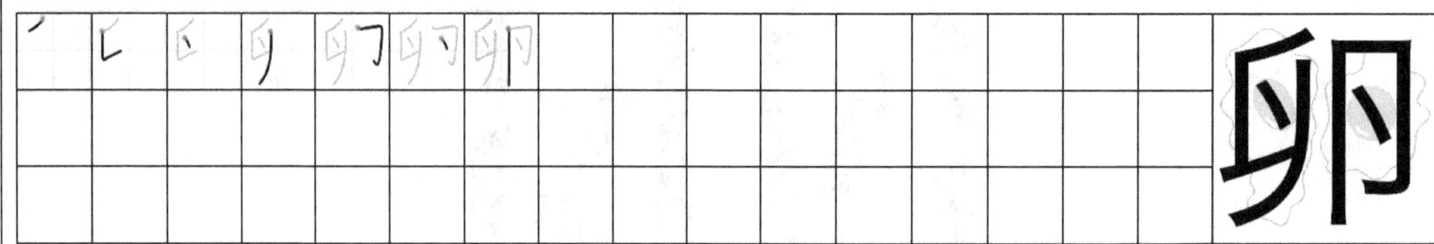

Kun (つ ぶ)

つぶ
粒　= Grain

卵 EGG, SPAWN, ROE

"Two eggs (卵) showing the yolk"

Kun (た ま ご)

たまご
卵　= Egg, eggs

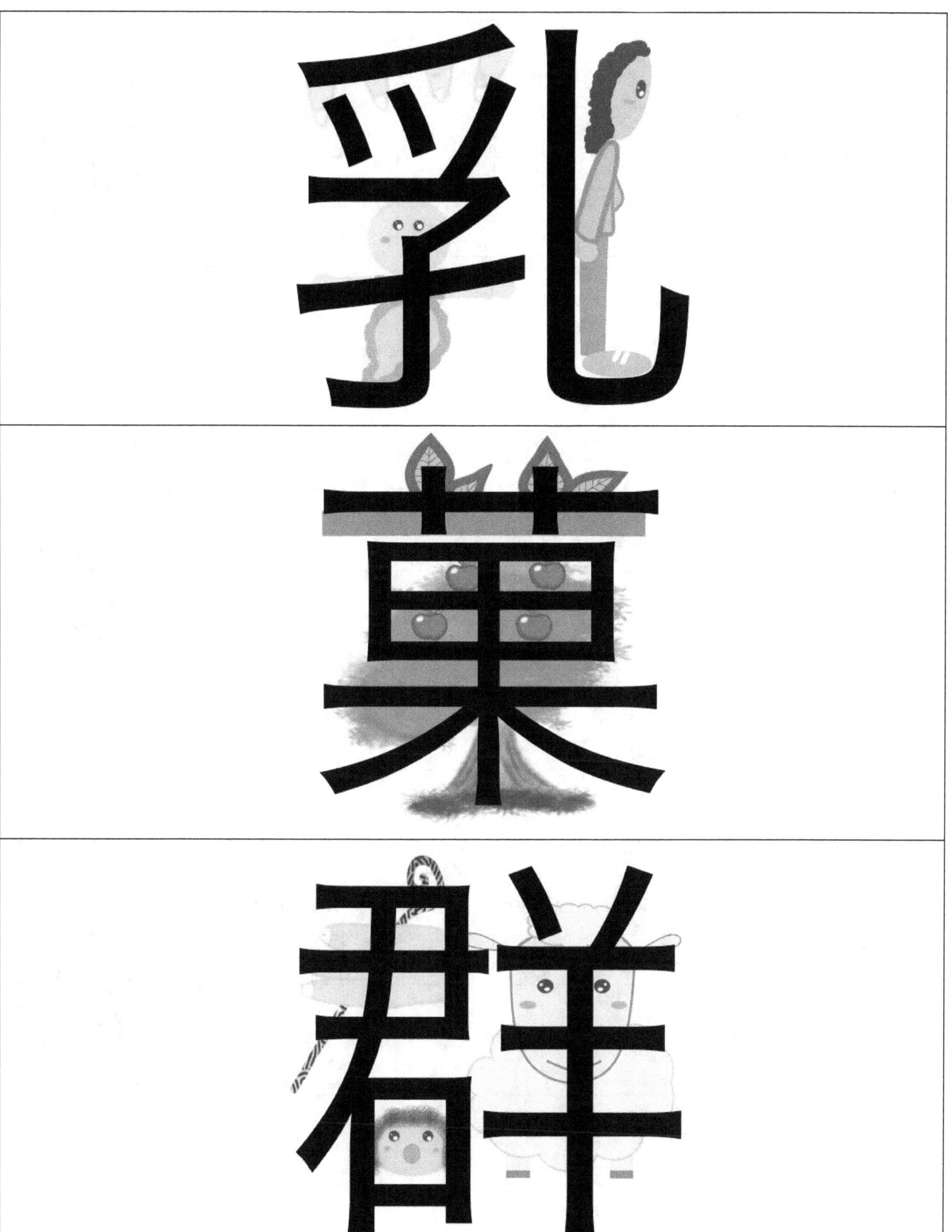

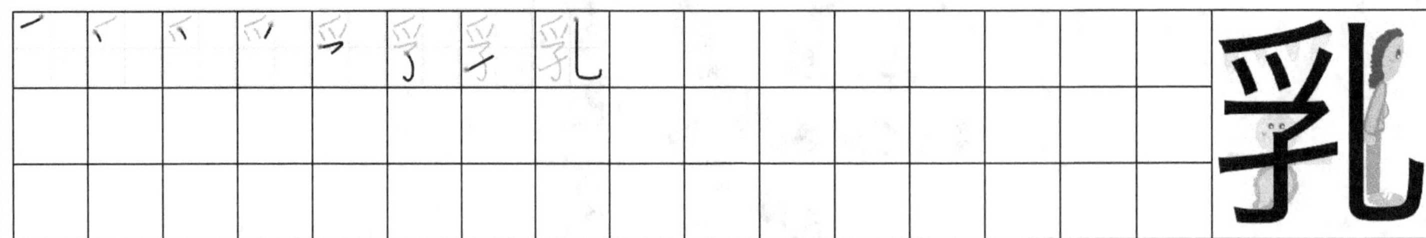

乳 MILK, BREASTS

"She bends (乚) to give milk (乳) to the child (子) she is holding in her hands (爫)

ON (ニュウ)

ぎゅうにゅう
牛　乳　= (Cow's) milk

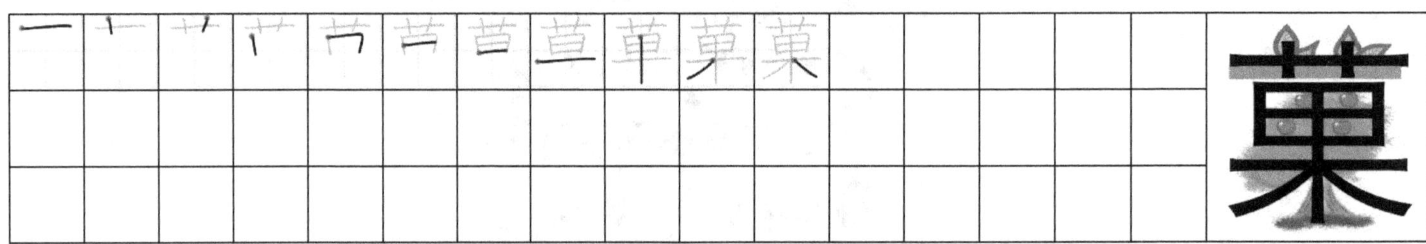

菓 FRUIT, CANDY, CAKES

"A lot of processes were carried out (果) to get fruits (菓) the way we know them today"

ON (カ)

かし
菓子 = Confectionery, sweets, candy

群 FLOCK, GROUP, CROWD

"This flock (群) of sheep (羊) belongs to the ruler (君)"

Kun (む)

む
群れ = Group, crowd, flock

CHAPTER 4: OBJECTS

畳	靴	帽	布	袋	装
54	55	56	57	58	59
環	宝	版	針	像	件
60	61	62	63	64	65
贈	財	誌	志	舟	窓
66	67	68	69	70	71
机	棒	枚	筒	符	封
72	73	74	75	76	77
巻	郵	爆			
78	79	80			

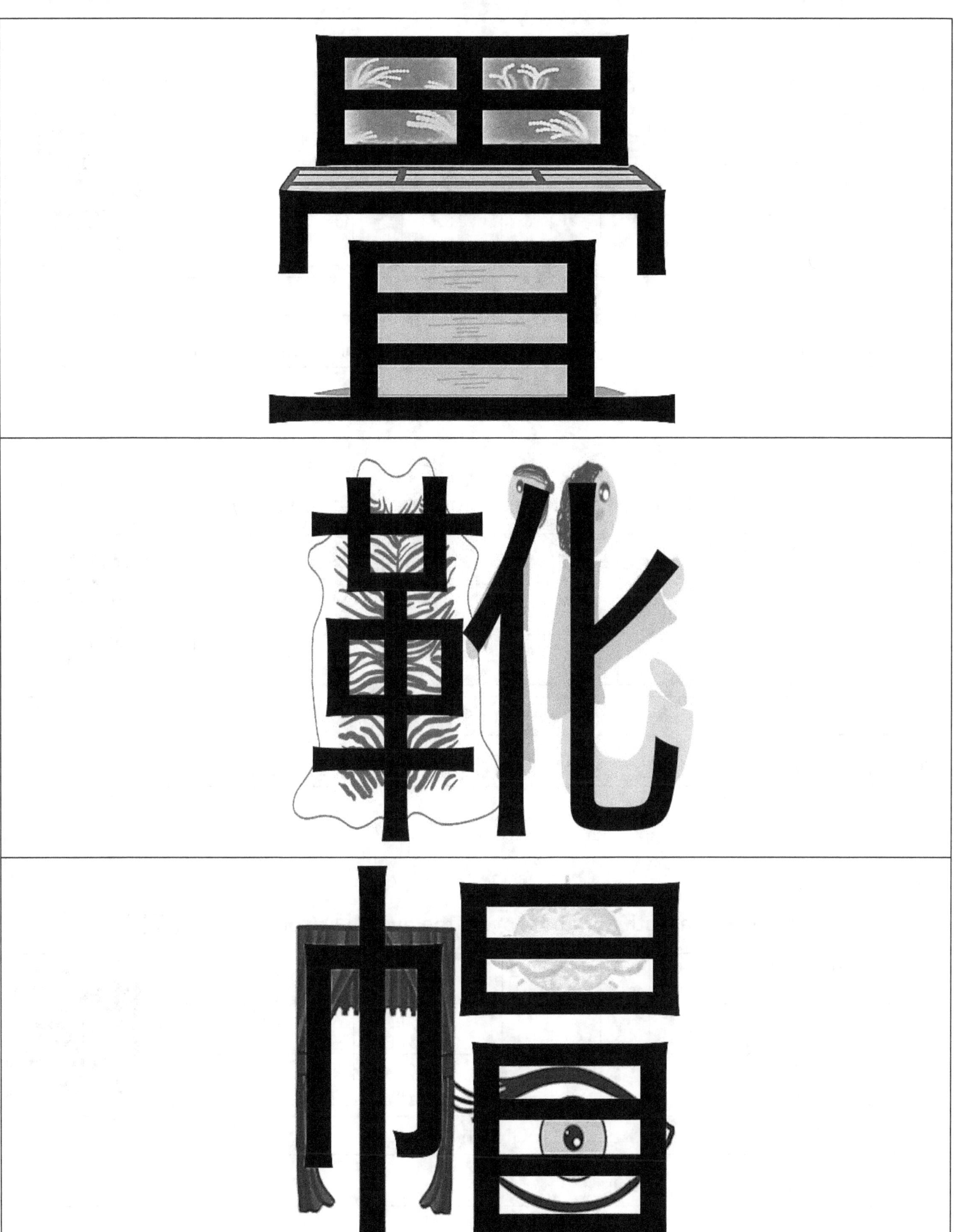

畳 TATAMI MAT, FOLD

"The ancestors (且) invented the tatami (畳) as a covering (冖) made out of rice (田) straw"

Kun (たたみ、たた)

たたみ 畳　= Tatami mat	たた 畳 む = To fold (clothes, umbrella)

靴 SHOES

"Leather (革) can take the form of (化) a shoe (靴)"

Kun (くつ)

くつ 靴　= Shoes, footwear	くつした 靴 下 = Socks, stockings

帽 CAP, HEADGEAR

"A cap (帽) is a cloth (巾) that covers the eyes (目) from the sun (日)"

ON (ボウ)

ぼうし 帽 子 = Hat, cap

布

袋

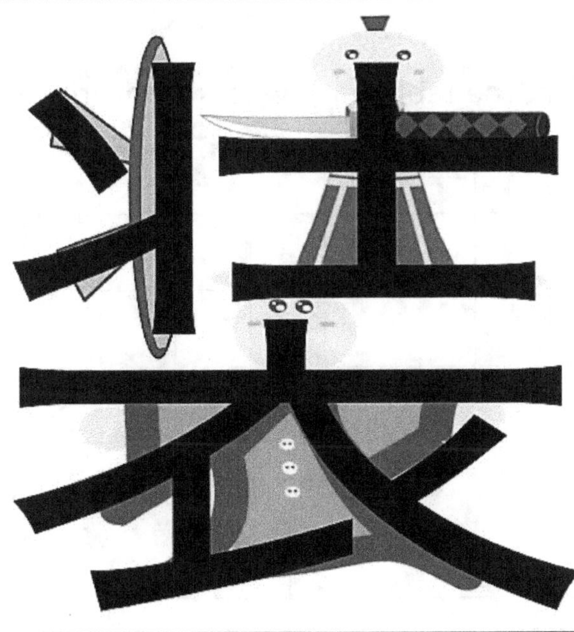

武装

布 CLOTH, DISTRIBUTE

"A hand (ナ) holding a cloth (布)"

ON (フ) | Kun (ぬの)

さいふ
財布 = Purse, wallet

ふとん
布団 = Futon

もうふ
毛布 = Blanket

ぬの
布 = Cloth

ざぶとん
座布団 = Cushion (Jap.)

ぶんぷ
分布 = Distribution

袋 SACK, BAG, POUCH

"The first bags (袋) were made out of cloth (衣) to substitute (代) a hand-carry"

Kun (ふくろ) | ODD (び)

てぶくろ
手袋 = Glove

ふくろ
袋 = Bag, sack

たび
足袋 = Japanese socks (with split toe), tabi

装 ATTIRE, DRESS

"The samurai (士), sitting at the table (爿), wears an attire (装) of very fine cloth (衣)"

ON (ソウ)

そうち
装置 = Equipment, installation

ほうそう
包装 = Packing, wrapping

ふくそう
服装 = Garments

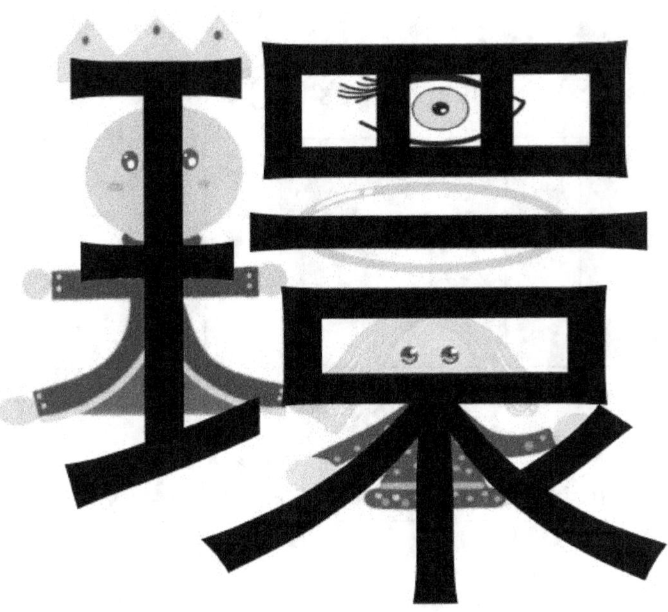

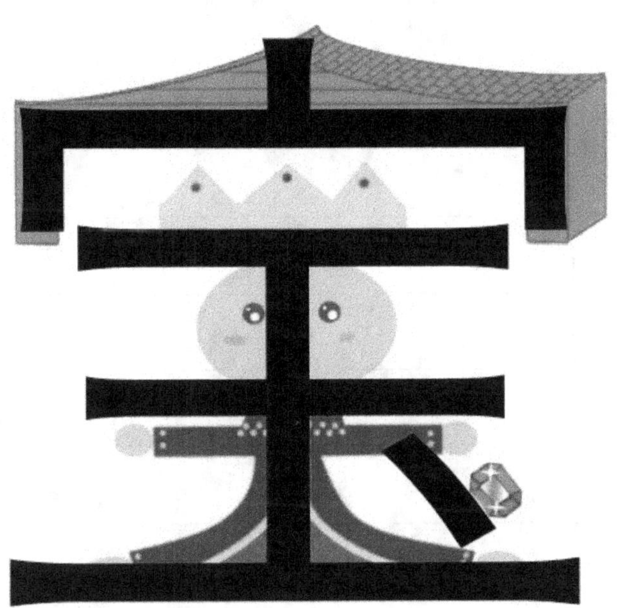

環 RING, CIRCLE, WHEEL

"The girl in pretty clothes (衣) opens her eyes (目) wide to look at the king's (王) ring (環)"

環

ON (カン)

かんきょう 環　境　= Circumstance, environment	じゅんかん 循　環　= Cycle, rotation

宝 TREASURE

"There is a treasure (宝) box full of jewels (玉) on the roof (宀)"

宝

ON (ホウ)　・　Kun (たから)

ほうせき 宝　石　= Gem, jewel	たから 宝　= Treasure

版 PRINTING BLOCK, EDITION, IMPRESSION

"This printing block (版) fragment (片) works by pressing it against (反) the surface"

版

ON (ハン)

しゅっぱん
出　版　= Publication

針

像

件

針 NEEDLE, PIN

"These ten (十) needles (針) are made of a strong metal (金)"

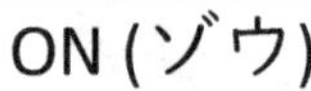

ON (シン)	Kun (はり)
しんろ 針 路 = Course, direction ほうしん 方 針 = Objective, plan, policy	はり 針 = Needle はりがね 針 金 = Wire

像 IMAGE, STATUE, FIGURE

"The person (イ) makes a statue (像) of an elephant (象)"

ON (ゾウ)

そうぞう
想 像 = Imagination

件 CASE, ITEM, AFFAIR

"The person (イ) counts the available items (件) to breed the cows (牛)"

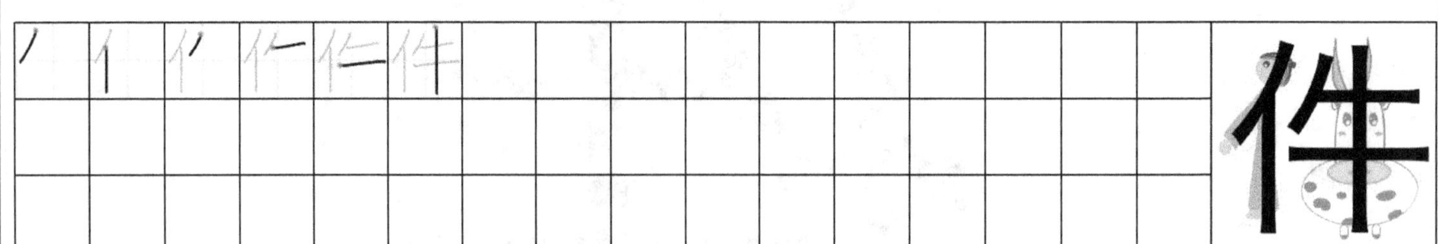

ON (ケン)

じけん 事 件 = Event, affair	じょうけん 条 件 = Conditions, terms

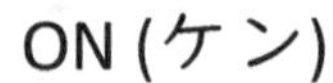

贈 PRESENTS, SEND, AWARD TO

"When you give money (貝) as a present (贈), you are adding layers (曾) to their wealth"

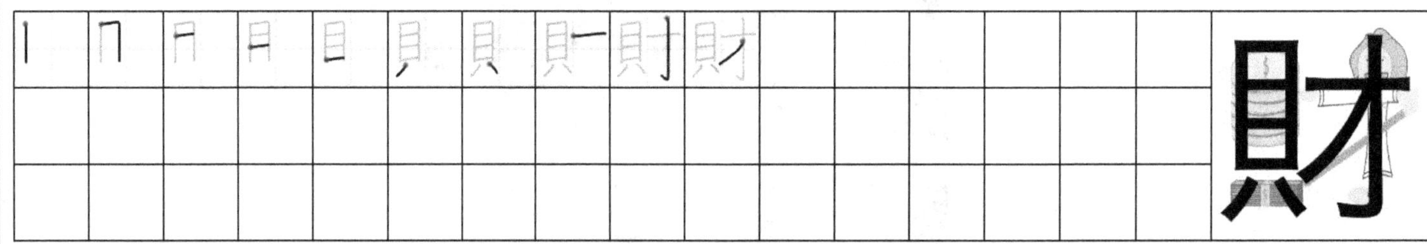

Kun (おく)

おく　もの	おく
贈り物 = Present, gift	贈る = To give to

Note: 曾 was originally layers of baskets, dishes and a steamer on top.

財 WEALTH, PROPERTY, MONEY

"If you are a genius (才) with money (貝) you can build good wealth (財)"

ON (サイ)

ざいさん	さいふ
財産 = Property, fortune	財布 = Purse, wallet

誌 DOCUMENT, RECORDS

"The samurai (士) wrote a document (誌) describing his intentions (志)"

ON (シ)

ざっし
雑誌 = Magazine, journal

志 INTENTION, PLAN, HOPES

"The samurai (士) keeps his intentions (志) in his heart (心)"

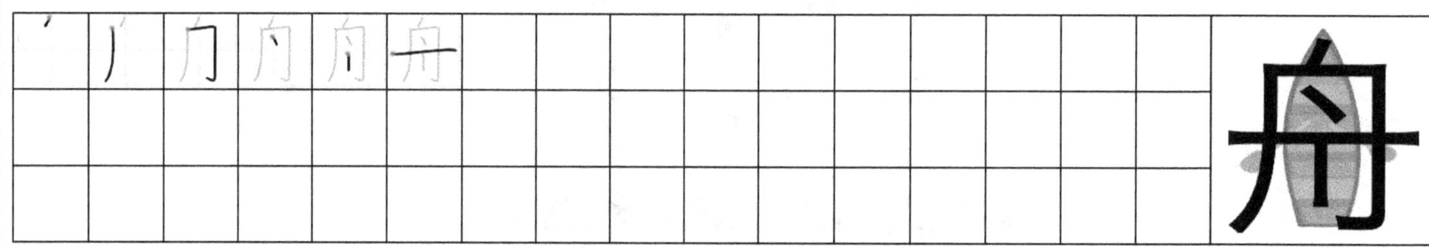

ON (シ)

い し
意志 = Will

舟 SHIP, BOAT

"Just the shape of a boat (舟)"

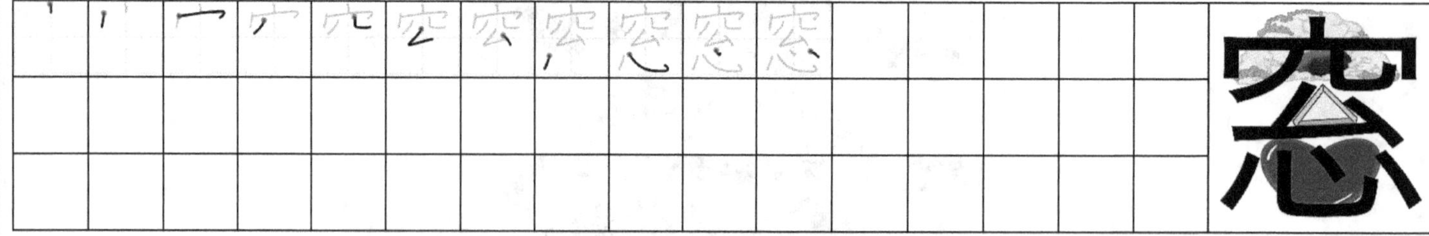

Kun (ふね)

ふね
舟 = Ship, boat

窓 WINDOW, PANE

"This place feels like a cave (穴), so I relax my heart (心) by looking outside the window (窓)"

Kun (まど)

まど	まどぐち
窓 = Window	窓 口 = Ticket window

机 DESK, TABLE

"I make tables (几) and desks (机) with wood (木)"

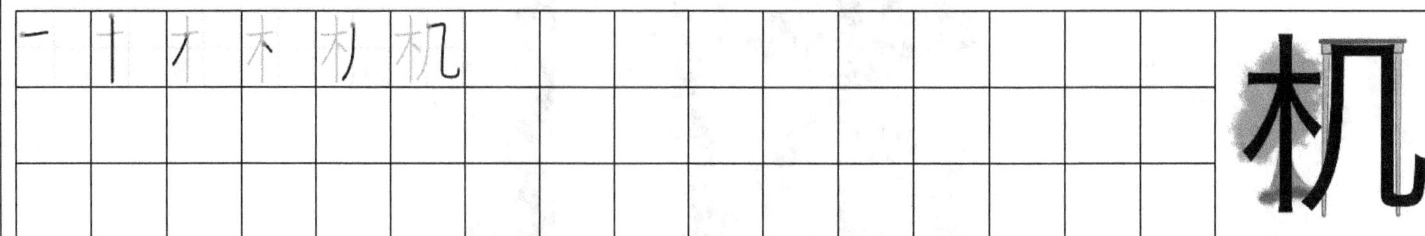

Kun (つくえ)

つくえ
机　= Desk

棒 POLE, ROD, STICK

"Make a pole (棒) out of wood (木) for your harvest offerings (奉)"

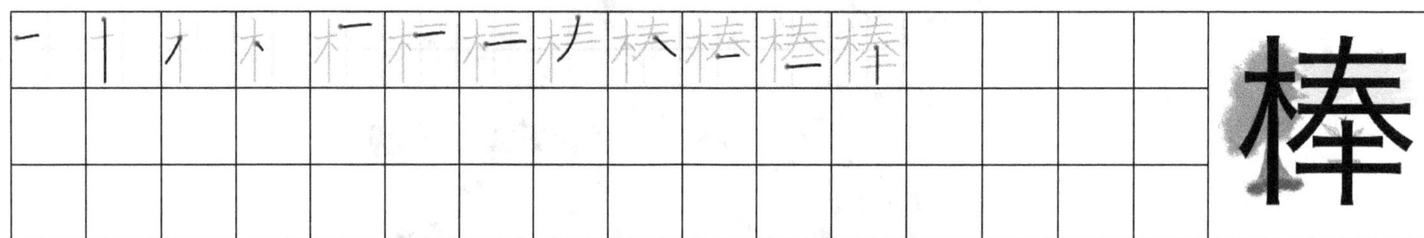

ON (ボウ)

どろぼう
泥　棒　= Thief, burglar

ぼう
棒　= Pole, rod, stick

枚 SHEET OF…, COUNTER (FLAT THIN OBJECTS)

"Hit (攵) the wood (木) in a way that you make thin sheets (枚)"

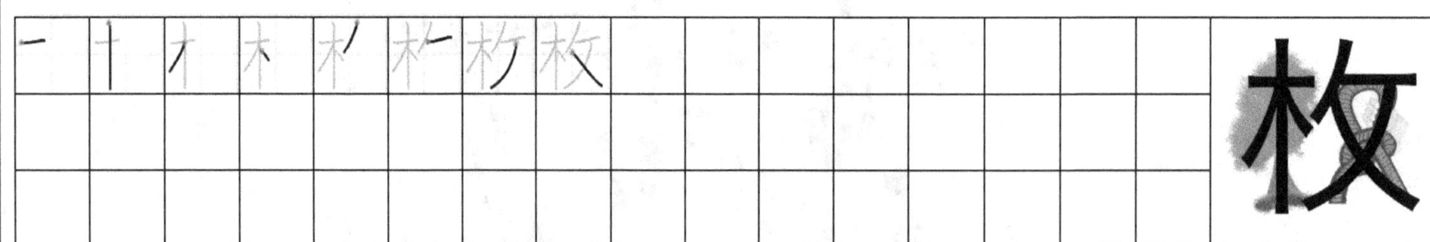

ON (マイ)

まいすう
枚　数　= The number of flat things

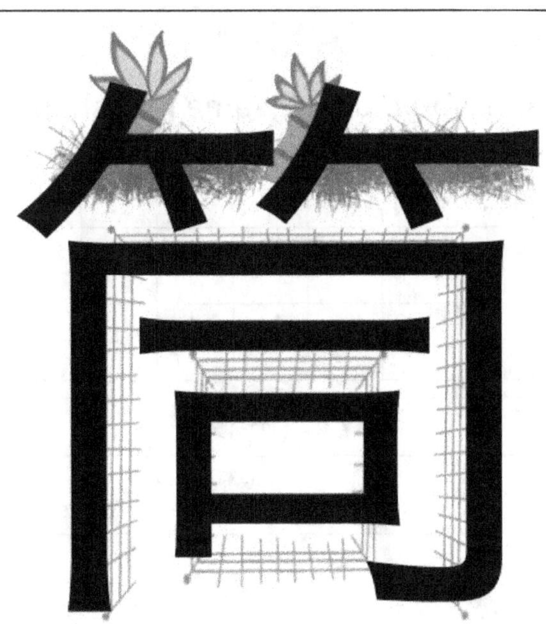

筒 CYLINDER, PIPE, TUBE

"A cylinder (筒) shape would be the same (同) shape of a bamboo (竹)"

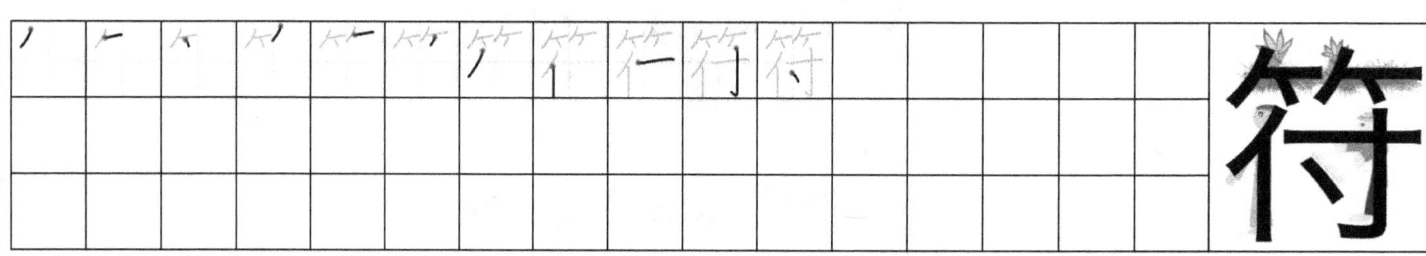

ON (トウ)

すいとう 水 筒 = Water bottle	ふうとう 封 筒 = Envelope

符 TOKEN, SIGN, MARK

"Bamboo (竹) tokens (符) used to be adhered (付) to contracts"

ON (フ)

きっぷ 切 符 = Ticket	ふごう 符 号 = Sign, mark, symbol

封 SEAL, CLOSING

"The ruler measures (寸) and adds a seal (封) to the boundaries of his land (圭)"

ON (フウ)

ふうとう 封 筒 = Envelope

巻 SCROLL, VOLUME, BOOK, ROLL UP, COIL

"Straighten (己) the old scrolls (巻) carefully with your hands (龹), so we can read them"

Kun (まき、ま)

ねまき 寝 巻　= Sleep-wear	ま 巻く = To wind, to coil

郵 MAIL

"I sent in the mail (郵) to the city (β) a plant with dropping leaves (垂)"

ON (ユウ)

ゆうそう 郵 送　= Mailing	ゆうびん 郵 便　= Postal service

Note: A plant with dropping leaves signified something going in a different direction, which is how it was related to mail.

爆 BOMB, BURST OPEN, POP

"A bomb (爆) exploded with violence (暴) and got everything on fire (火)"

ON (バク)

ばくはつ 爆 発　= Explosion, detonation

CHAPTER 5: PLACES & LOCATION

庁	床	宅	宇	境	壁
81	82	83	84	85	86
城	塔	域	署	郊	隅
87	88	89	90	91	92
裏	蔵	劇	段	欧	途
93	94	95	96	97	98
片	奥	頂	軒	挟	河
99	100	101	102	103	104
営	泉				
105	106				

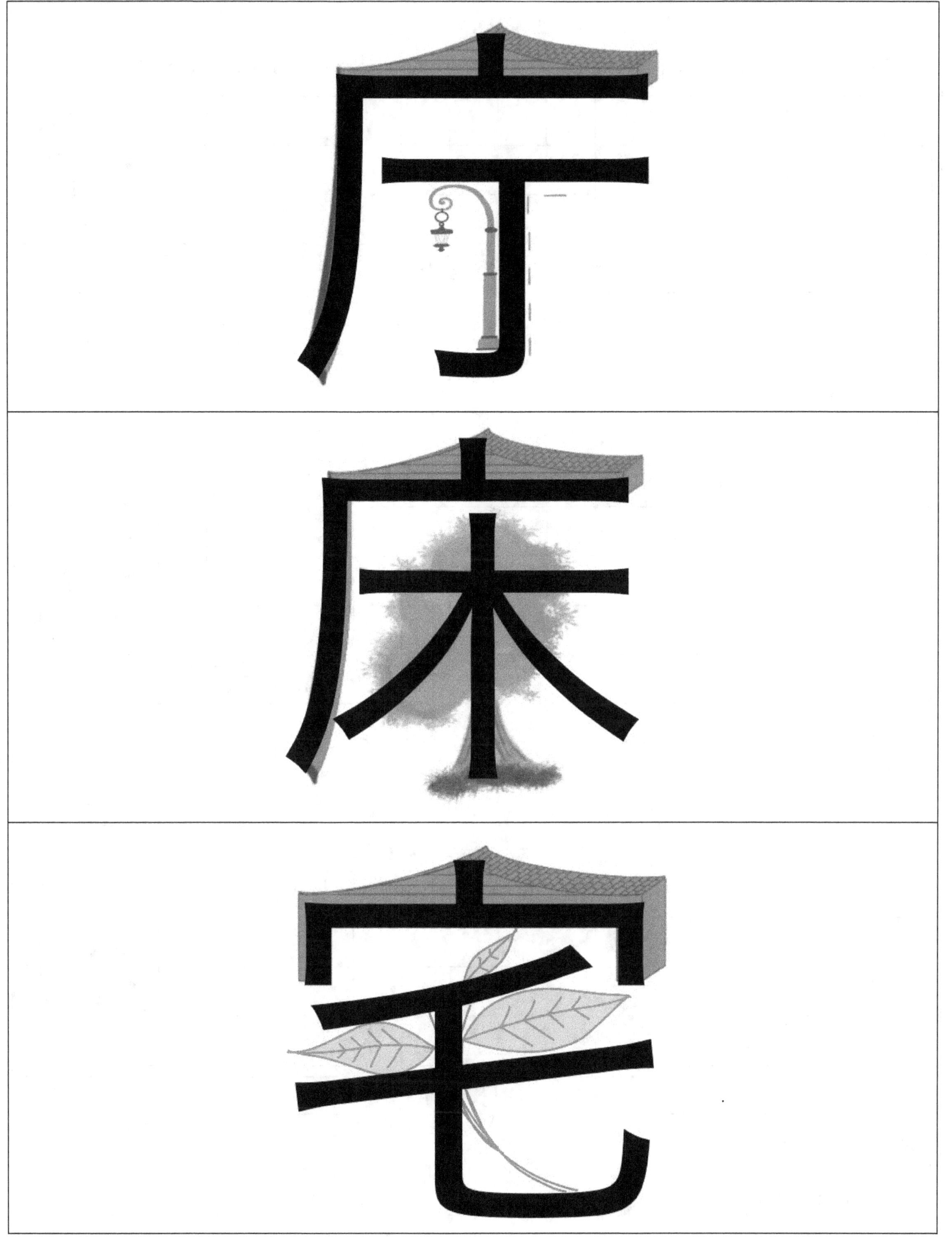

庁 GOVERNMENT OFFICE

"The government office (庁) is located on the same street (丁) as the shelter tent (广)"

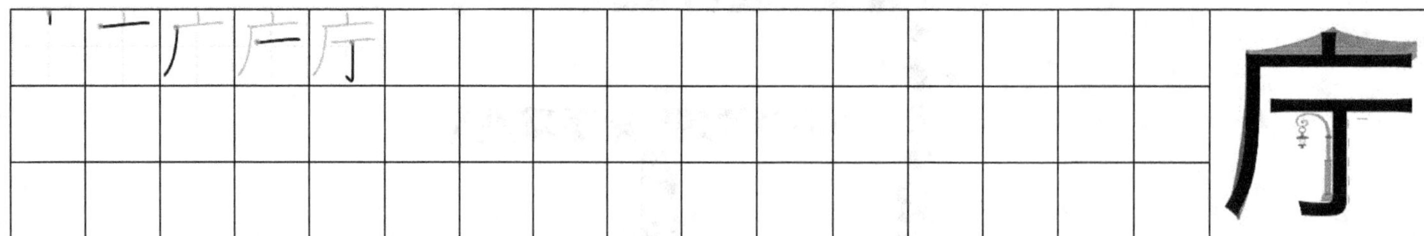

ON (チョウ)	
かんちょう 官 庁 = Government office	けんちょう 県 庁 = Prefectural office

床 BEDDING, FLOOR, PADDING

"The padding (床) inside this tent (广) is made of wood (木)"

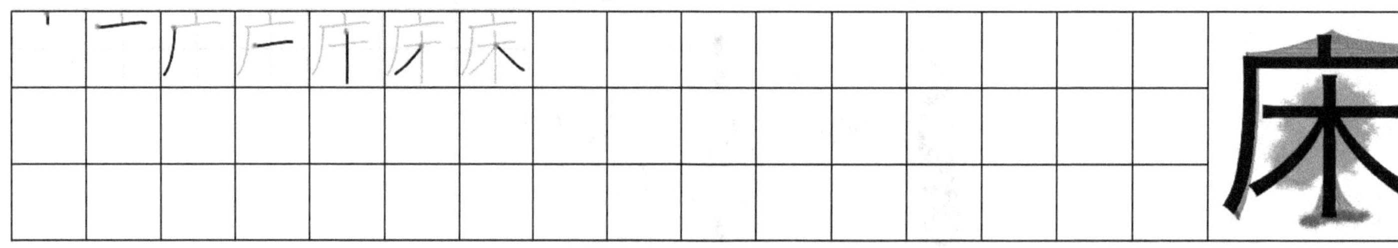

ON (ショウ)	Kun (とこ、ゆか)	
きしょう 起 床 = Getting out of bed, rising	とこ ま 床 の間 = Alcove とこや 床屋 = Barber	ゆか 床 = Floor

Note: The original kanji had the radical of "wooden plank", which makes more sense to its meaning.

宅 HOME, HOUSE, RESIDENCE

"This is the home (宅) to very unique tree leaves (毛)"

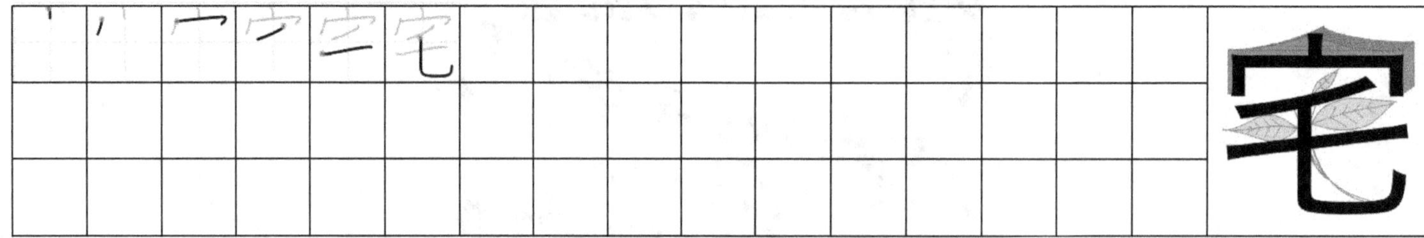

ON (タク)	
きたく 帰 宅 = Returning home	じゅうたく 住 宅 = Residence
じたく 自 宅 = One's home	たく 宅 = House, home

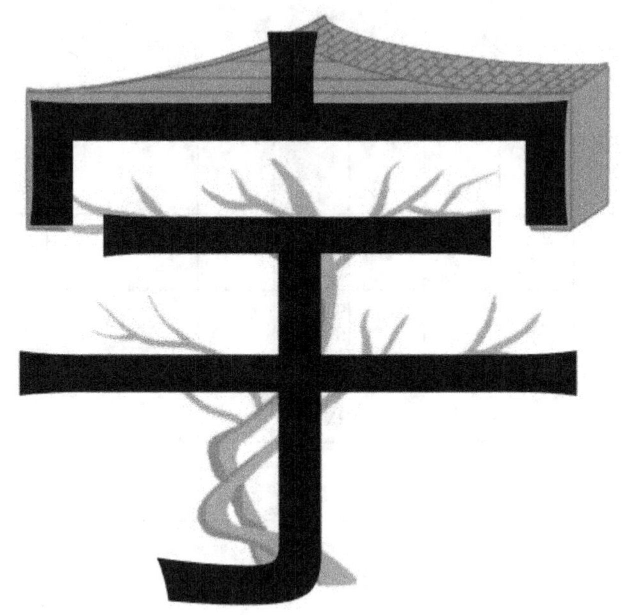

宇

境

壁

宇 ROOF, HOUSE, HEAVEN

"The roof (宇) is dry (干)"

ON (ウ)

うちゅう
宇 宙 = Universe

境 BORDER, BOUNDARY

"Stand (立) on this ground (土) to watch the border (境) so the enemy doesn't get in"

ON (キョウ)		Kun (さかい)
かんきょう 環 境 = Circumstance	こっきょう 国 境 = National border	さかい 境 = Border, boundary
きょうかい 境 界 = Boundary		

壁 WALL, FENCE

"As punishment (辟), criminals would face the wall (壁) with knees on the ground (土) and then get marked with a tattooing needle (辛)"

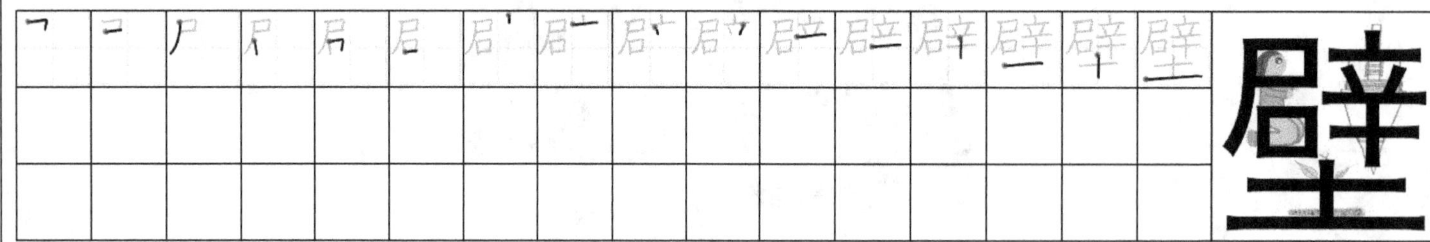

Kun (かべ)

かべ
壁 = Wall

城

塔

城

城 CASTLE

"The castle's (城) grounds (土) are guarded by soldiers with halberds (戈)"

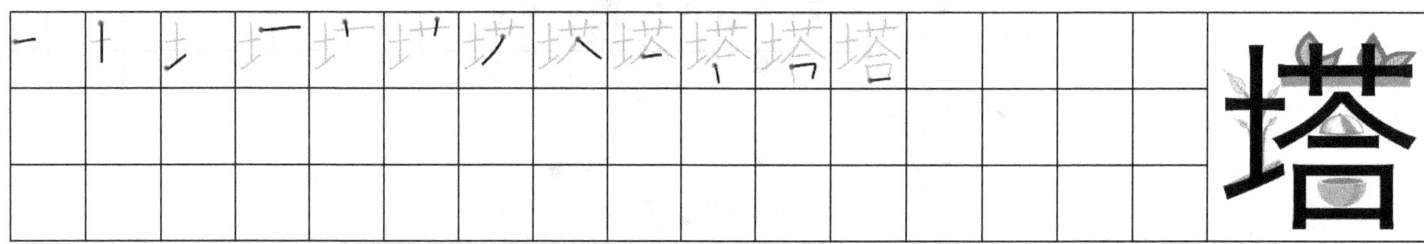

Kun (しろ)

しろ
城　= Castle

塔 TOWER, PAGODA

"The answer (答) lies on the grounds (土) of this tower (塔)"

ON (トウ)

とう
塔　= Tower, pagoda

域 REGION, LIMITS, RANGE

"Use your halberds (戈) around the enclosure (口) of this region (域) to defend its grounds (土)"

ON (イキ)

くいき
区 域　= Limits, boundary

ちいき
地 域　= Area, region

りゅういき
流　域　= (River) basin

署 SIGNATURE, GOVT OFFICE

"The government office (署) is run by a net (罒) of people (者) with political power"

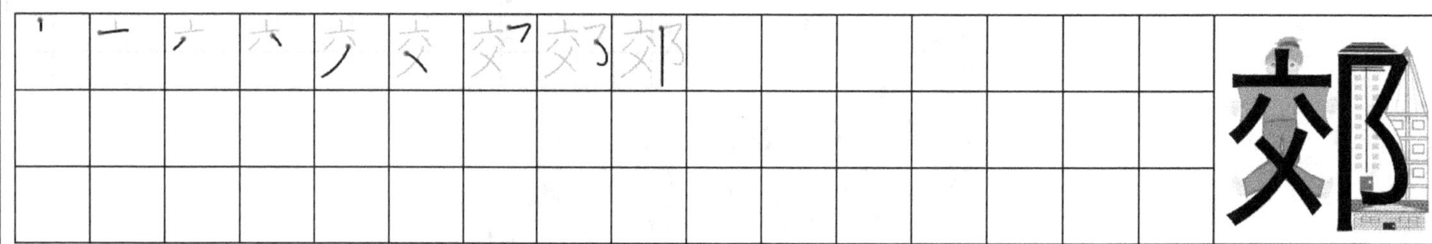

ON (ショ)

しょめい 署 名 = Signature	しょうぼうしょ 消 防 署 = Fire station

郊 OUTSKIRTS, SUBURBS

"People mingle (交) in the outskirts (郊) of the city (阝)"

ON (コウ)

こうがい
郊 外 = Suburb, outskirts

隅 CORNER, NOOK

"The monkey (禺) hides in a corner (隅) at the bottom of the hill (阝)"

Kun (すみ)

すみ
隅 = Corner, nook

"This village (里) believes it is lucky to wear your clothes (衣) the wrong side (裏)"

一 ナ 一 一 一 一 一 一 一 一 一 一 一

Kun (うら)

うら 裏 = Reverse side, back	うらぎ 裏 切る = To betray
うらがえ 裏 返 す = To turn inside out	うらぐち 裏 口 = Backdoor

蔵 STOREHOUSE, HIDE, OWN

"The retainer's (臣) halberd (戈) is inside the storehouse (蔵) by the tall grass (艹)"

一 一 艹 艹 芦 芦 芦 芦 芦 芦 茂 蔵 蔵 蔵

ON (ゾウ)

ちょぞう 貯 蔵 = Storage, preservation	れいぞうこ 冷 蔵 庫 = Refrigerator

劇 DRAMA, PLAY

"The play (劇) is about a pig (豕) fighting a tiger (虍) with a knife (刂)"

一 一 广 广 卢 卢 虍 虐 虏 虏 虏 虏 慮 劇

ON (ゲキ)

えんげき 演 劇 = Play (theatrical)	げきじょう 劇 場 = Theatre
げき 劇 = Drama, play	ひげき 悲 劇 = Tragedy

段

欧

途

段 STEPS, STAIRS

"The hand uses a tool (殳) to forge the stairs (段)"

ON (ダン)

いちだん 一 段 = Much more, more	しゅだん 手 段 = Means, way	ねだん 値 段 = Price, cost
かいだん 階 段 = Stairs	だんかい 段 階 = Grade, state	ふだん 普 段 = Usual, normal

欧 EUROPE

"A lot of countries in Europe (欧) lack (欠) districts (区)"

ON (オウ)

おうべい
欧 米 = Europe & America

途 ROUTE, WAY

"This path (辶) is the route (途) to the surplus (余) of wood (木)"

ON (ト)

ちゅうと 中 途 = In the middle	とちゅう 途 中 = On the way
とたん 途端 = Just (now)	ようと 用 途 = Usefulness

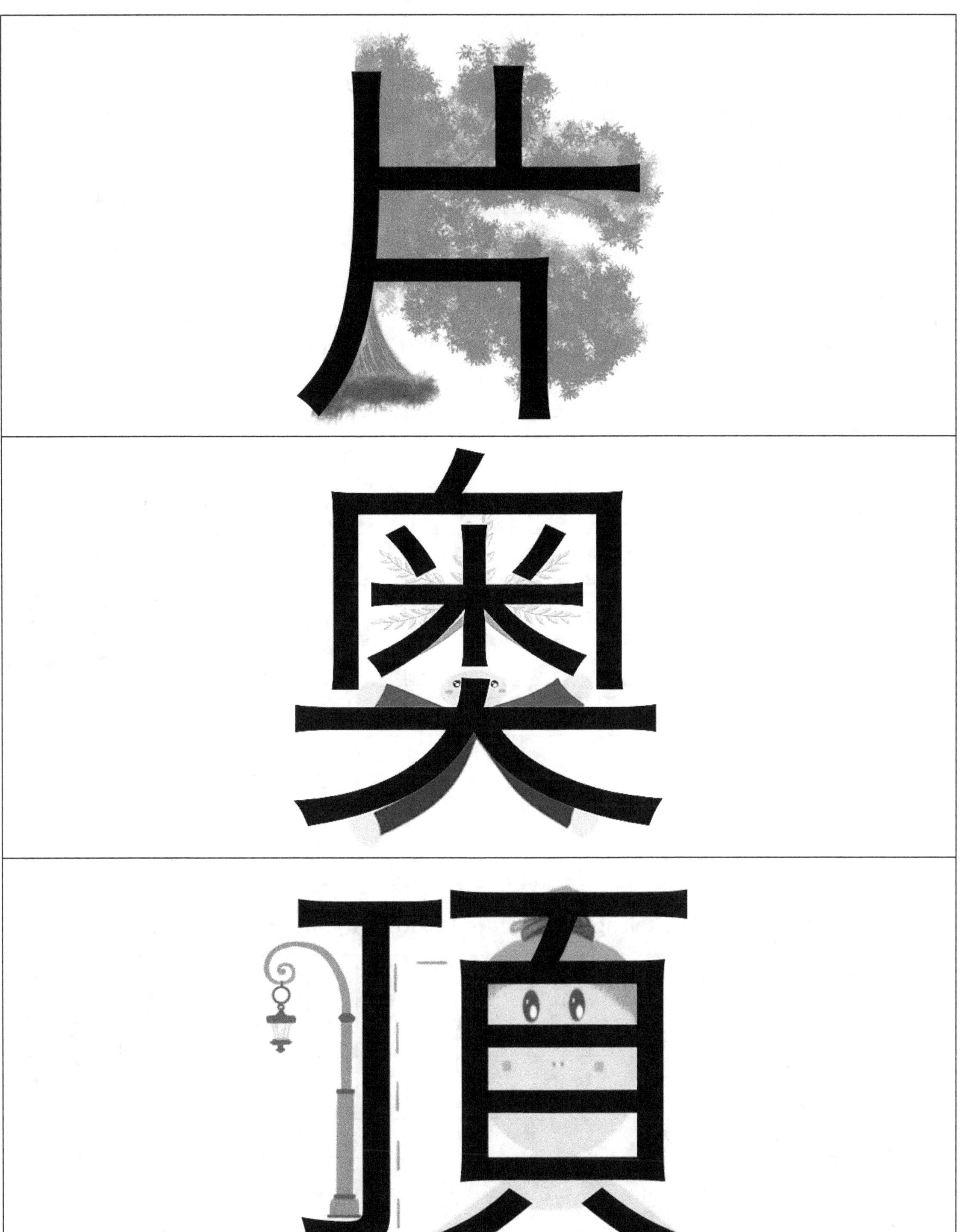

片 ONE-SIDED, RIGHT-SIDE

"The right-side (片) of a tree"

On (ヘン)	Kun (かた)		
はへん 破片 = Fragment	かたかな 片仮名 = Katakana かたづ 片付く = To put in order	かたづ 片付ける = To tidy up かたみち 片道 = One-way (trip)	かたよ 片寄る = To be partial

奥 HEART, INTERIOR

"Big (大) grains of rice (米) used to be offered to the gods in the interior (奥) of the house"

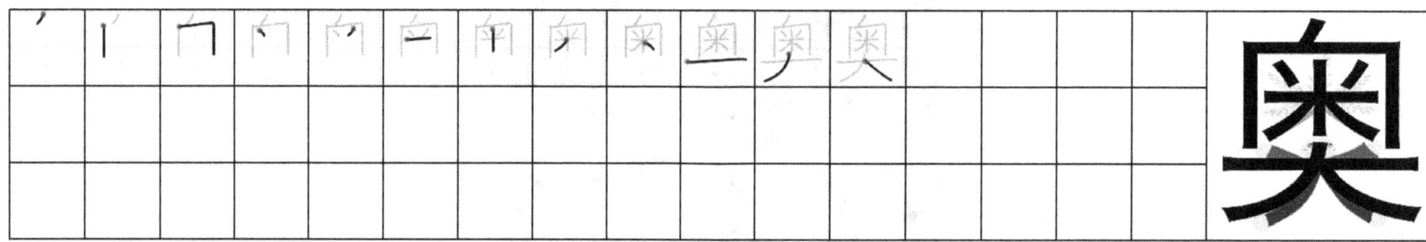

Kun (おく)
おく 奥 = Interior, inner part

頂 PLACE ON THE HEAD, RECEIVE, TOP

"My head (頁) is telling me to get to the top (頂) of that street (丁)"

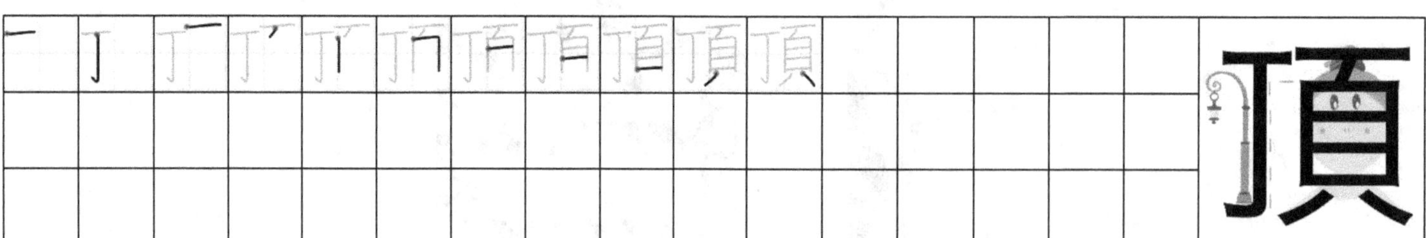

ON (チョウ)	Kun (いただ)
ちょうじょう 頂上 = Top, summit ちょうてん 頂点 = Top, summit	いただ 頂く = To receive

軒 EAVES, COUNTER (HOUSES)

"The eaves (軒) of the cart (車) shall always remain dry (干)"

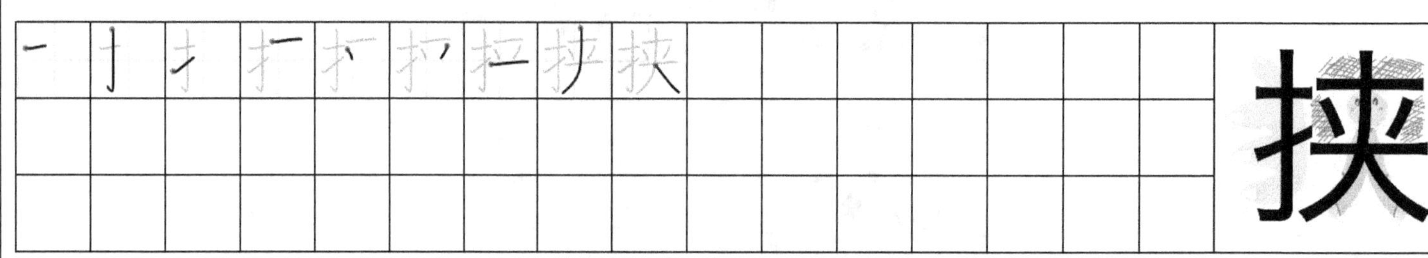

ON (ケン)	Kun (のき)
けん 軒 = Counter for buildings (esp. houses)	のき 軒 = Eaves

挟 PINCH, BETWEEN

"Squeeze (夹) the kids in between (挟) your two hands (扌)"

Kun (はさ)	
はさ 挟 まる = To get between	はさ 挟 む = To interpose, to hold between

河 RIVER

"Is it possible (可) for a river (河) to sing?"

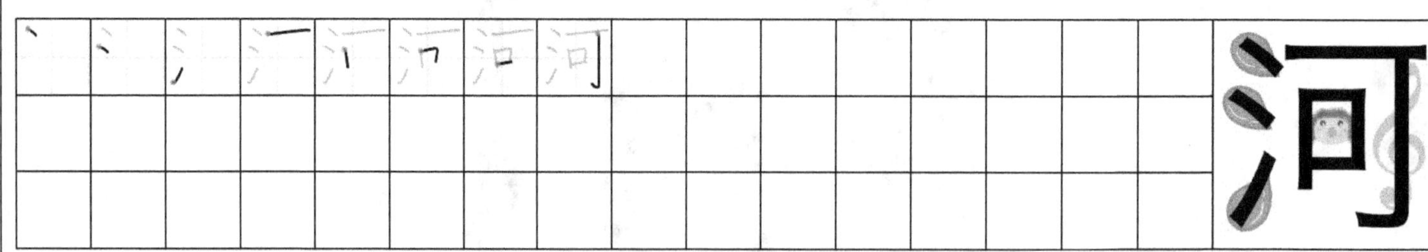

ON (ガ)	Kun (かわ)
うんが 運 河 = Canal, waterway	かわ 河 = River, stream

常

泉

営 OCCUPATION, CONDUCT (BUSINESS)

"Use fire (⺍) to light up the military rooms (呂) as it is time to conduct business (営)"

ヽ	ヽ	⺍	⺍	兯	兴	営	営	営	営	営				

ON (エイ)

えいぎょう 営 業　= Business, trade	けいえい 経 営　= Management

泉 SPRING, FOUNTAIN

"The water (水) in the fountain (泉) looks white (白)"

′	′	冂	白	白	白	泉	泉	泉						

ON (セン) / Kun (いずみ)

おんせん 温 泉　= Hot spring	いずみ 泉　= Spring, fountain

Note: Originally the kanji was water coming out from a cave.

CHAPTER 6: ABSTRACT

修	価	任	賃	貿	資
107	108	109	110	111	112
販	仮	報	職	香	婚
113	114	115	116	117	118
故	務	政	格	権	雑
119	120	121	122	123	124
判	余	券	状	適	況
125	126	127	128	129	130

修 DISCIPLINE, MASTER

"This person (亻) trains discipline (修) by not cutting his hair (彡) or by being hit (攵) when making a mistake"

ON (シュウ)

けんしゅう	しゅうせい
研 修 = Training	修 正 = Amendment, correction
しゅうぜん	しゅうり
修 繕 = Repair, mending	修 理 = Repairing

価 PRICE, VALUE

"The person (亻) sets a high price (価) for the cover (覀)"

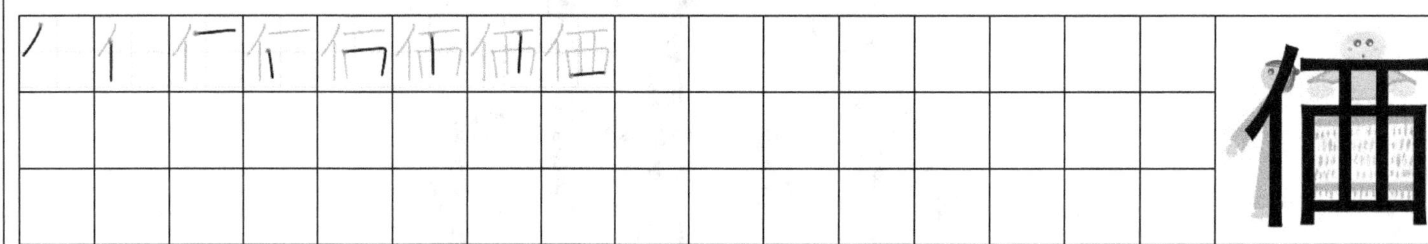

ON (カ)

かかく	こうか	ひょうか
価格 = Price, value	高 価 = High price	評 価 = Valuation, appraisal
かち	ていか	ぶっか
価値 = Value	定 価 = Established price	物 価 = Prices (in general)

任 DUTY, RESPONSIBILITY

"This person's (亻) responsibility (任) is to carry the loaded pole (壬)"

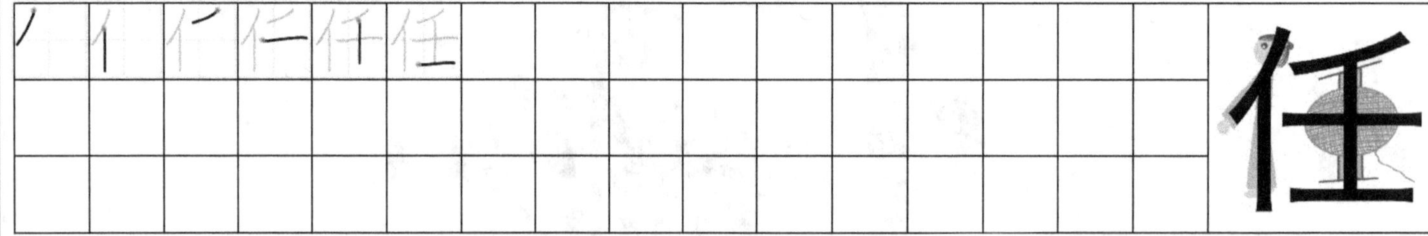

ON (ニン)　　　　　　　　　　Kun (まか)

しゅうにん	まか
就 任 = Inauguration	任 せる = To entrust (e.g. a task) to another
せきにん	
責 任 = Responsibility	

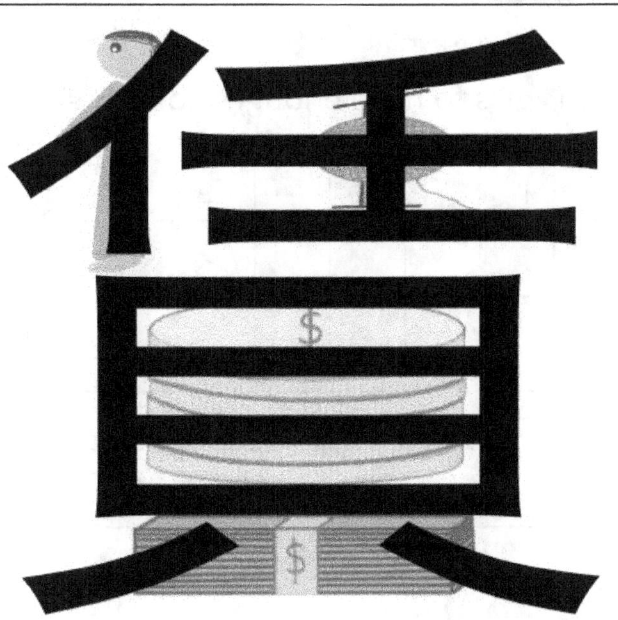

賃 FARE, FEE, HIRE, WAGES

"Your responsibility (任) is to have enough money (貝) to pay the fees (賃)"

ON (チン)

やちん
家賃 = Crime

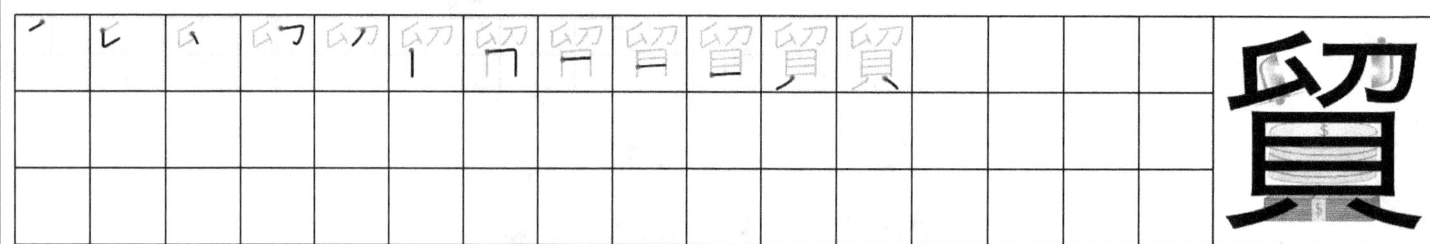

貿 TRADE, EXCHANGE

"In a financial trade (貿) the monies (貝) are divided into two (卯) parts"

ON (ボウ)

ぼうえき
貿易 = Trade (foreign)

Note: The original element for "divide into two" was a representation of an animal cut in half.

資 ASSETS, CAPITAL, FUNDS, RESOURCES

"The next (次) step with money (貝) is growing the capital (資)"

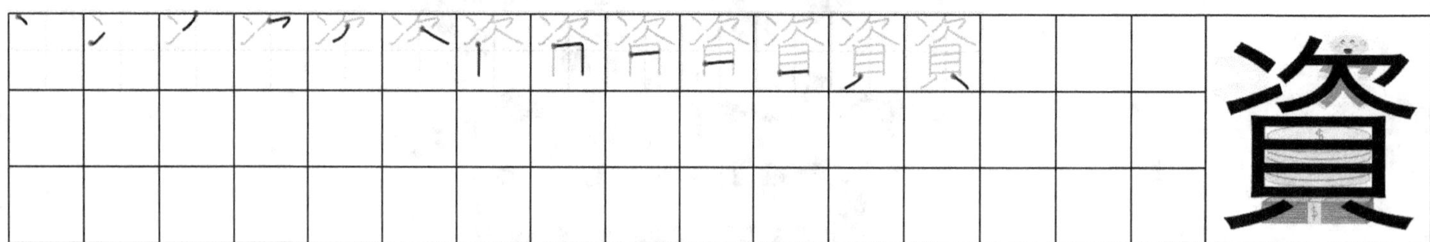

ON (シ)

しげん
資源 = Resources

しほん
資本 = Funds, capital

しりょう
資料 = Materials, data

販 TRADE, MARKETING

"The man against (反) the cliff is trading (販) his money (貝)"

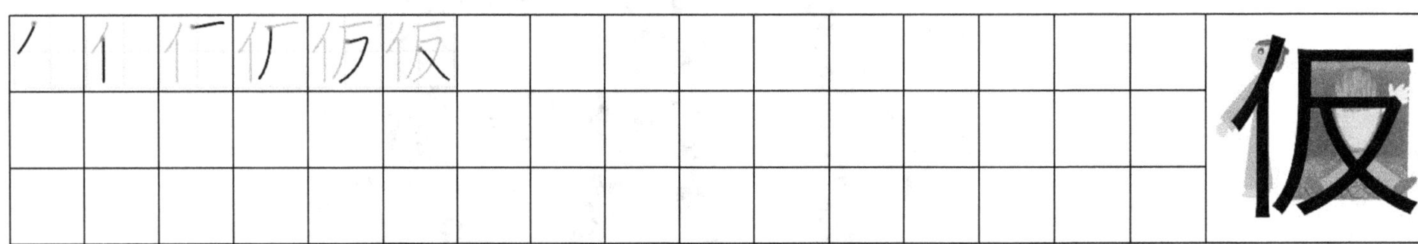

ON (ハン)

はんばい
販 売 = Sale

仮 TEMPORARY, INTERIM

"In the interim (仮), the person (亻) stands against (反) the cliff to attack intruders"

ON (カ)

おく　がな
送 り 仮 名 = Okurigana

かてい
仮 定 = Supposition

ひらがな
平 仮 名 = Hiragana

かたかな
片 仮 名 = Katakana

かな
仮 名 = Kana

ふ　がな
振 り 仮 名 = Furigana

報 REPORT, NEWS, REWARD

"News (報) say that crime is under control (艮), and that is happiness (幸)"

ON (ホウ)

じょうほう
情 報　= Information, (military) intelligence

ほうこく
報 告 = Report, information

でんぽう
電 報 = Telegram

よほう
予 報 = Forecast, prediction

Note: Originally the kanji were handcuffs and someone subduing as a meaning of "to judge"

職

香

婚

職 EMPLOYMENT, WORK

"The soldier's work (職) is to be ready with his halberd (戈) to any sound (音) that his ears (耳) hear"

ON (ショク)

しゅうしょく
就 職 = Finding employment

しょくぎょう
職 業 = Occupation

しょくば
職 場 = Place of work

しょくにん
職 人 = Worker, tradesman

香 SMELL, PERFUME

"The sun (日) helps release the smell (香) of the grain (禾) during harvest season"

ON (コウ)

こうすい
香 水 = Perfume

Kun (かお)

かお
香 り = Aroma, scent

婚 MARRIAGE

"When the sun (日) raises, this woman's (女) family (氏) will celebrate her marriage (婚)"

ON (コン)

けっこん
結 婚 = Marriage

りこん
離 婚 = Divorce

こんやく
婚 約 = Engagement

故 INTENTIONALLY, REASON, CAUSE

"Old (古) customs were followed as norms, otherwise that was a reason (故) to get hit (攵)"

	ON (コ)		Kun (ふる)
じこ 事故 = Accident	こきょう 故 郷 = Home town, birthplace		ふるさと 故 郷 = Home town, birthdplace
こしょう 故 障 = Break-down			

務 TASK, DUTIES

"In war times, the task (務) was to be strong (力) using the halberd (矛) and hitting (攵) the enemies"

	ON (ム)		Kun (つと)
ぎむ 義務 = Duty, obligation	じむ 事務 = Business, office work		つと 務 め = Service, duty
こうむ 公 務 = Official business			つと 務 める = To serve, to work (for)

政 GOVERNMENT, POLITICS

"The government (政) can feel like a whip hitting (攵) us to correct (正) us"

ON (セイ)	
せいじ 政治 = Politics	せいふ 政府 = Government
せいとう 政 党 = Political party	

格 STATUS, RANK, CAPACITY

"Each (各) type of wood (木) has a different capacity (格) for what you can make with it"

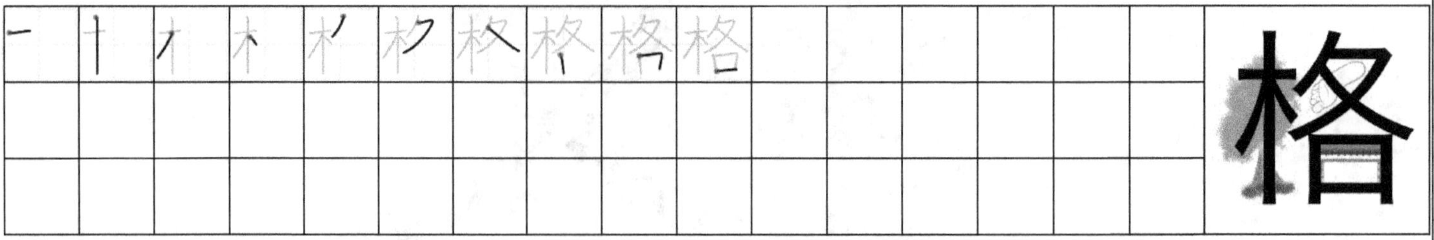

ON (カク)

かかく 価格 = Price, value	ごうかく 合格 = Success	どうかく 同格 = The same rank
かくべつ 格別 = Exceptional	せいかく 性格 = Character, personality	

権 AUTHORITY, POWER

"Small birds (隹) don't have as much authority (権) over nests on trees (木) as big birds do"

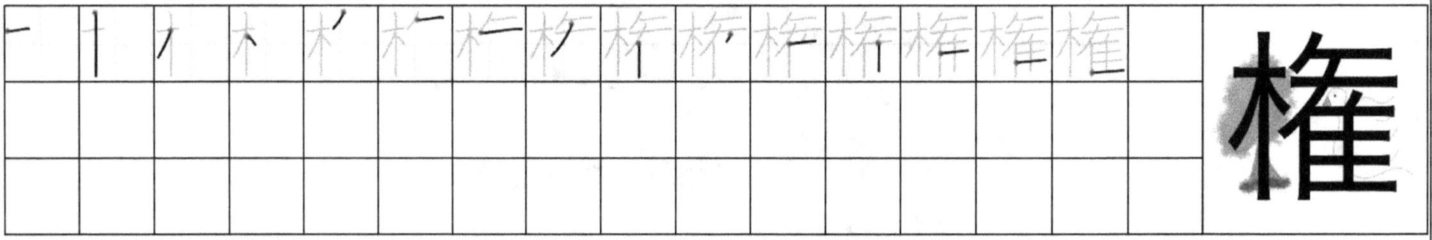

ON (ケン)

けんり
権利 = Privilege, right

雑 MISELLANEOUS

"There are nine (九) miscellaneous (雑) birds (隹) on that tree (木)"

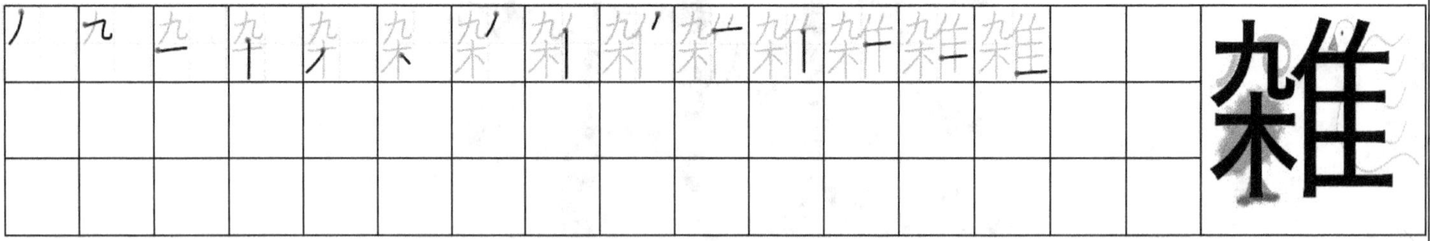

ON (ザツ、ゾウ)

こんざつ 混雑 = Confusion, congestion	ざっし 雑誌 = Magazine, journal	ぞうきん 雑巾 = Dust cloth
ざつおん 雑音 = Noise, interference	ふくざつ 複雑 = Complex	

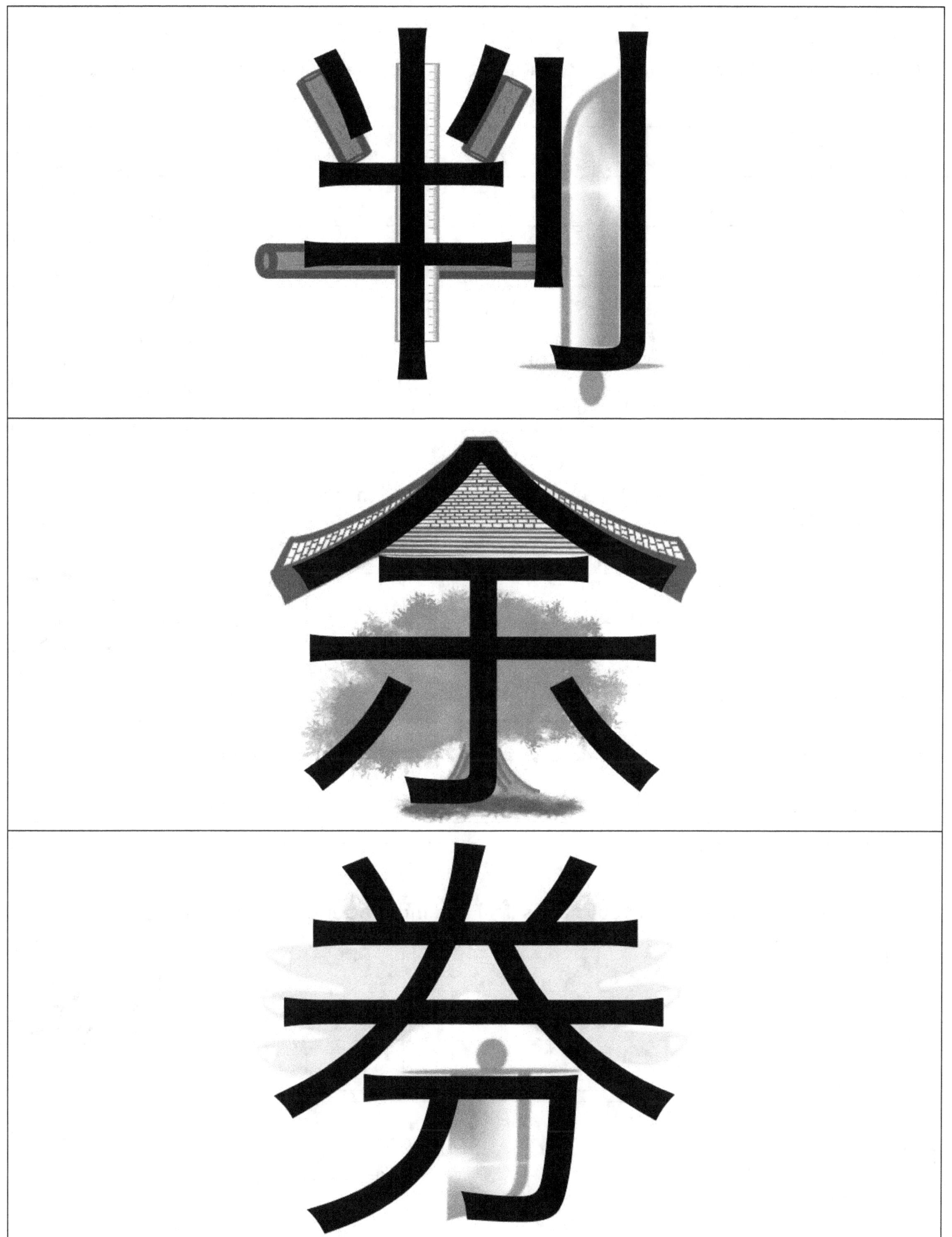

判 JUDGEMENT, STAMP, SEAL

"Contracts were cut in half (半) and given to each party. If the contract was broken, the case was taken to judgement (判)"

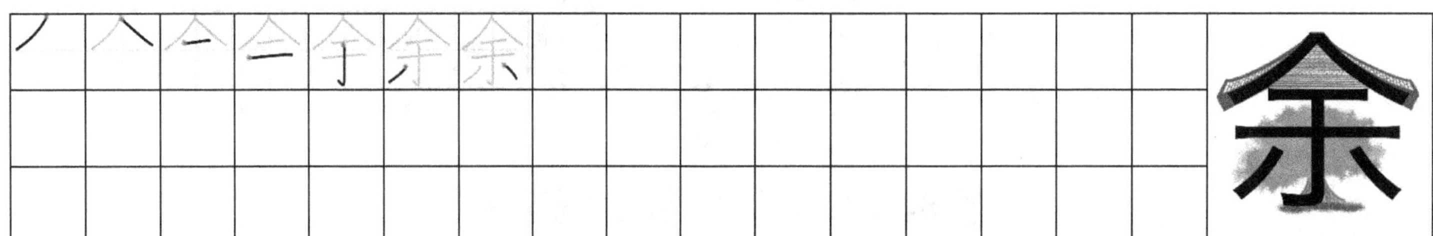

ON (ハン)

さいばん 裁 判 = Trial, judgement	はんこ 判 子 = Seal (signature)	はんだん 判 断 = Decision	ひょうばん 評 判 = Fame, reputation
しんぱん 審 判 = Trial, judgement	はんじ 判 事 = Judge	ひはん 批 判 = Criticism	

余 TOO MUCH, SURPLUS, REMAINDER

"There is too much (余) wood (木) in the house"

ON (ヨ) / Kun (あま)

ON (ヨ)		Kun (あま)
よけい 余 計 = Too much	よぶん 余 分 = Extra, excess	あま 余 り = (Not) very, (not) much
よそ 余所 = Another place	よゆう 余 裕 = Surplus	あま 余 る = To remain, to be left over

券 TICKET, BOND

"Grab a knife (刀) in your hands (龹) and indent our contract bond (券)"

ON (ケン)

ていきけん 定 期 券 = Commuter pass	けん 券 = Ticket, bond, coupon
かいすうけん 回 数 券 = Book of tickets	

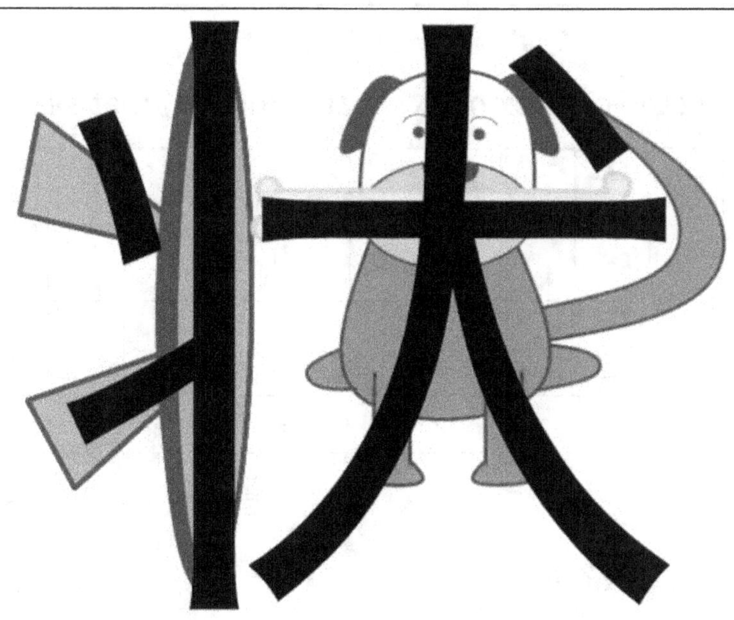

状 STATUS QUO, CONDITIONS

"We are checking the condition (状) of the dog (犬) that's laying on the table (爿)"

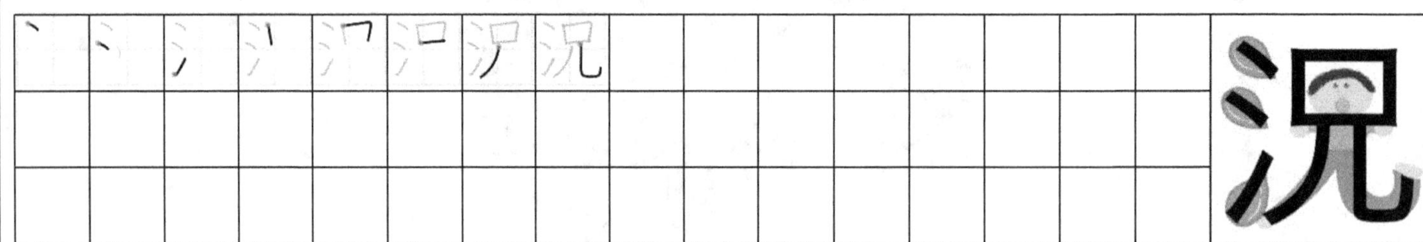

ON (ジョウ)

げんじょう
現 状 = Status quo

しょうじょう
症 状 = Symptoms

じょうきょう
状 況 = Situation, state of affairs

じょうたい
状 態 = Situation

適 SUITABLE, OCCASIONAL

"A legitimate person (商) would guide us through a suitable (適) path (辶)"

ON (テキ)

てきかく
適 確 = Precise, accurate

てきせつ
適 切 = Pertinent, appropriate

てき
適 する = To fit

てきど
適 度 = Moderate

てきとう
適 当 = Fitness

てきよう
適 用 = Applying

かいてき
快 適 = Pleasant

況 CONDITION, SITUATION

"Get some water (氵) to the older brother (兄) to ease his condition (況)"

ON (キョウ)

じょうきょう
状 況 = State of affairs, situation

CHAPTER 7: ABSTRACT PART II

術	禁	際	領	乱	因
131	132	133	134	135	136
効	警	能	補	富	犯
137	138	139	140	141	142
税	幅	党	寸	夢	総
143	144	145	146	147	148

術

禁

際

術 ART, SKILL, TECHNIQUE

"When you go (行) through here, you'll notice how much skill (術) it takes to grow millets (朮)"

ON (ジュツ)

がくじゅつ 学 術 = Science, scholarship	げいじゅつ 芸 術 = (Fine) art
ぎじゅつ 技 術 = Art, technique, technology	しゅじゅつ 手 術 = Surgical operation

禁 PROHIBITION, BAN

"It is prohibited (禁) to enter the altar (示) in the sacred forest (林)"

ON (キン)

きんえん 禁 煙 = No smoking!	きんし 禁 止 = Prohibition

際 OCCASION, EDGE, ADVENTUROUS

"Let's make of this festival (祭) by the hill (阝) an occasion (際) to get close to the gods"

ON (サイ)

こうさい 交 際 = Company, society	じっさい 実 際 = Practical, reality
こくさい 国 際 = International	さい 際 = On the occasion of

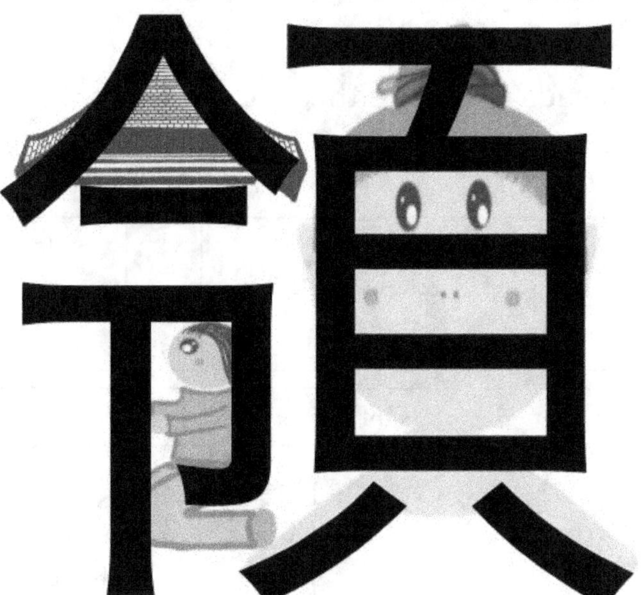

領 JURISDICTION, TERRITORY, REIGN

"The government heads (頁) have the jurisdiction (領) to create laws (令)"

ON (リョウ)

だいとうりょう 大 統 領 = President	りょうじ 領 事 = Consul
ようりょう 要 領 = Outline, point	りょうしゅう 領 収 = Receipt (of money)

乱 RIOT, WAR, DISTURB

"Before a riot (乱) starts, let us correct all those who bend (乚) to the enemy and whose tongues (舌) speak rebellion"

ON (ラン)

こんらん 混 乱 = Disorder, chaos	らんぼう 乱 暴 = Violence

因 CAUSE, FACTOR, DEPEND ON

"Here you can see a big (大) person depending on (因) the enclosure (口) of his bed to sleep"

ON (イン)	Kun (よ)
げんいん 原 因 = Cause, origin	よ 因 る = To come from, to be caused by

効 EFFICACY, MERIT, BENEFIT

"For everything you do, mix (交) intellect and strength (力) and it will show efficacy (効)"

ON (コウ)		Kun (き)
こうか 効果 = Effect	ゆうこう 有効 = Valid	き 効く = To be effective
こうりょく 効力 = Efficacy		

警 ADMONISH, COMMANDMENT

"Please respect (敬) the words (言) of commandment (警)"

ON (ケイ)

けいかん 警官 = Policeman	けいさつ 警察 = Police
けいこく 警告 = Warning, advice	けいび 警備 = Defense, guard

能 TALENT, ABILITY

"The kanji of talent (能) was originally the kanji of bear (熊), hence the similarity"

ON (ノウ)

かのう 可能 = Possible	ちのう 知能 = Intelligence	さいのう 才能 = Talent	げいのう 芸能 = Public entertainment
きのう 機能 = Function	のうりつ 能率 = Efficiency	のうりょく 能力 = Ability	せいのう 性能 = Ability, efficiency

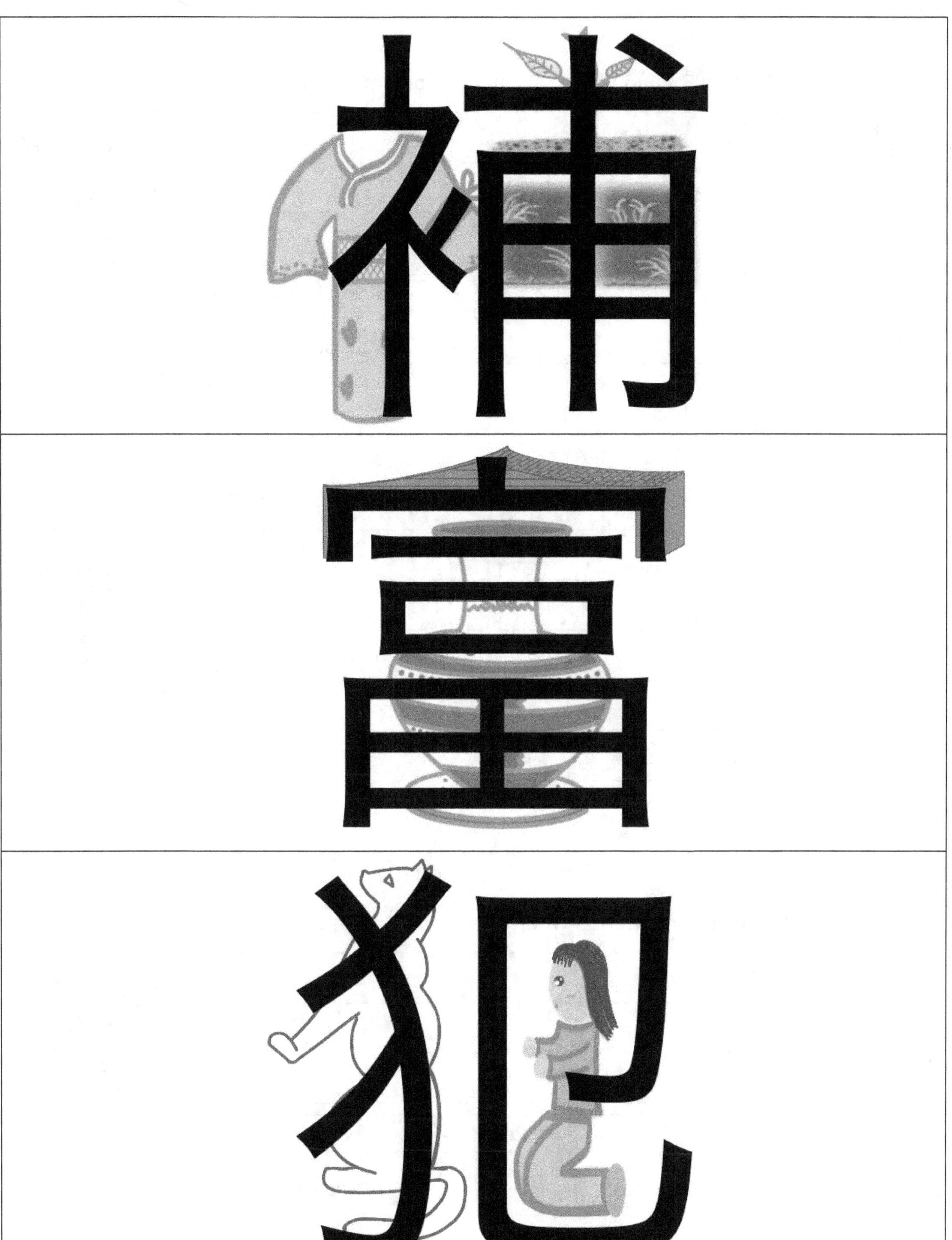

補 SUPPLEMENT, SUPPLY, COMPENSATE

"Clothes (ネ) and plants (甫) are a supplement (補) to humans"

ON (ホ)		Kun (おぎな)
こうほ		おぎな
候補 = Candidate		補 う = To compensate for

富 WEALTH, ABUNDANT

"Under that roof (宀) there are vessels (畐) full of wealth (富)"

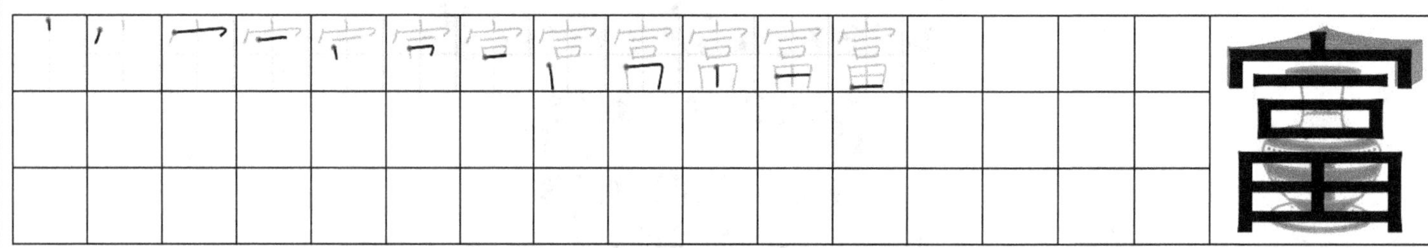

ON (フ)
ほうふ
豊富 = Abundance, plentiful

犯 CRIME, SIN, OFFENSE

"She was kneeling down (㔾) when the beast (犭) committed the crime (犯)"

ON (ハン)	
はんざい	ぼうはん
犯罪 = Crime	防犯 = Prevention of crime
はんにん	
犯人 = Offender	

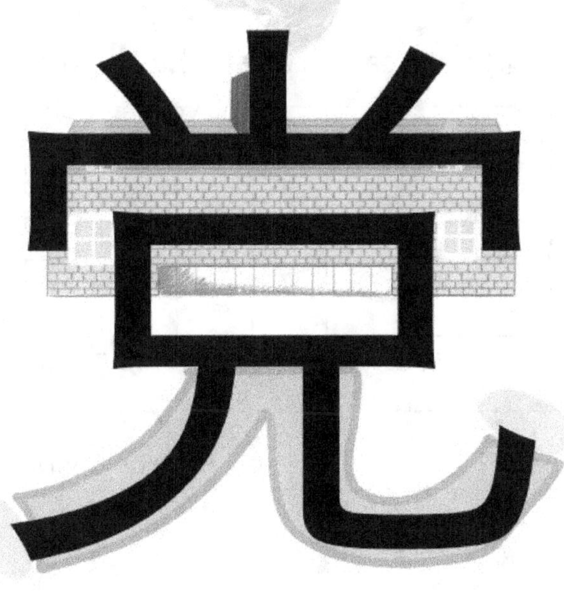

税 TAX, DUTY

"The older brother (兄) pays the taxes (税) of the grain (禾) harvest"

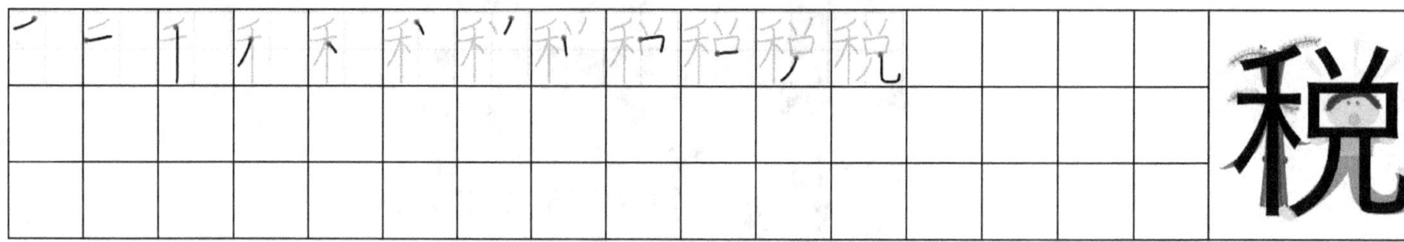

ON (ゼイ)

かぜい
課税 = Taxation

ぜいかん
税 関 = Customs house

ぜいきん
税 金 = Tax, duty

めんぜい
免 税 = Tax exepmtion

幅 WIDTH, HANGING SCROLL

"Make the cloth (巾) of enough width (幅) to cover the wine container (畐)"

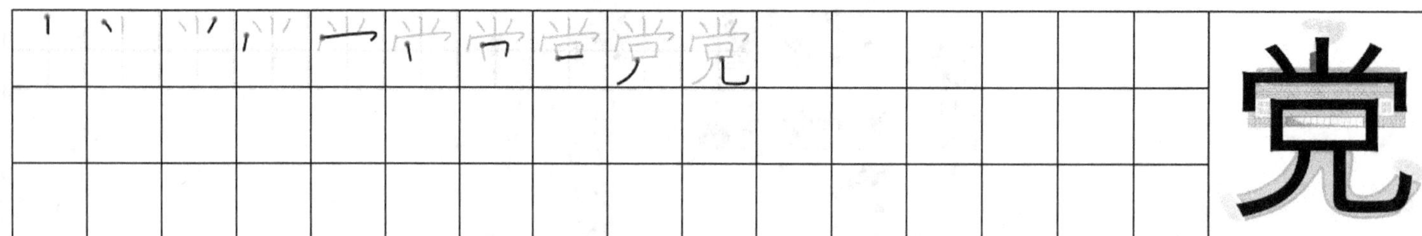

Kun (はば)

はば
幅 = Width

党 PARTY, FACTION, CLIQUE

"A high status (尚) political party (党) has high end members"

ON (トウ)

せいとう
政 党 = (member of) political party

とう
党 = Party (political)

寸

夢

総

寸 MEASUREMENT, TENTH OF A SHAKU

"These measurements (寸) were made with a ruler"

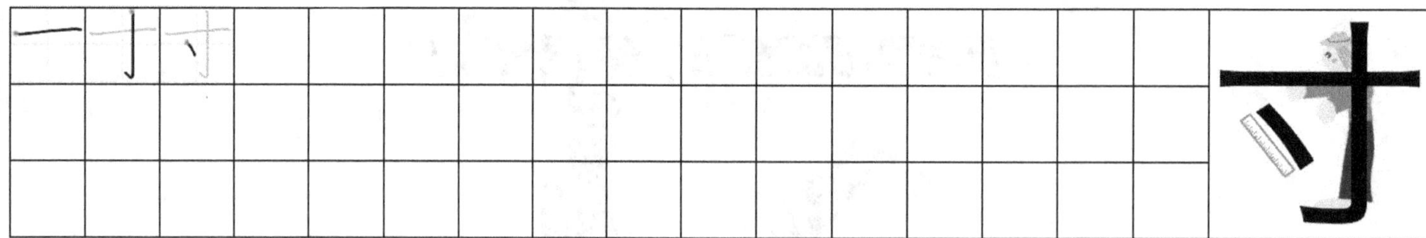

ON (スン)

すんぽう
寸 法 = Measurement, size, dimension

夢 DREAM, VISION

"You cover (冖) your eyes (罒) at night (夕) to sleep well and have sweet dreams (夢)"

ON (ム)	Kun (ゆめ)

むちゅう
夢 中 = Ecstasy

ゆめ
夢 = Dream

総 WHOLE, GENERAL, FULL

"My whole (総) heart (心) is broken and sewn together by threads (糸)"

ON (ソウ)

そうりだいじん
総 理 大 臣 = Prime minister

CHAPTER 8: FEELINGS

恥	恵	怒	志	悩	憎
149	150	151	152	153	154
績	情	精	眠	罪	非
155	156	157	158	159	160
疲	痛	勢	圧	互	湿
161	162	163	164	165	166
技	批	独	欲	専	敬
167	168	169	170	171	172

恥

恵

怒

恥 SHAME, DISHONOR

"When you feel shame (恥), your ears (耳) become red, and your heart (心) rate increases"

Kun (は)

は
恥ずかしい = Ashamed, embarrassing

恵 FAVOR, BLESSING, GRACE

"Be the grace (恵) of your heart (心) all around you, like a thread in a spindle (亩)"

ON (ケイ、エ)	Kun (めぐ)
おんけい 恩 恵 = Grace, favor ちえ 知恵 = Wisdom, wit, sagacity	めぐ 恵 まれる = To be blessed with

怒 ANGRY, BE OFFENDED

"After the mistreatment, the slave's (奴) heart (心) became very angry (怒)"

Kun (おこ)

おこ
怒 る = To get angry, to be angry

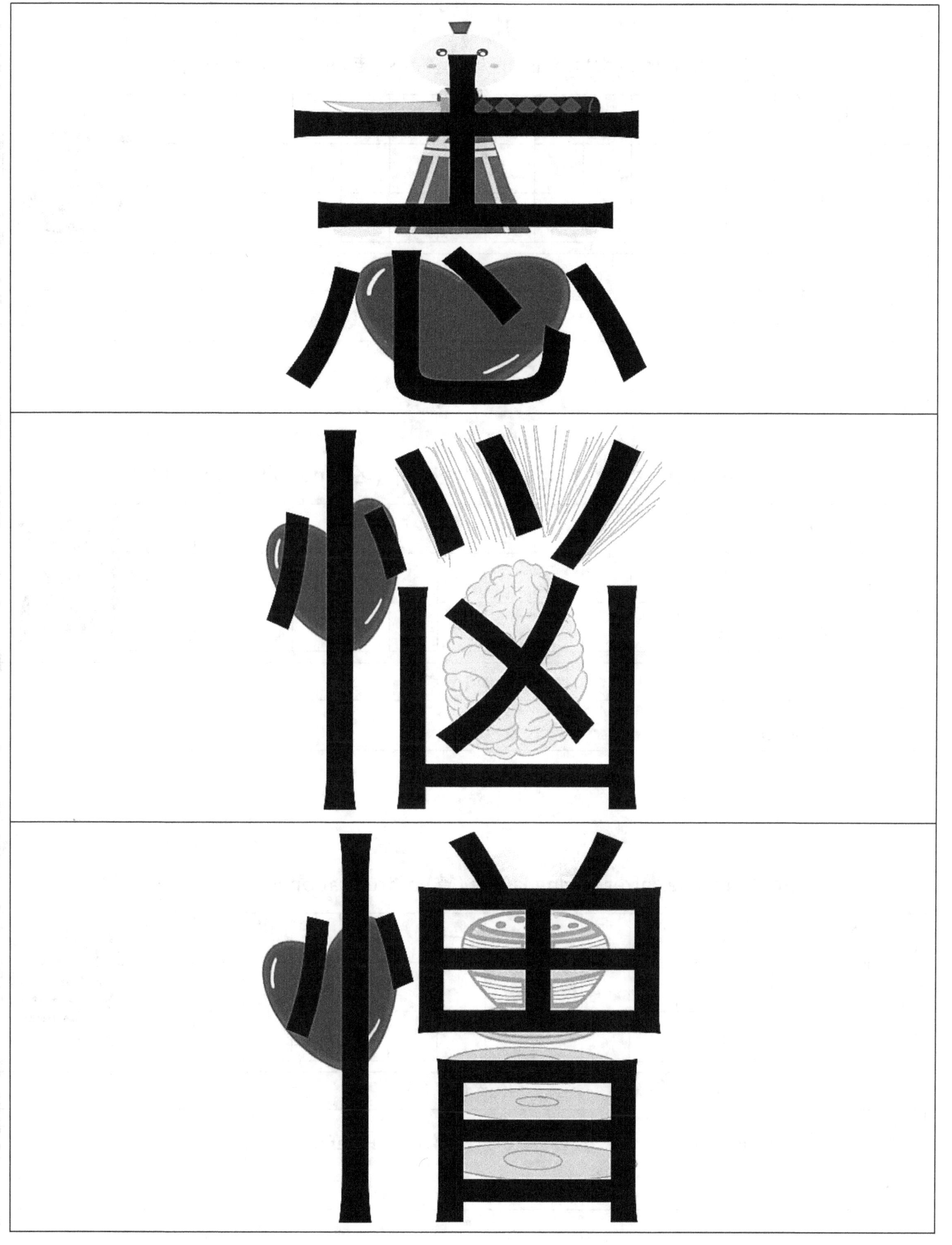

志 INTENTION, PLAN, HOPES

"The samurai (士) holds his intentions (志) in his heart (心)"

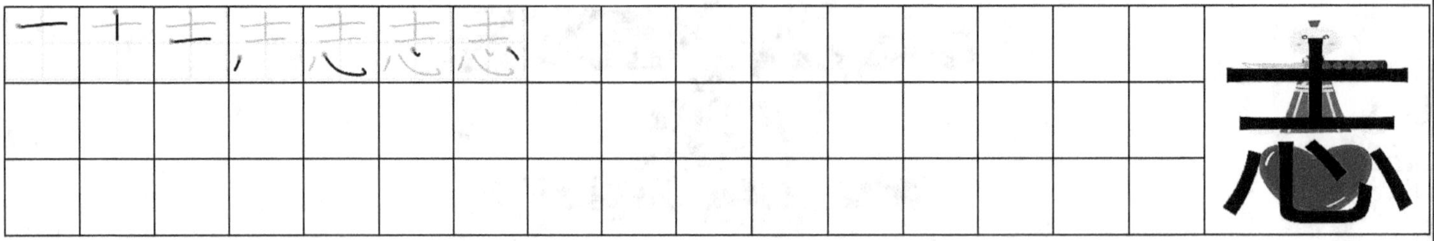

ON (シ)

いし
意志 = Will, intention

悩 TROUBLE, WORRY, IN PAIN

"Troubles (悩) are very painful to the brain (囟) and to the heart (忄)"

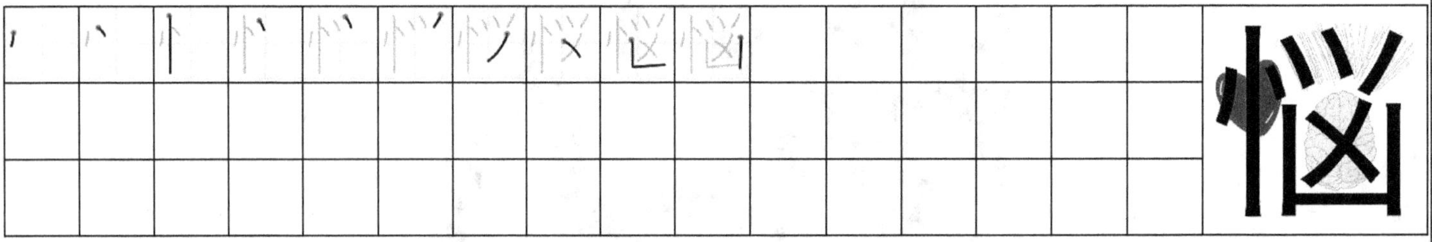

Kun (なや)

なや
悩 む = To be worried

憎 HATE, DETEST

"Hate (憎) comes after having layers (曾) of frustration in your heart (忄)"

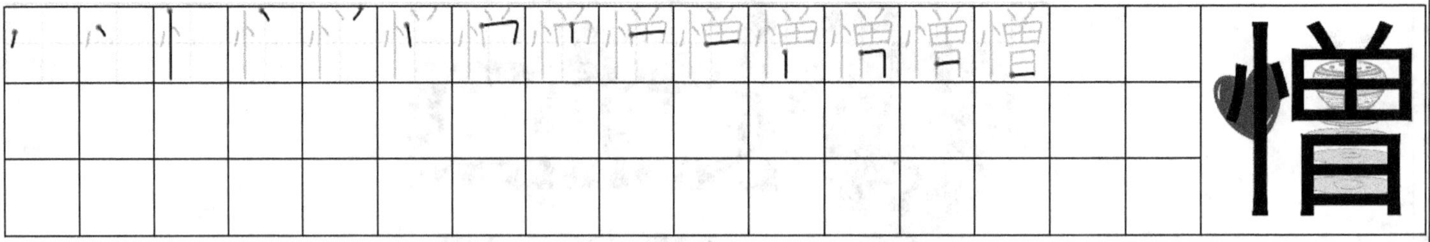

Kun (にく)

にく
憎 らしい = Hateful

にく
憎 む = To hate

にく
憎 い = Hateful, poor-looking

績 ACHIEVEMENTS, EXPLOITS

"When you are responsible (責) of threading (糸) your own path, your achievements (績) are great"

ON (セキ)

こうせき	じっせき	せいせき
功 績 = Merit, meritorious deed	実 績 = Achievements	成 績 = Results, grades

情 FEELINGS, EMOTION, PASSION

"New emotions (情) in one's heart (忄) can be as refreshing as blue (青) moon"

ON (ジョウ)

じじょう	かんじょう	ゆうじょう	じゅんじょう
事 情 = Circumstances	感 情 = Emotion	友 情 = Fellowship	純 情 = Pure heart
じょうほう	くじょう	あいじょう	ひょうじょう
情 報 = Information	苦 情 = Complaint	愛 情 = Affection	表 情 = Facial expression

精 EXCELLENCE, VITALITY, GHOST

"The excellence (精) of rice grains (米) depends on how green (青) the plant looks"

ON (セイ)

せいしん	せいぜい
精 神 = Mind, soul	精 々 = At the most

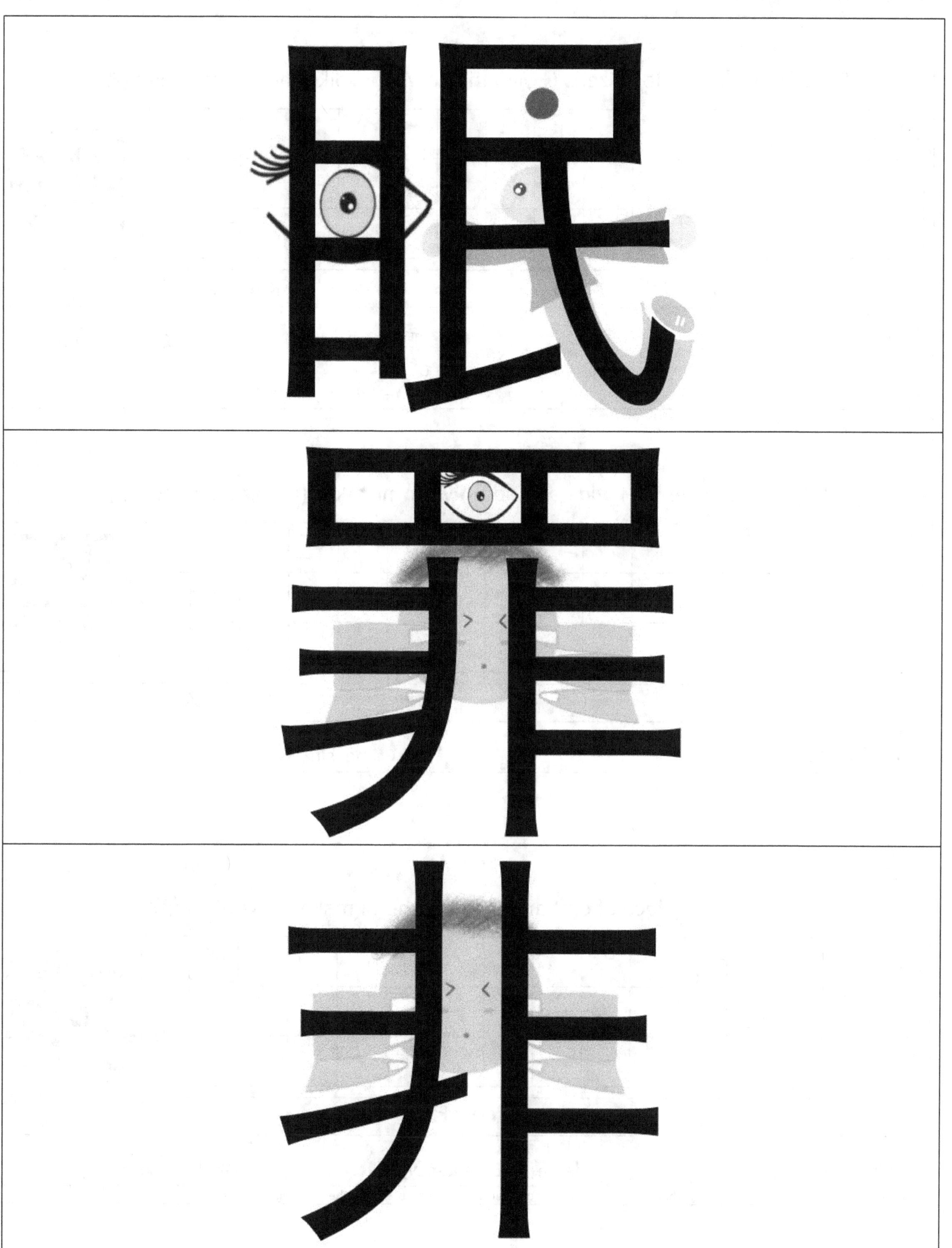

眠 SLEEP, DROWSY

"The eyes (目) of the citizens (民) in this town look like they never sleep (眠)"

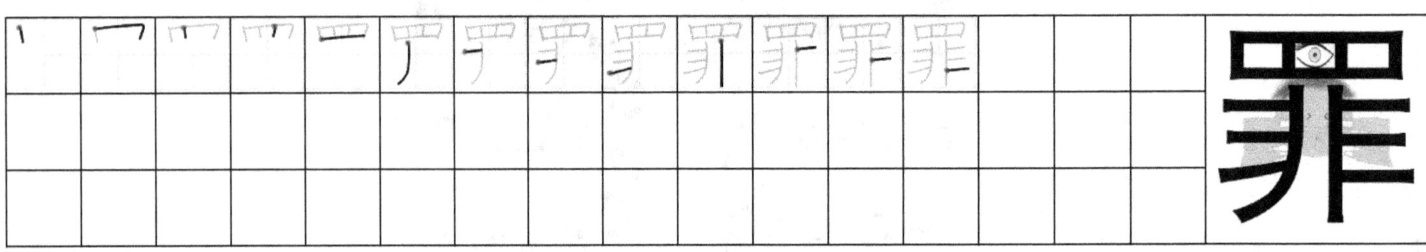

ON (ミン)	Kun (ねむ)	
すいみん 睡 眠 = Sleep	いねむ 居 眠 り = Dozing ねむ 眠 い = Sleepy, drowsy	ねむ 眠 る = To sleep

罪 CRIME, SIN, GUILT

"Open your eyes (罒) wide and admit your mistakes (非) and crimes (罪)"

ON (ザイ)	Kun (つみ)
はんざい 犯 罪 = Crime	つみ 罪 = Crime, sin

非 MISTAKE, INJUSTICE

"I cover my face of embarrassment when I make a mistake (非)"

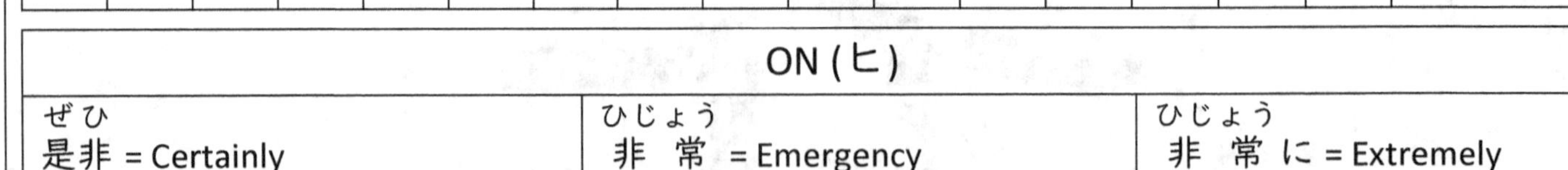

ON (ヒ)		
ぜひ 是非 = Certainly	ひじょう 非 常 = Emergency	ひじょう 非 常 に = Extremely

Note: The kanji was originally two wings that were never together or against each other, therefore the meaning of "no good"

疲 EXHAUSTED, TIRE, WEARY

"I'm so tired (疲) that I feel the pain (疒) all over my skin (皮)"

Kun (つか)	
つか 疲 れ = Tiredness	つか 疲 れる = To get tired

痛 PAIN, HURT, DAMAGE

"I'm in pain (痛) when I have to use the stairs to pass through (甬)"

ON (ツウ)	Kun (いた)
くつう 苦痛 = Agony	いた 痛 い = Painful
ずつう 頭痛 = Headache	いた 痛 み = Pain, ache

勢 FORCES, ENERGY

"All his energy (勢) and strength (力) go into planting (埶) and harvesting"

ON (セイ)	Kun (いきお)
おおぜい 大 勢 = Great number of people	いきお 勢 い = Force, vigor
しせい 姿 勢 = Attitude, posture	

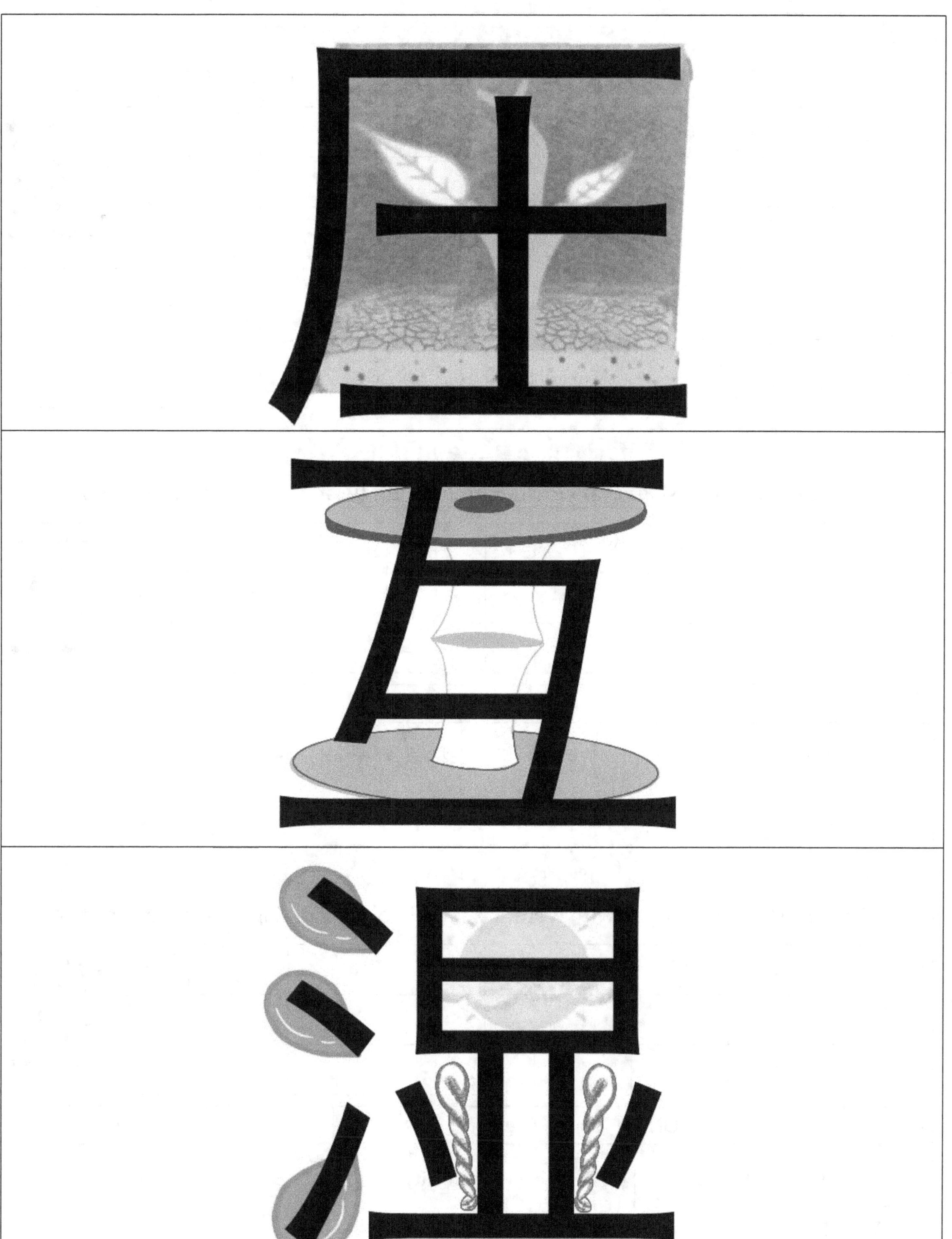

圧 PRESSURE, OVERWHELM

"The cliff (厂) puts pressure (圧) on the ground (土) below"

一 丆 厂 圧 圧

ON (アツ)

あっしゅく 圧 縮 = Compression, pressure	けつあつ 血 圧 = Blood pressure
きあつ 気 圧 = Atmospheric pressure	

互 MUTUALLY, RECIPROCALLY

"A tool having two sides that would mutually (互) twist a thread to make a rope"

一 匚 丂 互

ON (ゴ) | Kun (たが)

ON (ゴ)	Kun (たが)
そうご 相 互 = Mutual	たが お 互 い = Each other たが 互 い = Mutual

湿 DAMP, WET, MOIST

"The silk (㢱) got wet (湿) with water (氵), and now it is drying under the sun (日)"

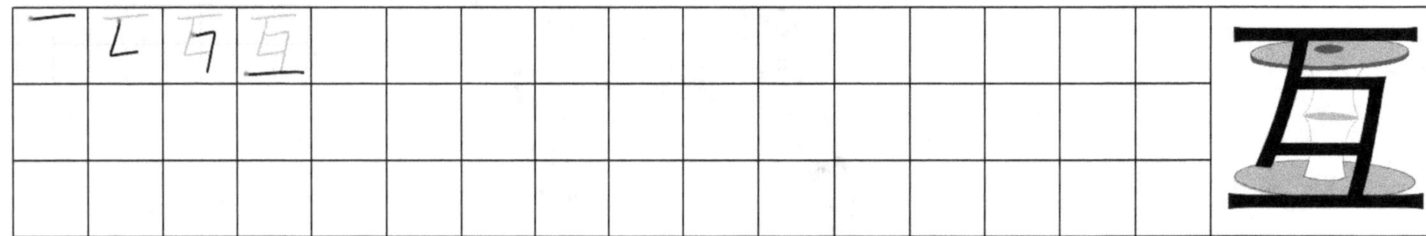

ON (シツ) | Kun (しめ)

ON (シツ)		Kun (しめ)
しっけ 湿 気 = Moisture, humidity	しつど 湿 度 = Level of humidity	しめ 湿 る = To be wet, to be damp
しっき 湿 気 = Moisture, humidity		

技

批

独

技 SKILL, ART, CRAFT, VOCATION

"I use my hands (扌) to turn twigs (支) into art (技)"

ON (ギ)

えんぎ
演 技 = Acting, performance

ぎし
技師 = Engineer, technician

ぎじゅつ
技 術 = Art, technique

きょうぎ
競 技 = Match, contest

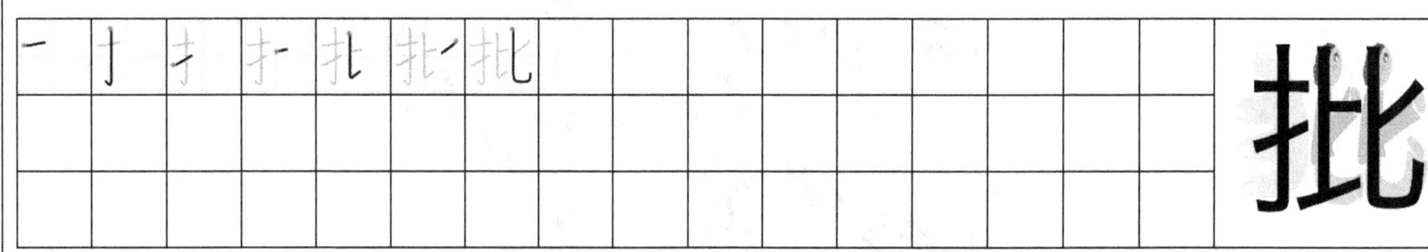

批 CRITICISM, STRIKE

"Criticism (批) happens when you use your hands (扌) to compare (比) others"

ON (ヒ)

ひはん
批 判 = Criticism

ひひょう
批 評 = Commentary, criticism

独 SINGLE, ALONE, GERMANY

"Some beasts (犭) and even insects (虫) would do anything to eat alone (独)"

ON (ドク)

どくしん
独 身 = Unmarried

どくとく
独 特 = Peculiarity

どくりつ
独 立 = Independence

Kun (ひと)

ひと
独 り = Alone, unmarried

ひと　ごと
独 り 言 = Monologue

欲

尊

敬

欲 LONGING, GREED, DESIRE

"A desire (欲) begins when you are lacking (欠) something, and everything feels like an empty valley (谷)"

ON (ヨク)	Kun (ほ)
しょくよく 食 欲 = Appetite (for food) よくば 欲 張り = Avarice, greed	ほ 欲しい = Wanted, wished for

専 SPECIALTY, EXCLUSIVE

"His specialty (専) is measuring (寸) the yarn and putting it in a spindle (甫)"

ON (セン)	
せんこう 専 攻 = Major subject, special study せんせい 専 制 = Despotism, autocracy	せんもん 専 門 = Specialty

敬 RESPECT, HONOR

"When the shepherd (苟) whips (攵), the sheep respect (敬) the commands"

ON (ケイ)		Kun (うやま)
けいい 敬 意 = Respect けいご 敬 語 = Honorific	そんけい 尊 敬 = Respect, esteem	うやま 敬 う = To show respect

CHAPTER 9: ADJECTIVES

紅	永	巨	狭	甘	辛
173	174	175	176	177	178
危	険	恐	忙	快	怖
179	180	181	182	183	184
尊	軟	善	柔	異	硬
185	186	187	188	189	190
難	確	豊	濃	汚	涼
191	192	193	194	195	196

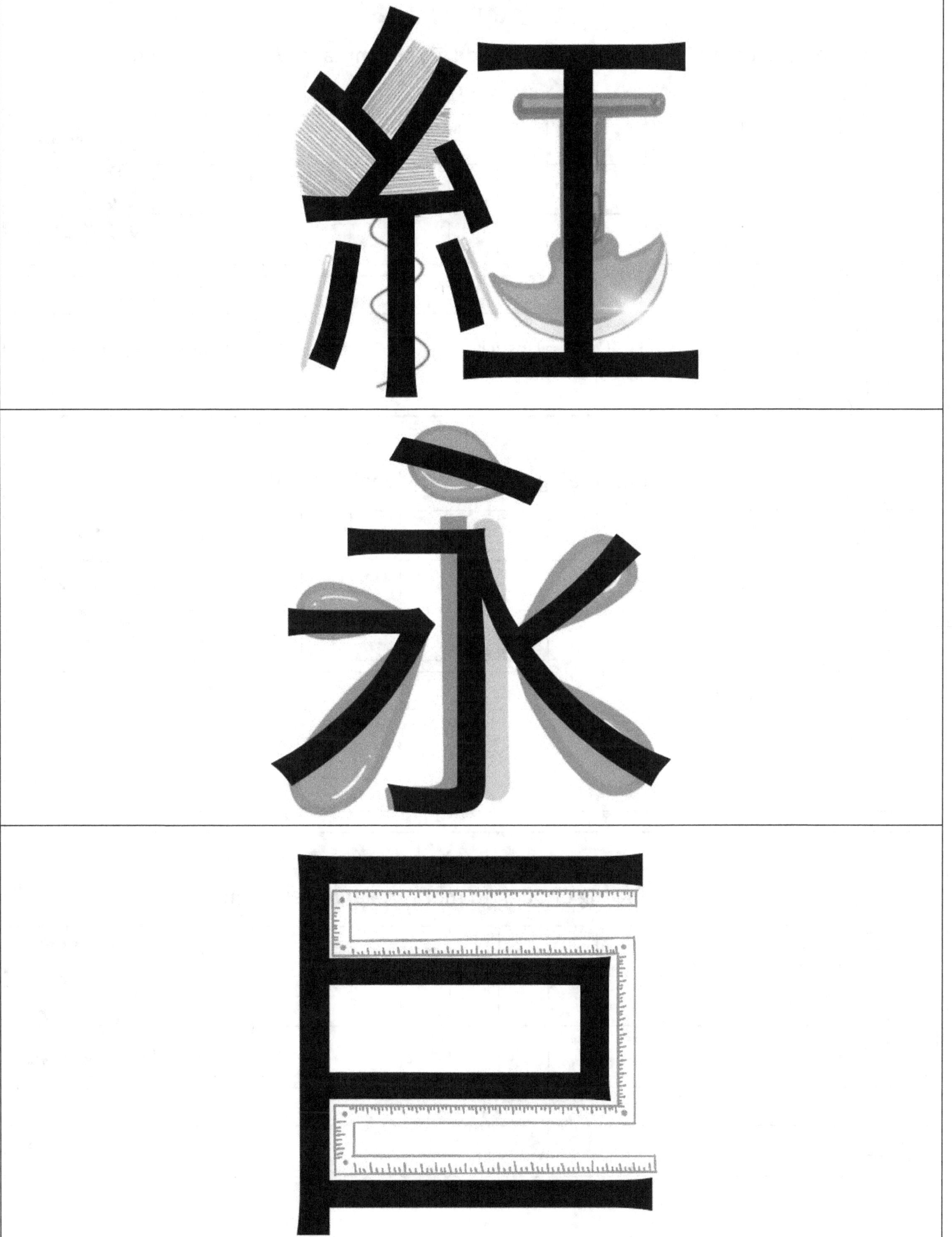

紅 DEEP RED, CRIMSON

"Before, the craft (工) of making deep red (紅) silk threads (糸) was done to bring prosperity"

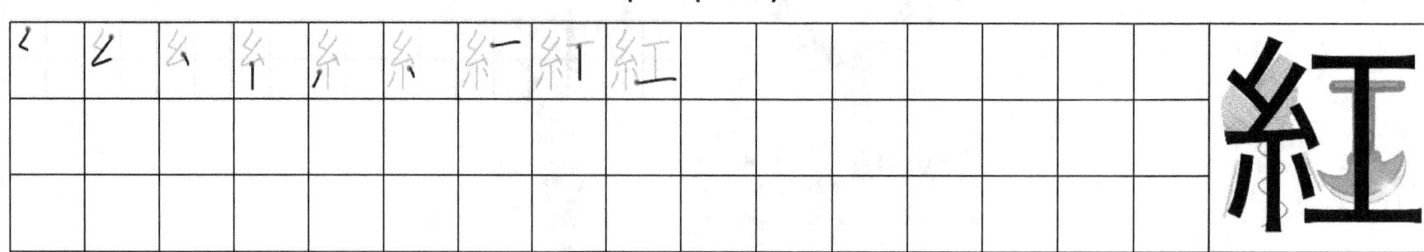

ON (コウ)	Kun (べに)	ODD (もみ)
こうちゃ 紅茶 = Black tea こうよう 紅葉 = Autumn colors	くちべに 口紅 = Lipstick	もみじ 紅葉 = (Japanese) Maple

永 ETERNITY, LONG

"Water (水) can go on for very long (永) paths"

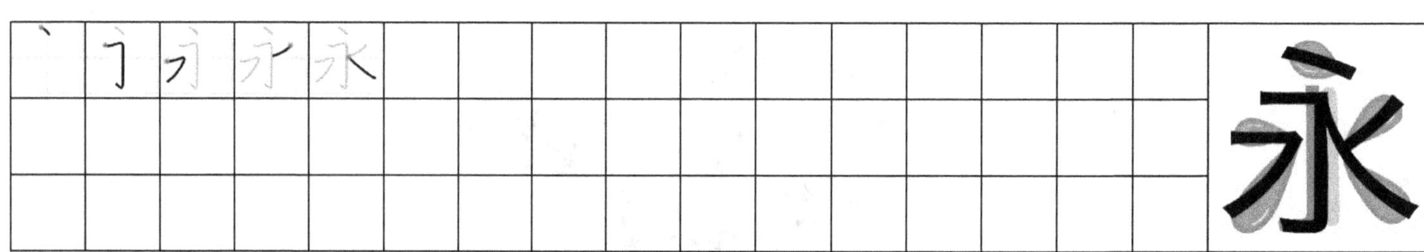

ON (エイ)	Kun (なが)
えいえん 永遠 = Eternity えいきゅう 永久 = Eternity	なが 永い = Long, lengthy

巨 BIG, GIGANTIC, LARGE

"This ruler is long enough to measure large (巨) items"

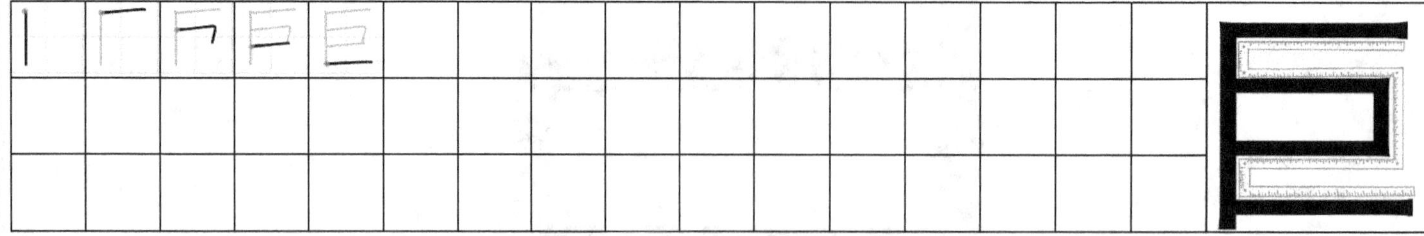

ON (キョ)
きょだい 巨大 = Huge, gigantic

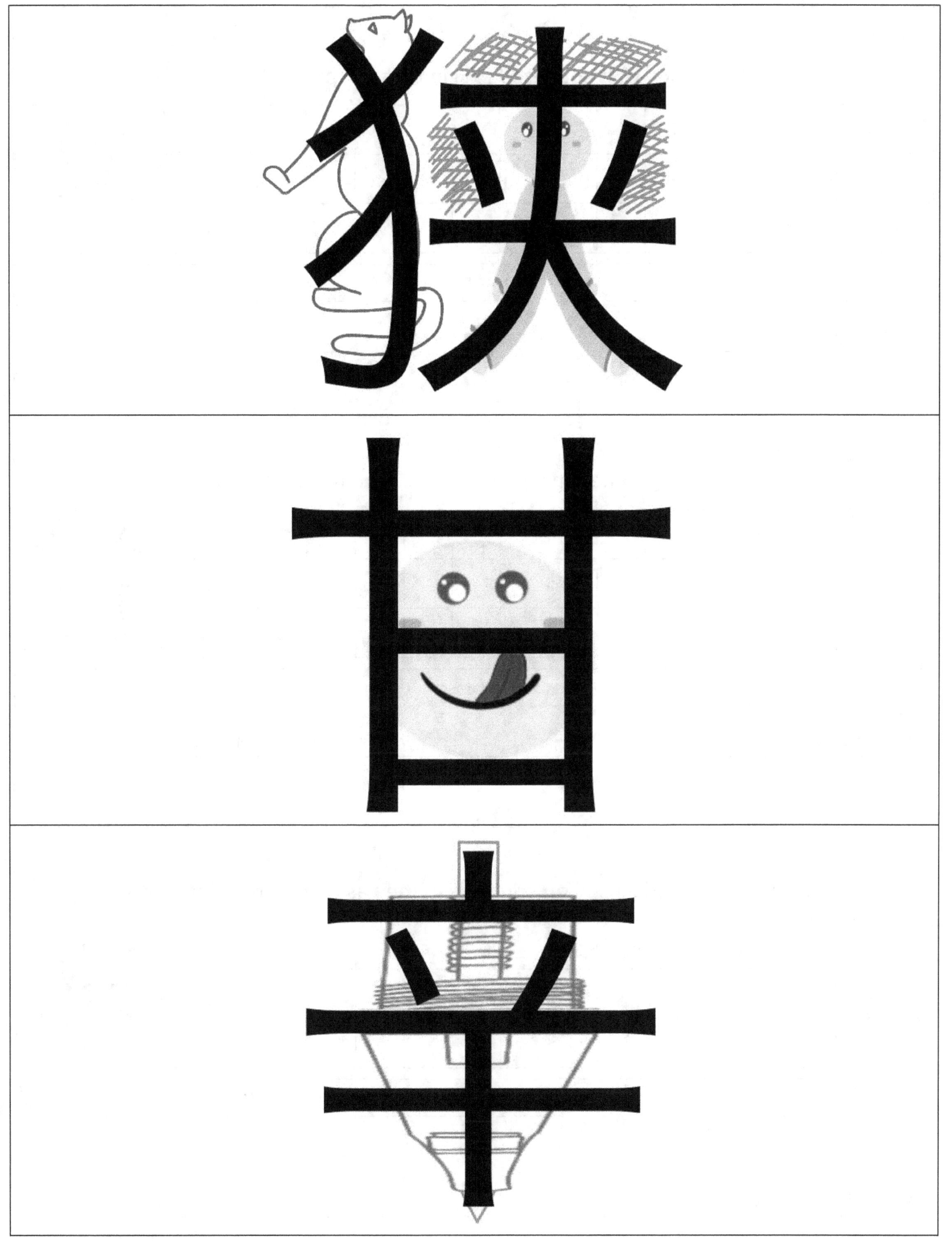

狭 NARROW, CRAMPED

"The beast (犭) is squeezed (夹) in that narrow (狭) space"

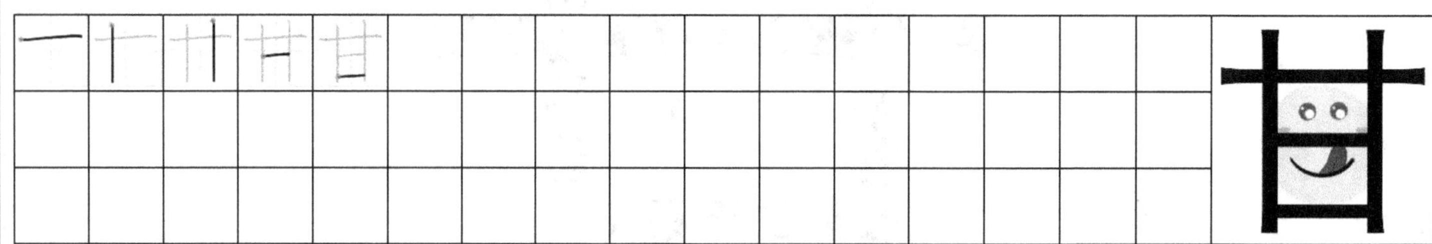

Kun (せま)

せま
狭 い ＝ Narrow

甘 SWEET, COAX, SUGARY

"I'm tasting something very sweet (甘) in my mouth (口)"

Kun (あま)

あま 甘 い ＝ Sweet	あま 甘 やかす ＝ To spoil, to pamper

辛 SPICY, BITTER, HOT, PAINFUL

"The tattooing needle used on criminals in the past was very painful (辛)"

Kun (から、つら)

から 辛 い ＝ Spicy しおから 塩 辛 い ＝ Salty (taste)	つら 辛 い ＝ Painful

危險

恐

危 DANGEROUS, FEAR

"A person is dangerously (危) bending (⺈) at the edge of a cliff (厂), and another person is kneeling (㔾) down below"

ON (キ)		Kun (あぶ、あや)	
きけん 危 険 = Danger		あぶ 危 ない = Dangerous	あや 危 うい = Dangerous

険 PRECIPITOUS, INACCESSIBLE PLACE

"The person examines (僉) how inaccessible (険) the hill (阝) is"

ON (ケン)	Kun (けわ)
きけん 危 険 = Danger ぼうけん 冒 険 = Adventure	けわ 険 しい = Inaccessible, precipitous

恐 FEAR, DREAD

"The person is curled up (凡) while working (工) on how to overcome the fears (恐) in his heart (心)"

ON (キョウ)	Kun (おそ)
きょうしゅく 恐 縮 = Being sorry, being ashamed きょうふ 恐 怖 = Fear, dread	おそ 恐 れる = To fear, to be afraid of おそ 恐 ろしい = Terrible, dreadful

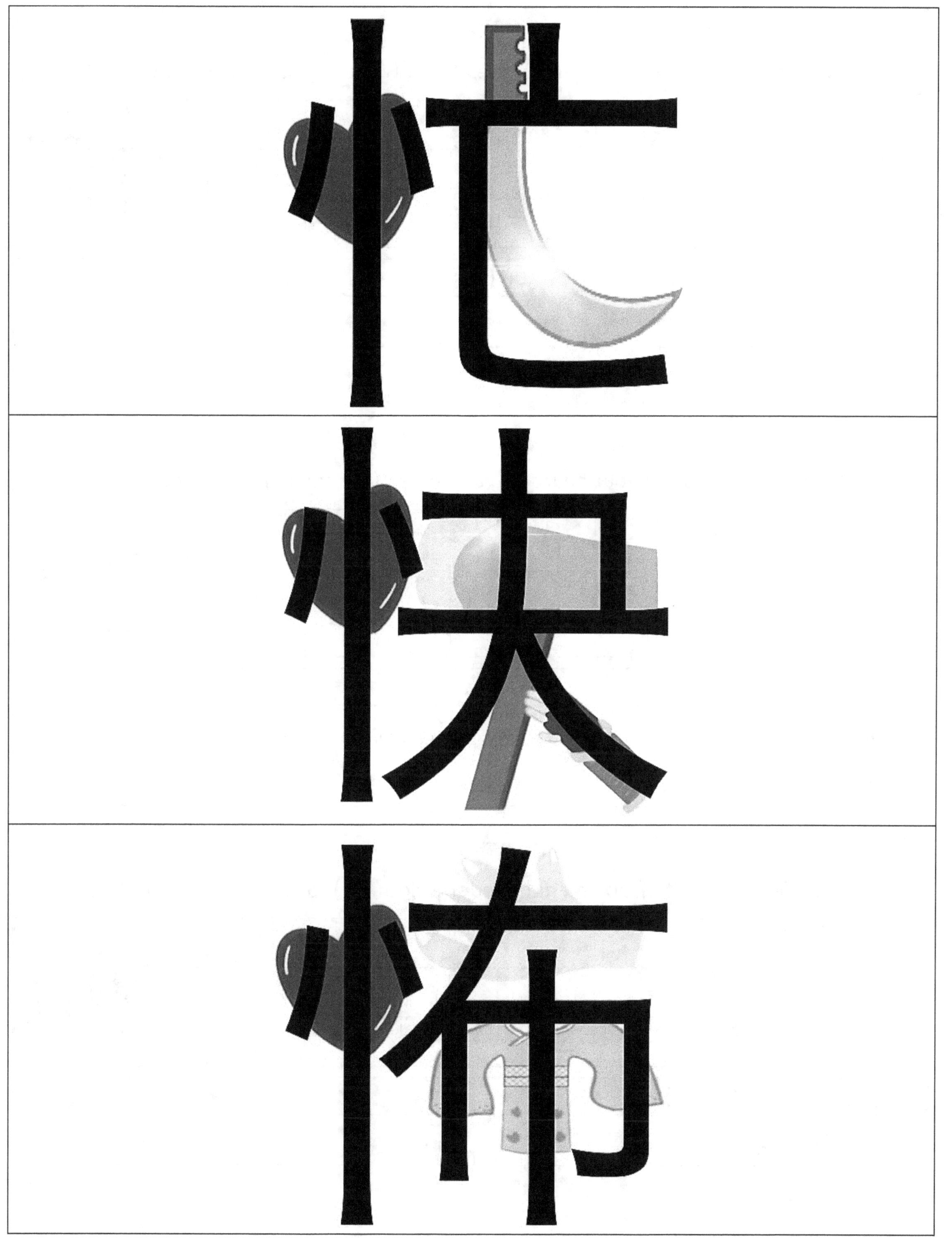

忙 BUSY

"When a person is very busy (忙), their heart (忄) and mind feel dead (亡)"

Kun (いそが)

いそが
忙 しい = Busy

快 PLEASANT, CHEERFUL

"Stay cheerful (快) in your heart (忄) and break (夬) any negative thoughts"

ON (カイ)

かいせい
快 晴 = Good weather

かいてき
快 適 = Pleasant, comfortable

ゆかい
愉 快 = Pleasant, happy

怖 DREADFUL, FEARFUL

"If you feel fearful (怖), go and hide under a cloth (布) to calm your heart (忄)"

ON (フ)

きょうふ
恐 怖 = Dread, fear

Kun (こわ)

こわ
怖 い = Scary

尊

軟

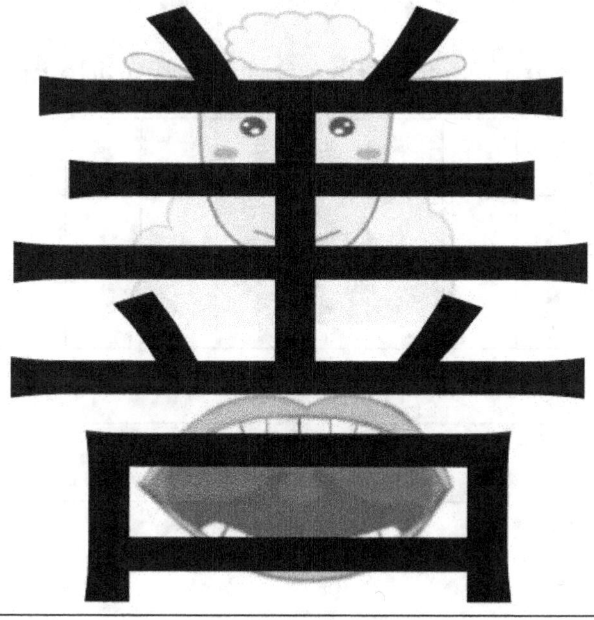

善

尊 PRECIOUS, REVERED, VALUABLE

"Measure (寸) a good amount of wine (酉) to offer it as something precious (尊) to the gods"

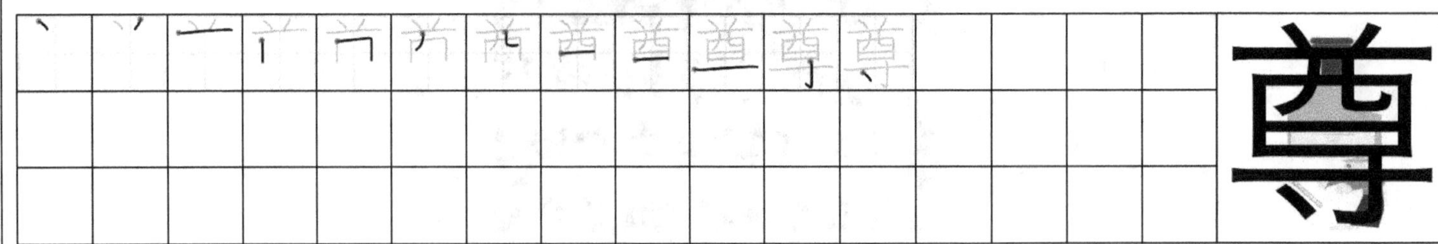

ON (ソン)

そんけい	そんちょう
尊 敬 = Respect, reverence	尊 重 = Respect, regard

軟 SOFT

"This car (車) lacks (欠) soft (軟) components for comfort"

Kun (やわ)

やわ
軟 らかい = Soft, tender

善 GOOD, VIRTUOUS

"A good (善) shepherd uses his mouth (口) to guide his sheep (羊)"

ON (ゼン)

かいぜん	ぜん
改 善 = Improvement	善 = Good, virtue

柔

異

硬

柔 TENDER, SOFTNESS

"A halberd (矛) can easily cut soft (柔) wood (木)"

Kun (やわ)

やわ
柔 らかい = Soft, tender

異 STRANGENESS, DIFFERENT, UNUSUAL

"The man with the mask (田) is strange (異), and together (共) with his personality, he can be scary"

ON (イ)	Kun (こと)
いじょう 異 常　= Abnormality	こと 異 なる = To differ

Note: In some kanjis the radical 田 was a man wearing a mask of a fierce expression from a deceased person. Another kanji that uses this radical is 鬼 (devil). Do not confuse with the radical of rice field (田).

硬 HARD, STIFF

"The bread got as hard (硬) as a stone (石), and it is getting late (更) to buy more"

ON (コウ)	Kun (かた)
こうか 硬貨　= Coin	かた 硬 い = Solid, hard

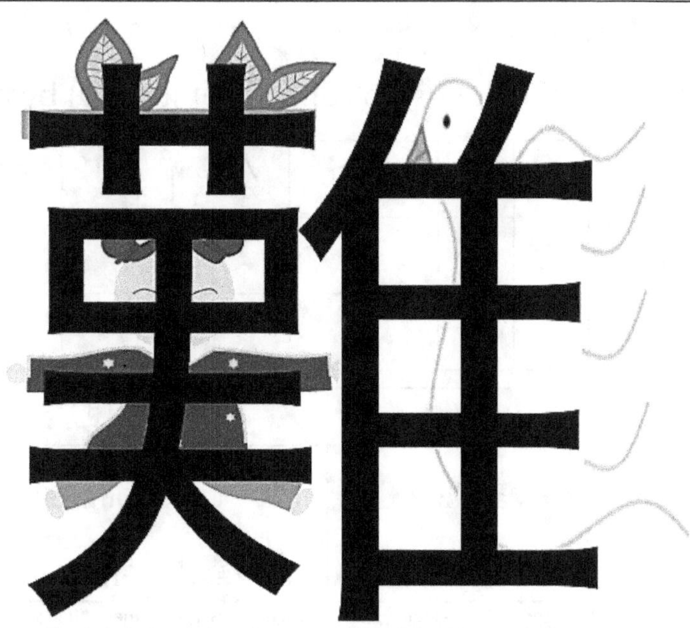

難 DIFFICULT, IMPOSSIBLE, TROUBLE

"It is very difficult (難) to capture a bird (隹) by hand"

ON (ナン)			Kun (むずか、がた、にく)	
こんなん 困 難 = Difficulty	さいなん 災 難 = Calamity		むずか 難 しい = Difficult	にく 〜 難 い = Difficult
とうなん 盗 難 = Theft			ありがた 有 難 い = Grateful	

Note: The element 莫 was only used for sound. But later, in Chinese only, they changed it for the element "hand", so that it would make more sense.

確 CERTAIN, FIRM, HARD, ASSURANCE

"When a bird (隺) flies they must be as firm (確) as a stone (石)"

ON (カク)			Kun (たし)
かくじつ 確 実 = Certain	かくりつ 確 率 = Probability	てきかく 的 確 = Precise	たし 確 か = Certain
かくにん 確 認 = Confirmation	せいかく 正 確 = Accurate	めいかく 明 確 = Distinct	たし 確 かめる = To ascertain

豊 BOUNTIFUL, RICH, ABUNDANT

"The harvest of beans (豆) and rice paddies (田) was abundant (豊)"

ON (ホウ)	Kun (ゆた)
ほうふ 豊 富 = Abundant, plentiful	ゆた 豊 か = Abundant

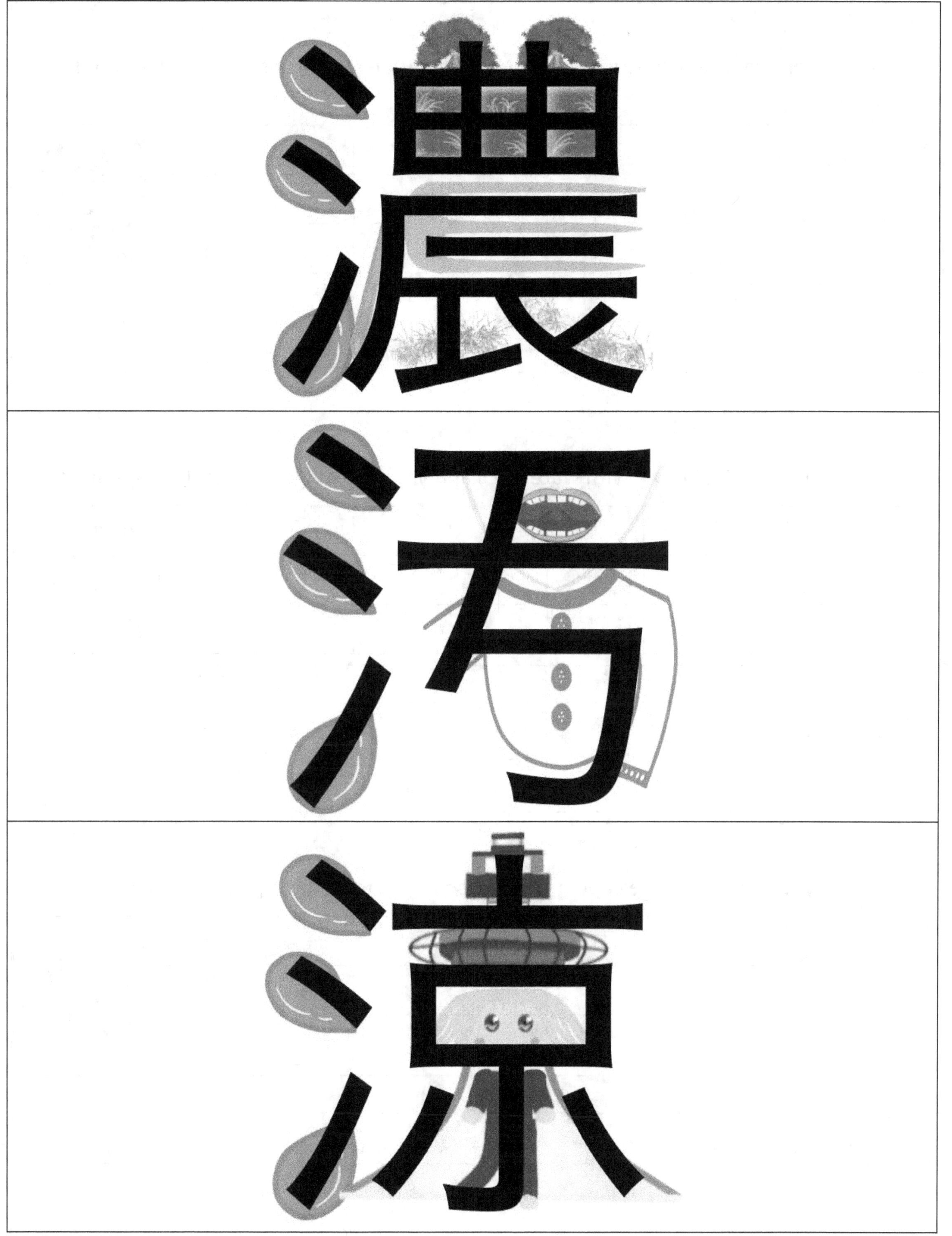

濃 DARK, THICK, UNDILUTED

"In the morning, in agriculture (農), you see undiluted (濃) drops of water (氵) on the crops"

ON (ノウ)	Kun (こ)
のうど 濃度 = Concentration	こ 濃い = Deep (color), dark

汚 DIRTY, POLLUTE

"Clean your dirty (汚) room with water (氵) and your breathing (丂) will be refreshing"

ON (オ)	Kun (よご、きたな)	
おせん 汚染 = Pollution	よご 汚す = To disgrace, to pollute よご 汚れる = To get dirty	きたな 汚い = Dirty, flithy

涼 REFRESHING, NICE AND COOL

"Spray water (氵) on the capital (京) city so it gets refreshing (涼) for everyone"

Kun (すず)	
すず 涼しい = Cool, refreshing	すず 涼む = To cool oneself

CHAPTER 10: ADJECTIVES II

簡	易	厚	暖	暴	普
197	198	199	200	201	202
純	鈍	鋭	若	薄	偉
203	204	205	206	207	208
込	逆	遅	貧	賢	珍
209	210	211	212	213	214

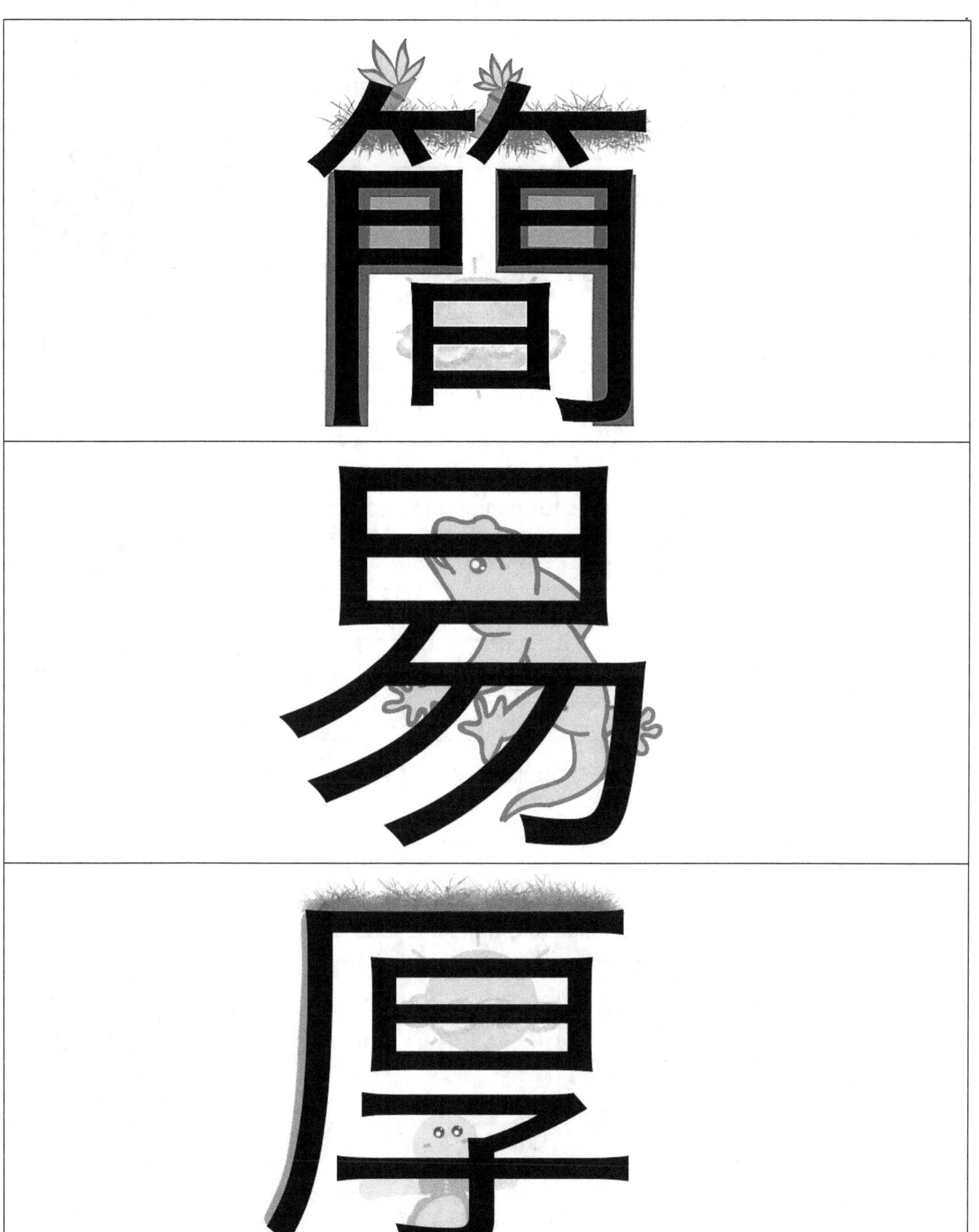

簡 SIMPLICITY, BREVITY

"You can see the sun (日) passing in brevity (簡) through the bamboo (⺮) doors (門)"

ON (カン)

かんたん
簡 単 = Simple, easy

易 EASY, SIMPLE

"It is easy (易) for lizards to change colors to protect themselves"

ON (イ、エキ) / Kun (やさ)

あんい
安 易 = Easy-going

ようい
容 易 = Easy, simple

ぼうえき
貿 易 = Trade (Foreign)

やさ
易 しい = Easy, plain

厚 THICK, CORDIAL

"The thick (厚) child (子) hides from the hot sun (日) under the cliff (厂)"

Kun (あつ)

あつ
厚 い = Cordial, thick

あつ
厚 かましい = Impudent

Note: In the ethymology, instead of a child and the sun, it was a very heavy a thick container under the cliff.

暖

暴

普

暖 WARMTH

"The helping hand (爫) of a friend (友) is warmer (暖) than the sun (日)"

ON (ダン)	Kun (あたた)	
おんだん 温 暖 = Warm, mild	あたた 暖 かい = Warm	あたた 暖 める = To warm
だんぼう 暖 房 = Heating (indoor)	あたた 暖 まる = To warm up	

暴 VIOLENT, OUTBURST, FORCE

"The sun (日) is violently (暴) drying everything, including the water (水)"

ON (ボウ)	Kun (あば)
らんぼう 乱 暴 = Rude, violent	あば 暴 れる = To act violently

Note: Originally rice instead of water

普 UNIVERSAL, GENERALLY

"It is universally (普) known that the sun (日) shines over everyone in the world"

ON (フ)	
ふきゅう 普 及 = Diffusion	ふつう 普 通 = Usually, generally
ふだん 普 段 = Usually, ordinarily	

純

鈍

鋭

純 INNOCENCE, GENUINE, PURITY

"We created genuine (純) silk threads (糸) at the camp (屯)"

ON (ジュン)

じゅんじょう
純 情 = Pure heart, innocence

たんじゅん
単 純 = Simple, plain

じゅんすい
純 粋 = Genuine, pure, true

鈍 DULL

"The metal (金) that was found in the camp (屯) was dull (鈍)"

Kun (にぶ、のろ)

にぶ
鈍 い = Dull (e.g. a knife)

のろ
鈍 い = Thickheaded

鋭 SHARP, POINTED, VIOLENT

"The older brother (兄) works with metal (金) to make it thin and sharp (鋭)"

Kun (するど)

するど
鋭 い = Pointed, sharp (blade, pain)

若 YOUNG, IMMATURE

"The grass (艹) I'm holding in my right hand (右) is known to make you young (若) again"

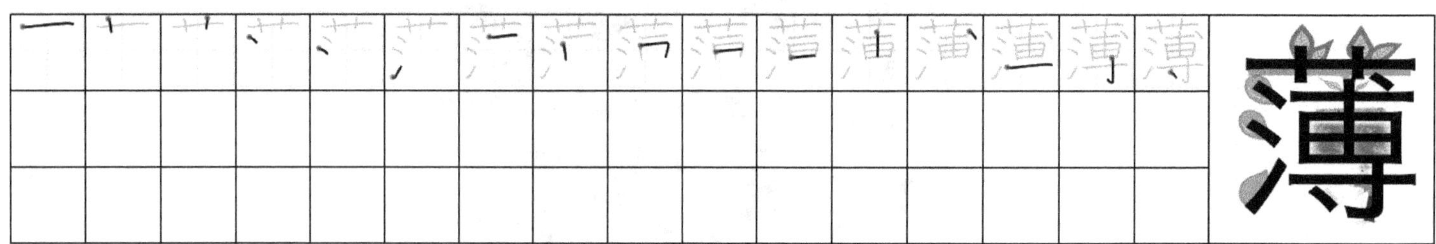

Kun (わか)

わか
若 い = Young, youthful

わかわか
若 々 しい = Youthful

Note: Originally a young woman dancing, but it lost its original shape over time.

薄 DILUTE, THIN, GRASS

"Morning dew is a thin (薄) layer of water (氵) on grass (艹) and plants (甫)"

Kun (うす)

うす
薄 い = Thin, watery

うすぐら
薄 暗 い = Gloomy

うす
薄 める = To dilute, to water down

偉 GREATNESS, ADMIRABLE, EXCELLENT

"The person (亻) guards (韋) his excellent (偉) reputation"

ON (イ)

いだい
偉 大 = Great, grand, magnificent

Kun (えら)

えら
偉 い = Great, eminent

込 CROWDED, MIXTURE

"When many people enter (入) through the same path (辶), it becomes crowded (込)"

ノ 入 入 入 込

Kun (こ)

突っ込む = To plunge into	溶け込む = To melt into	払い込む = To deposit	申し込む = To apply for
人込み = Crowd of people	引っ込む = To draw back	飛び込む = To jump in	

逆 REVERSE, INVERTED

"When a person is disobedient (屰) they go in reverse (逆) in their life path (辶)"

丶 ソ 丷 亡 屮 屰 屰 逆 逆

ON (ギャク) / Kun (さか)

ON (ギャク)	Kun (さか)	
逆 = Reverse	逆さ = Reverse	逆らう = To go against
	逆様 = Inverted	

遅 SLOW, LATE

"Go slow (遅) as there is the corpse (尸) of a sheep (羊) in this path (辶)"

フ 一 尸 尸 尸 尹 屖 屖 犀 犀 遅 遅

ON (チ) / Kun (おく、おそ)

ON (チ)	Kun (おく、おそ)
遅刻 = Lateness, late coming	遅れる = To be late, to be delayed
	遅い = Late, slow

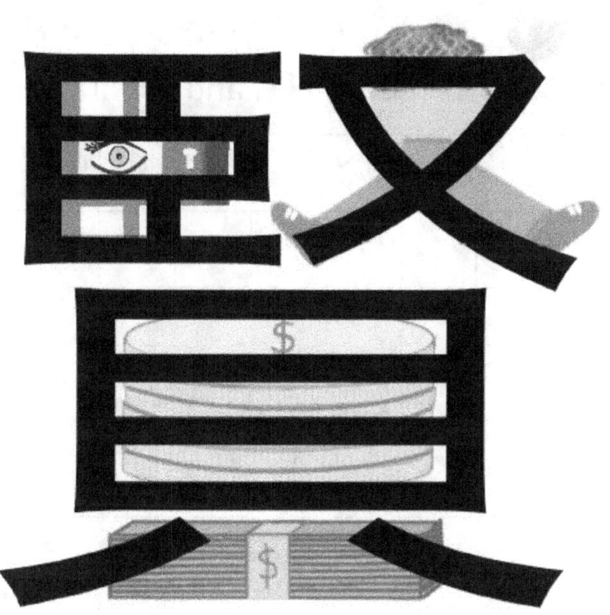

貧 POVERTY, POOR

"Dividing (分) all your money (貝) to just pay debt makes you poor (貧) quick"

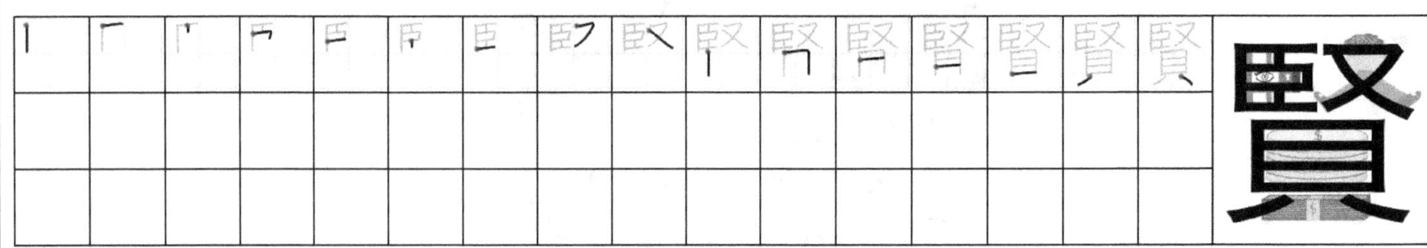

Kun (まず)

まず 貧 しい = Poor, needy	びんぼう 貧 乏 = Poor

賢 INTELLIGENT, WISDOM, WISE

"Be intelligent (賢) with money (貝) and you'll give a wise (臤) life"

Kun (かしこ)

かしこ
賢 い = Wise, clever

珍 RARE, STRANGE

"The king (王) contemplates a rare (珍) shiny jewel"

Kun (めずら)

めずら
珍 しい = Unusual, rare

CHAPTER 11: MATH & TIME

久	旧	幼	常	暮	晩
215	216	217	218	219	220
零	諸	並	偶	複	双
221	222	223	224	225	226
程	率	均	杯	匹	冊
227	228	229	230	231	232
個	齢	歳			
233	234	235			

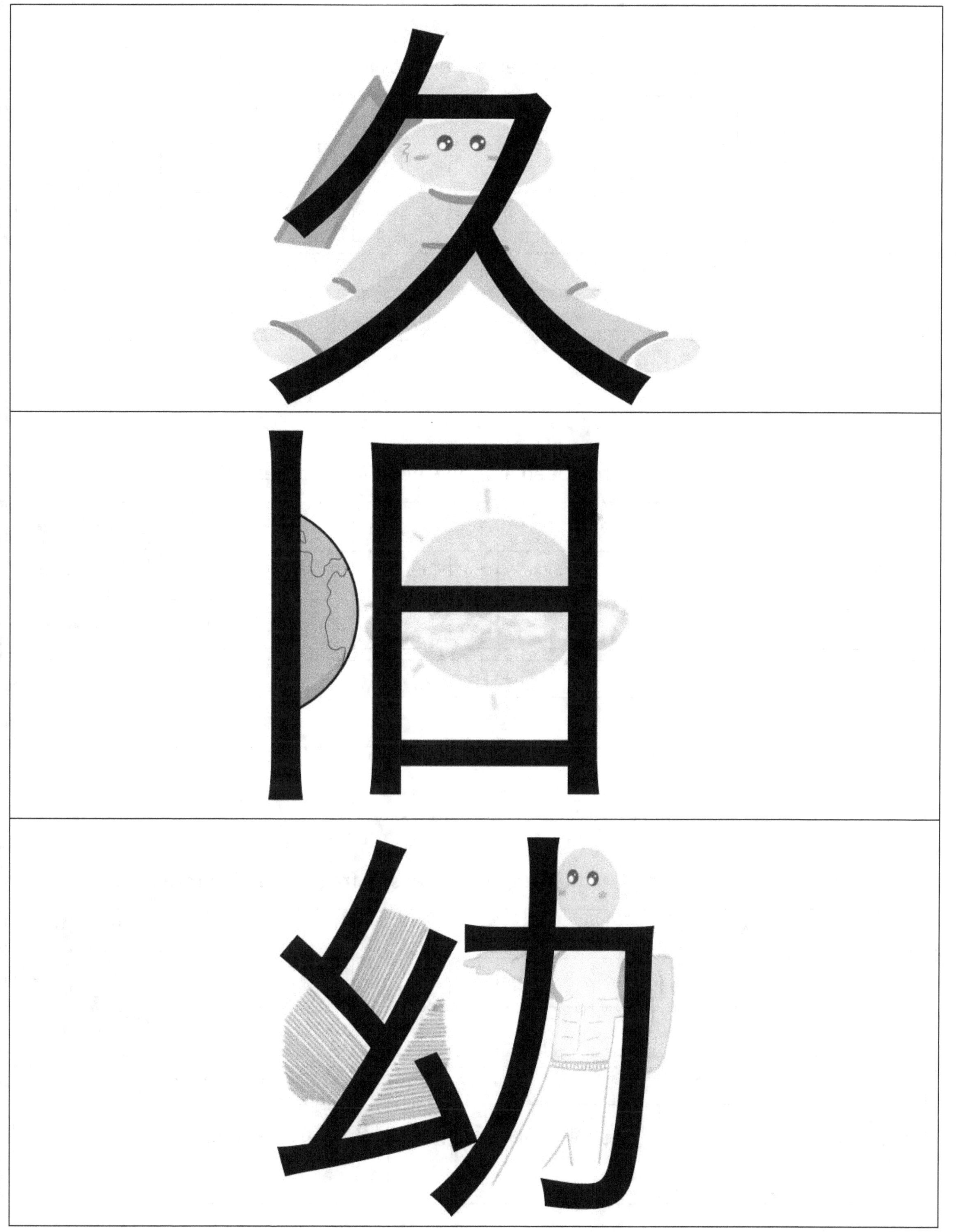

久 LONG TIME, OLD STORY

"The person (人) has been suffering for a long time (久)"

ノ　ク　久

ON (キュウ)	Kun (ひさ)
えいきゅう 永 久　= Eternity	ひさ 久 しぶり = After a long time

旧 FORMER, OLD TIMES

"The sun (日) has been around since the old times (旧)"

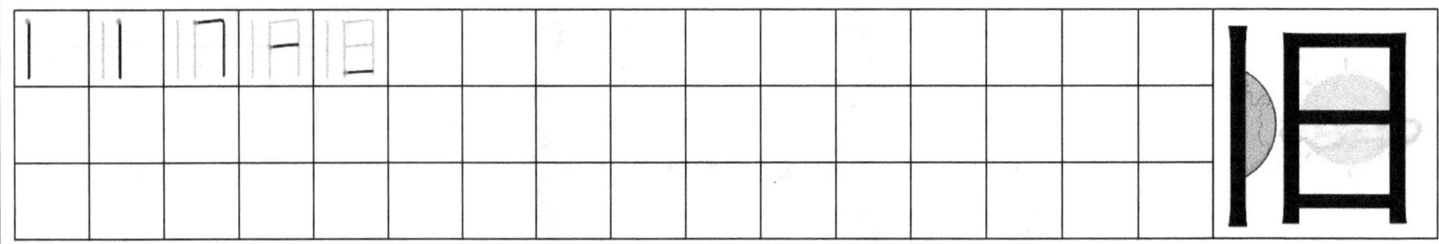

ON (キュウ)
きゅう 旧　= Ex-, former

幼 INFANCY, CHILDHOOD

"During my childhood (幼) my strength (力) was as fragile as a fine thread (幺)"

ON (ヨウ)		Kun (おさな)
ようち 幼 稚 = Infancy	ようちえん 幼 稚 園 = Kindergarten	おさな 幼 い = Very young
ようじ 幼 児 = Infant, young child		

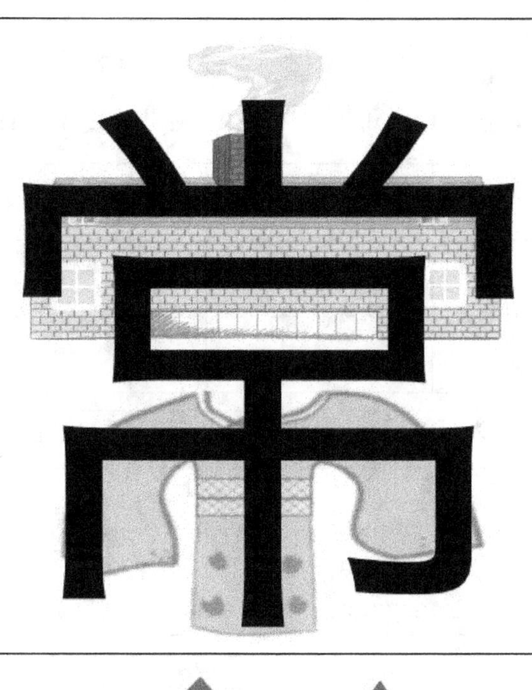

常

暮

晚

常 USUAL, ORDINARY, ALWAYS

"People from high status (尚) would always (常) wear fancy clothes (巾)"

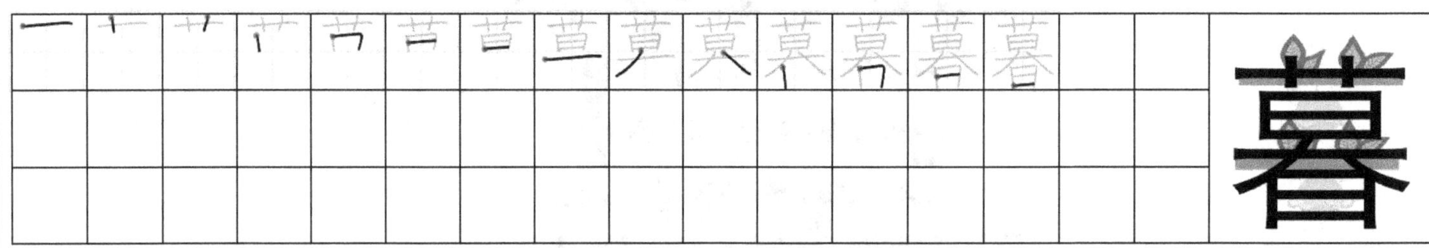

ON (ジョウ)

いじょう
異 常 = Abnormality

じょうしき
常 識 = Common sense

にちじょう
日 常 = Ordinary

ひじょう
非 常 = Emergency

ひじょう
非 常 に = Extremely

Kun (つね)

つね
常 に = Always

暮 EVENING, TWILIGHT, MAKE A LIVING

"In this evening (暮) you can see the sun's (日) sunset behind the grass (艹)"

Kun (く)

く
暮らし = Living, livelihood

く
暮らす = To live, to get along

く
暮れ = Year end, sunset

く
暮れる = To get dark, to end

晩 NIGHTFALL, NIGHT

"Don't make excuses (免) and study during the day (日) and during the night (晩)"

ON (バン)

ばん
晩 = Evening

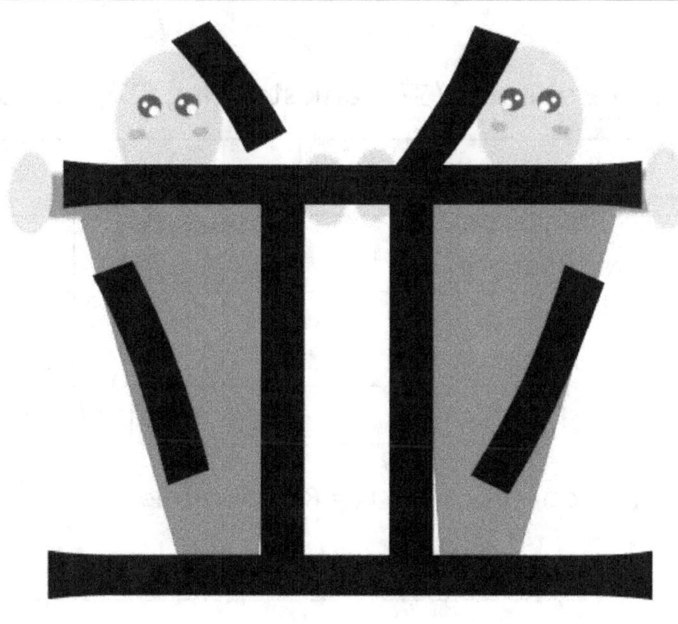

零 ZERO, NOTHING

"Someone not following orders (令) had to kneel under the rain (雨) at zero (零) degrees"

ON (レイ)

れい 零 = Zero	れいてん 零 点 = Zero (points, marks), no marks

諸 VARIOUS, MANY, SEVERAL

"She is a someone (者) who knows many (諸) random words (言)"

ON (ショ)

しょ
諸 = (Prefix) Various

並 ROW, RIVAL, EQUAL

"Two people of equal (並) rank standing (立) side by side"

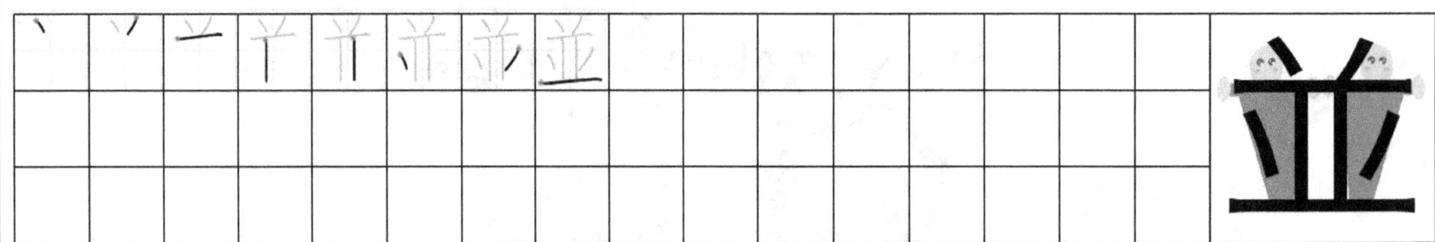

ON (ヘイ)	Kun (なみ、な)	
へいこう 並 行 = (going) side by side, concurrent	なみき 並 木 = Roadside tree なら 並 ぶ = To line up	なら 並 べる = To line up

偶

複

双

偶 EVEN NUMBER, ACCIDENTALLY, SAME KIND

"A person (亻) and a monkey (禺) share the same kind (偶) of DNA"

	ON (グウ)		Kun (たま)
ぐうぜん 偶 然	= (by) chance, unexpectedly, coincidence	たまたま 偶 々	= Occasionally, unexpectedly
ぐうすう 偶 数	= Even number	たま 偶	= Infrequent

複 DUPLICATE, DOUBLE

"My garments (ネ) are in duplicate (複) quantities so I don't repeat (复) clothes"

	ON (フク)	
ふくざつ 複 雑 = Complexity, complication		ふくすう 複 数 = Plural, multiple
ふくしゃ 複 写 = Copying, duplication		

双 PAIR, SET

"Two hands (又) are the same as a pair (双) of hands"

	Kun (ふた)
ふたご 双 子 = Twins	

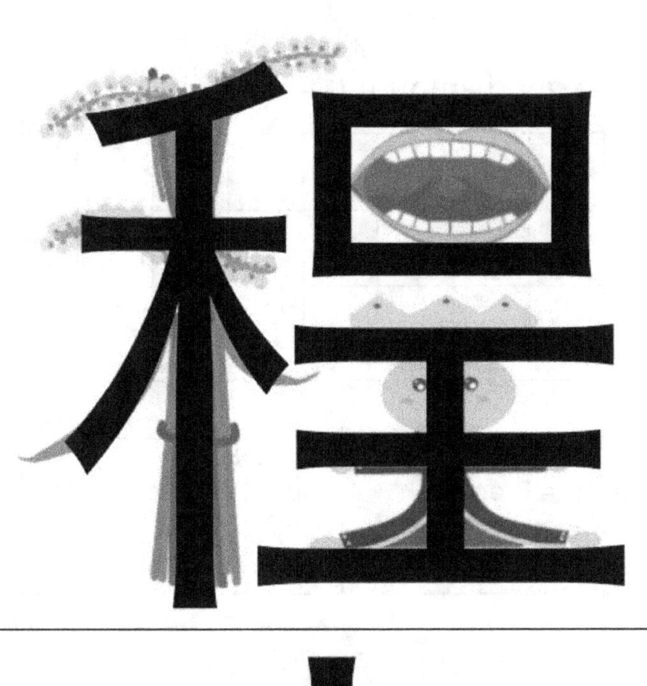

程

率

均

程 EXTENT, DEGREE, LAW, AMOUNT

"You must offer (呈) a good amount (程) of grain (禾) harvest to the gods"

ON (テイ)		Kun (ほど)	
ていど 程 度 = Degree, amount	かてい 過 程 = Process	さきほど 先 程 = A moment ago	ほど 程 = Degree
ほうていしき 方 程 式 = Equation	にってい 日 程 = Agenda	なるほど 成 程 = I see, indeed	

率 RATE, RATIO, LEAD

"Just like pulling threads (幺) firmly will make them stronger, leading (率) people firmly will make them stronger"

ON (リ ツ)		
りつ 率 = Rate, ratio	のうりつ 能 率 = Efficiency	かくりつ 確 率 = Probability

均 LEVEL, AVERAGE

"Level (均) the soil (土) evenly (二) by wrapping (勹) your hand around it and spreading it"

ON (キン)
へいきん 平 均 = Equilibrium

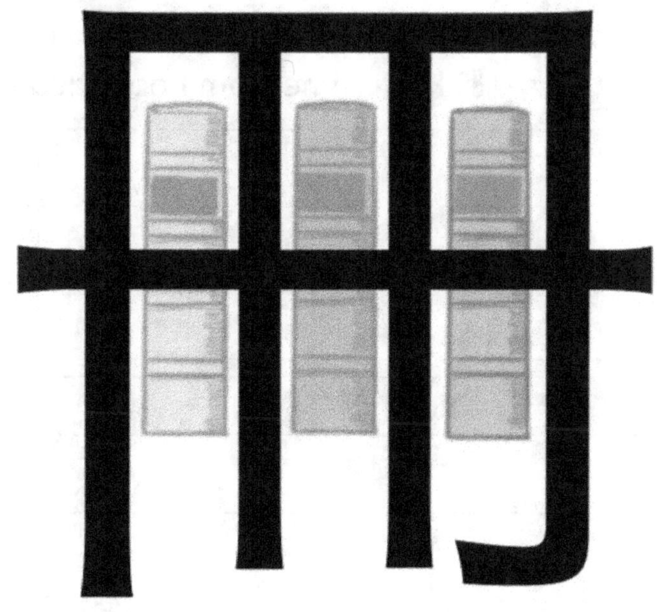

杯 COUNTER (CUPFULS), TOAST

"A toast (杯) used to be done using calyx (不) shaped cups made of wood (木)"

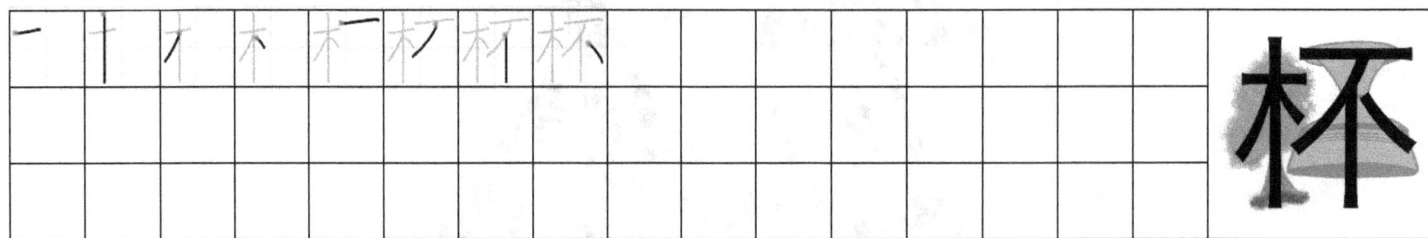

ON (パイ)

かんぱい
乾 杯　= Toast (drink)

匹 COUNTER FOR SMALL ANIMALS

"This counter for small animals (匹) kanji looks like a cat looking at you"

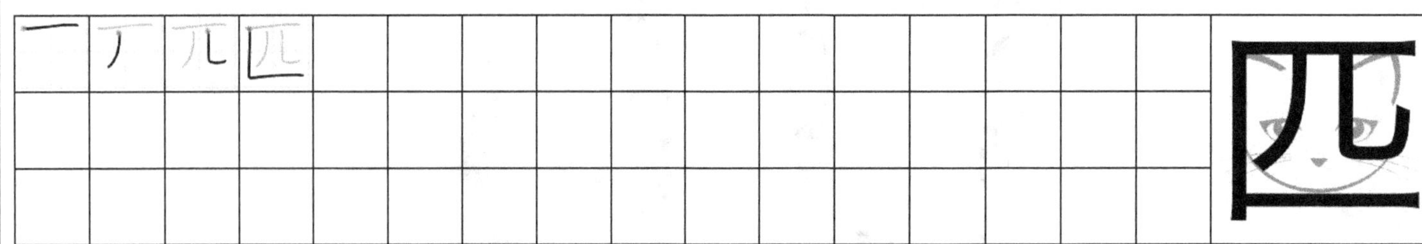

Kun (ひき)

ひき
匹　= Counter for small animals

冊 COUNTER FOR BOOKS, TOME

"This counter for books (冊) kanji came from books tied together"

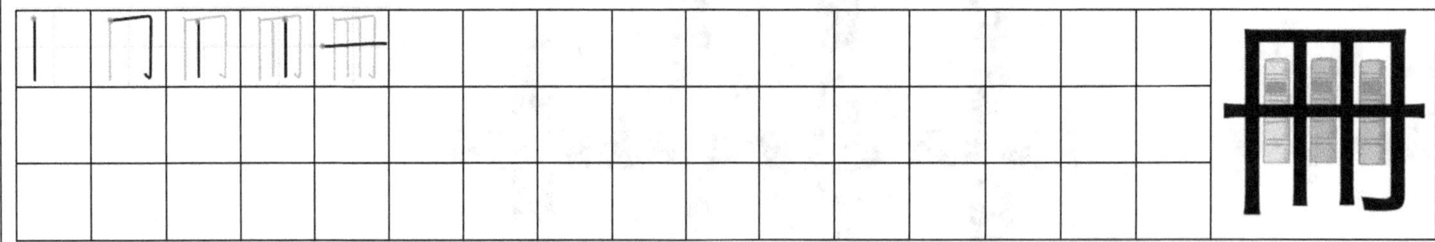

Kun (さつ)

さつ
冊　= Counter for volumes, books

個 INDIVIDUAL, COUNTER (ARTICLES)

"This person (イ) is a very solid (固) individual (個)"

ON (コ 、 カ)

こじん
個人 = Individual

こたい
個体 = An individual

かしょ
個所 = Passage, place

齢 AGE

"The decree (令) is to use teeth (歯) to obtain the age (齢) of certain specimens"

ON (レイ)

ねんれい
年 齢 = Age

歳 AGE, OCCASION

"On occasion (歳), we stop (止) collecting harvest, and instead we raise our halberds (戉) to say thank you"

ON (サイ)

さい
歳 = ~ Years-old

ばんざい
万 歳 = Hurrah, cheers

ODD (チ)

はたち
二十歳 = 20 years old

CHAPTER 12: SPEECH

可	再	条	姓	則	制
236	237	238	239	240	241
規	値	略	翌	編	層
242	243	244	245	246	247
律	御	肯	演	基	論
248	249	250	251	252	253
講	評	詞			
254	255	256			

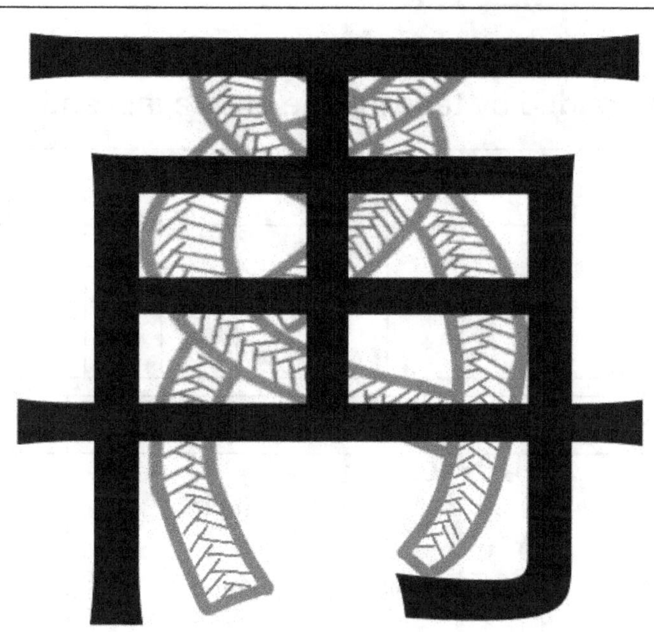

可 CAN, PASSABLE, DO NOT

"Can (可) you open your mouth (口) and sing?"

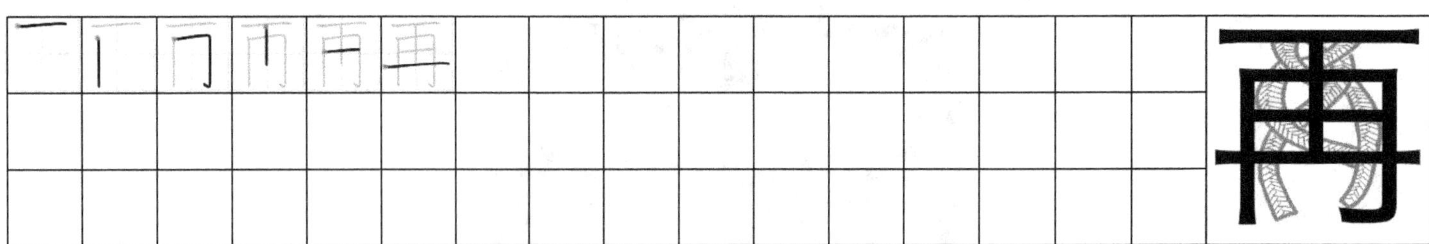

ON (カ)

かけつ 可 決 = Approval	きょか 許 可 = Permission	か 可 = Passable
かのう 可 能 = Possible, feasible	ふか 不可 = Wrong, bad	

再 AGAIN, TWICE

"A rope gets braided by tangling the ends again and again (再)"

ON (サ、サイ) | Kun (ふたた)

さらいげつ 再 来 月 = Month after next	さらいねん 再 来 年 = Year after next	ふたた 再 び = Once more
さらいしゅう 再 来 週 = Week after next	さいさん 再 三 = Again and again	

条 ARTICLE, CLAUSE

"Write an article (条) about a gigantic foot (夂) stepping on a tree (木)"

ON (ジョウ)

じょうけん
条 件 = Condition, requirement

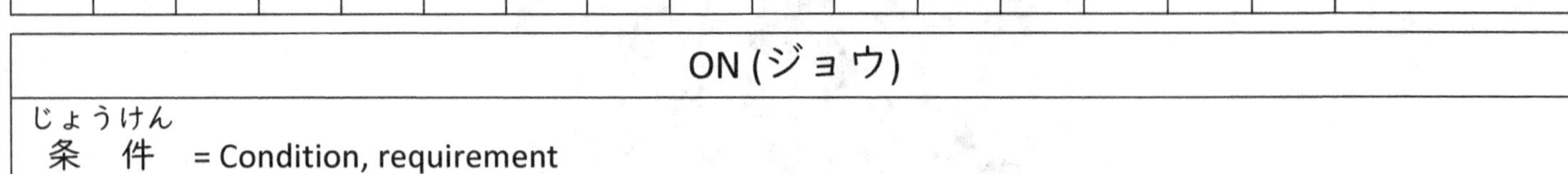

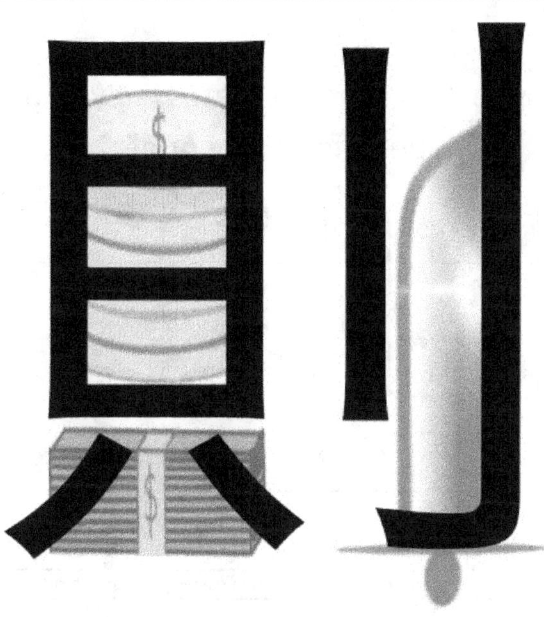

姓 SURNAME

"The woman (女) takes a new surname (姓) as she starts a new life (生)"

ON (セイ)

せい
姓 = Surname

則 RULE, LAW

"The rule (則) was: having a sword (刂) meant status, as you needed enough money (貝) to be able to buy one"

ON (ソク)

きそく 規 則 = Rule, regulations	ほうそく 法 則 = Law	ふきそく 不 規 則 = Irregularity

Note: Originally it was a vessel for sacrificial meat that was shared by everyone. The vessel signified the rules that everyone had to abide by.

制 SYSTEM, LAW, RULE

"The law (制) is to prune red (朱) poisonous leaves"

ON (セイ)

せいげん 制 限 = Restriction	せいさく 制 作 = Work (film, book)	せいど 制 度 = System
せんせい 専 制 = Despotism	たいせい 体 制 = Order, system	

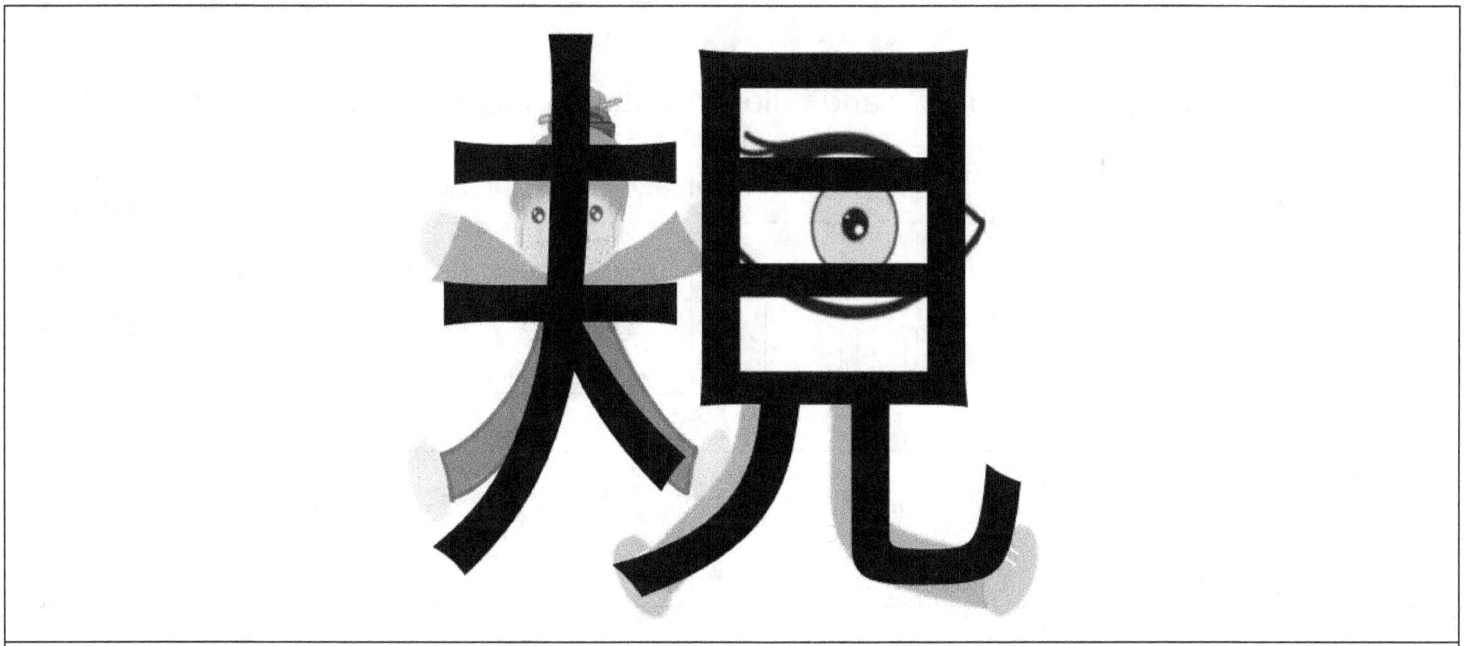

規

値

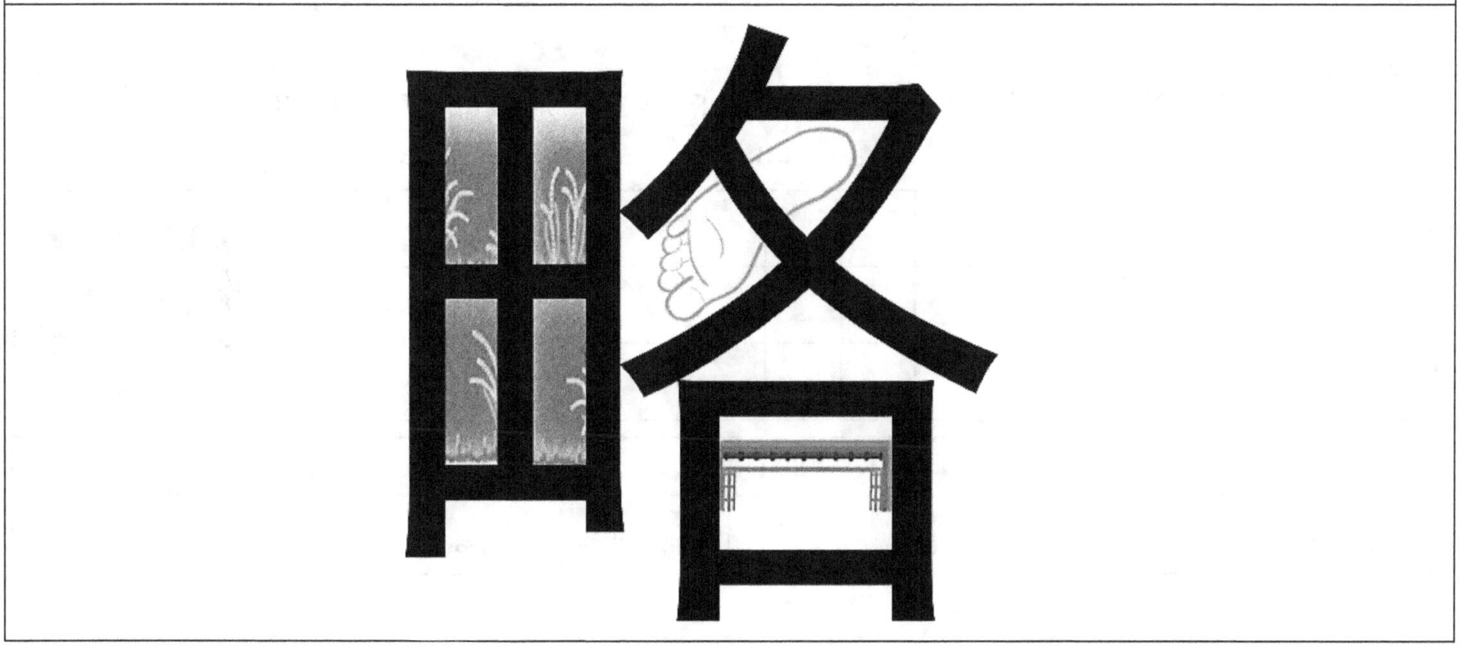

略

規 STANDARD, MEASURE

"Before a family had to watch (見) and follow the standards (規) set by the husband (夫)"

ON (キ)

きじゅん
規 準 = Standard

きそく
規 則 = Regulations

きりつ
規 律 = Order

じょうぎ
定 規 = (Measuring) ruler

ふきそく
不 規 則 = Irregularity

値 PRICE, COST, VALUE

"Before a purchase, a person (イ) would look straight (直) at the cost (値)"

ON (チ)

かち
価 値 = Value, worth

Kun (ね)

ね
値 = Value, price

ねだん
値 段 = Price, cost

略 ABBREVIATION, OMISSION, OUTLINE

"It is important to distribute every (各) rice paddy (田) fairly with no omission (略) of anyone"

ON (リャク)

しょうりゃく
省 略 = Omission

りゃく
略 す = To abbreviate

翌 NEXT, THE FOLLOWING

"The bird with long feathers (羽) flies next (翌) to that person standing up (立)"

ON (ヨク)

よくじつ
翌日 = Next day

編 COMPILATION, KNIT, BRAID, EDITING

"Beyond this door (戸) there are compilations (編) of tomes (冊) bound by threads (糸)"

ON (ヘン)	Kun (あ)	ODD (アミ)
たんぺん 短編 = Short (e.g. story, film) へんしゅう 編集 = Editing, compliation	あ 編む = To knit, to braid	あみもの 編物 = Knitting

層 STRATUM, SOCIAL CLASS

"A stratum (層) is just layers (曽) of divisions for people"

ON (ソウ)

いっそう
一層 = Much more, still more

こうそう
高層 = High-rise (building)

たいそう
大層 = Very, extremely

律 LAW, REGULATION

"Use the brush (聿) to write the laws (律) and the correct path (彳) everyone must follow"

ON (リツ)

きりつ	ほうりつ
規律 = Order, law	法律 = Law

御 HONORABLE, GOVERN

"It is honorable (御) to obey road (彳) signs such as the stop (止) sign"

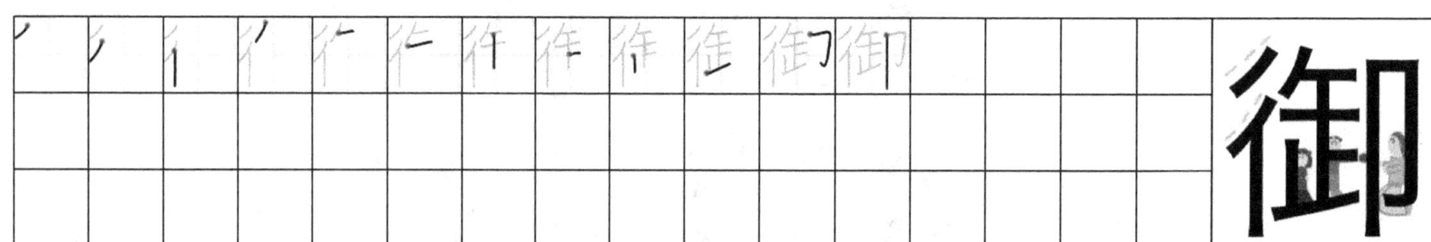

ON (ゴ)

ご	ごはん
御 = Honorific	御飯 = Meal
ごちそう	ごめん
御馳走 = Treating (someone)	御免 = Your pardon

Kun (お、おん)

おじぎ	おんちゅう
御辞儀 = Bow	御中 = And Company
	お
	御 = Honorific

肯 AGREEMENT, CONSENT

"Before any agreements (肯), I will get all my body parts (月) to stop (止) and think"

ON (コウ)

こうてい
肯定 = Positive, affirmation

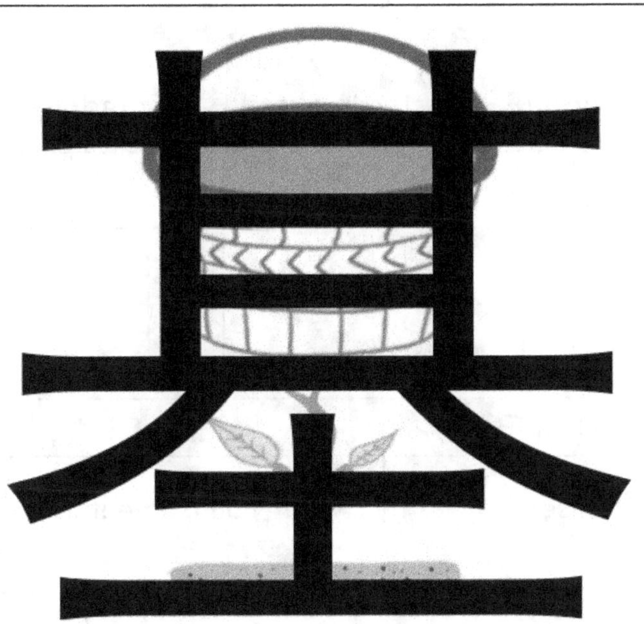

演 PERFORMANCE, ACT, PLAY

"The water (シ) performance (演) is called: The sign of the Tiger (寅)"

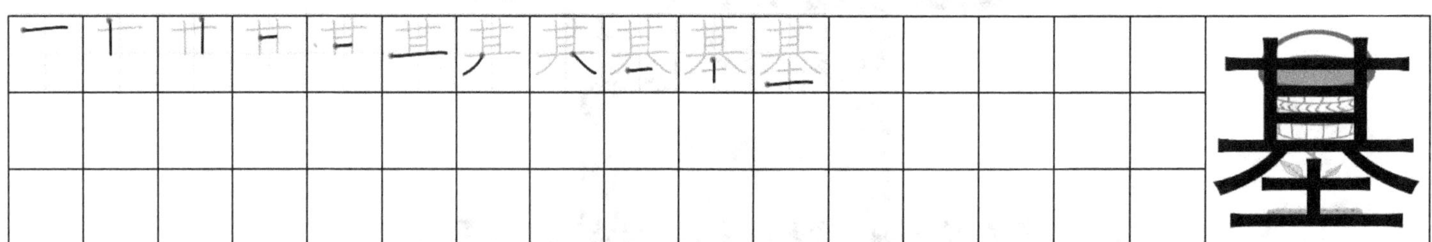

ON (エン)		
えんぎ 演 技 = Acting, performance	えんぜつ 演 説 = Speech, address	こうえん 講 演 = Lecture, address
えんげき 演 劇 = Play (theatrical)	えんそう 演 奏 = Musical performance	

基 FOUNDATION, FUNDAMENTALS

"The foundation (基) of this basket (其) is made of soil (土)"

ON (キ)			Kun (もと)
きじゅん 基 準 = Standard	きち 基 地 = Base	きほん 基 本 = Foundamentals	もと 基 = Basis
きそ 基 礎 = Foundation	きばん 基 盤 = Foundation		もと 基 づく = To be based on

論 ARGUMENT, DISCOURSE

"When you read books (冊) your words (言) become arguments (論) with logic"

ON (ロン)			
がいろん 概 論 = Intro, outline	ひょうろん 評 論 = Criticism	ろん 論 じる = To argue	ろんそう 論 争 = Controversy
ろんぶん 論 文 = Thesis	もちろん 勿 論 = Of course	ろん 論 ずる = To argue	ぎろん 議 論 = Argument, discussion

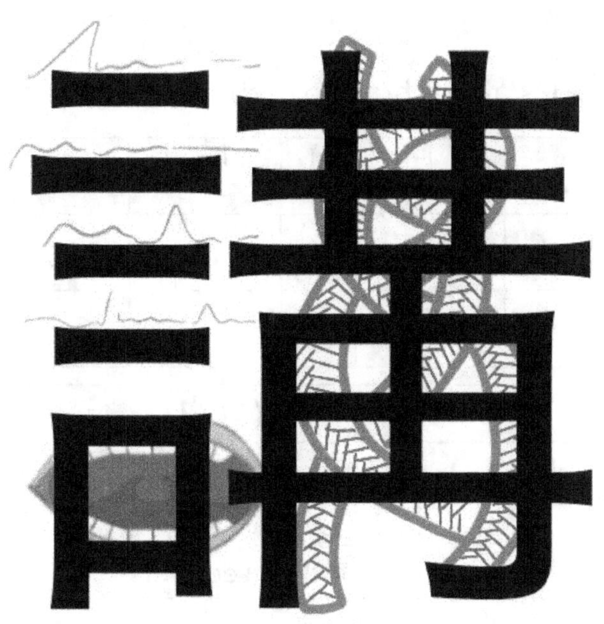

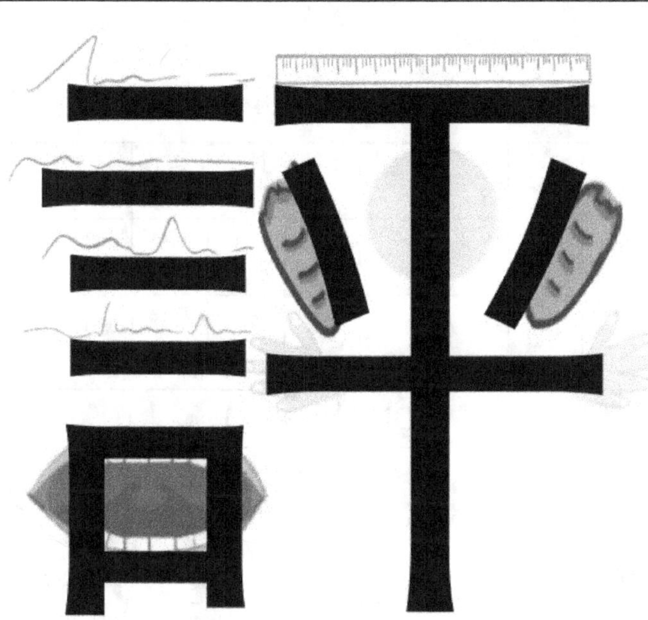

講 LECTURE, CLUB

"This lecture (講) is about how speech (言) connects people together (冓)"

ON (コウ)

きゅうこう 休 講 = Cancellation (lecture, class)	こうぎ 講 義 = Lecture	こうどう 講 堂 = Auditorium
こうえん 講 演 = Lecture	こうし 講 師 = Lecturer	

評 EVALUATE, COMMENT

"Make sure to say (言) an unbiased and peaceful (平) comment (評)"

ON (ヒョウ)

ひひょう 批 評 = Criticism, review	ひょうばん 評 判 = Fame, reputation
ひょうか 評 価 = Valuation, appraisal	ひょうろん 評 論 = Criticism, critique

詞 PART OF SPEECH, WORDS, POETRY

"When my boss (司) says (言) something, it sounds like anything but poetry (詞)"

ON (シ) / ODD (フ)

けいようし 形 容 詞 = i-adjective	だいめいし 代 名 詞 = Pronoun	ふくし 副 詞 = Adverb	せりふ 台 詞 = Speech, remarks
けいようどうし 形 容 動 詞 = Adjectival noun	どうし 動 詞 = Verb	めいし 名 詞 = Noun	

CHAPTER 13: VERBS PART I

占	与	咲	干	示	比
257	258	259	260	261	262
承	了	存	在	増	埋
263	264	265	266	267	268
較	輸	般	昇	乾	療
269	270	271	272	273	274
容	寝	寄	戻	突	破
275	276	277	278	279	280
支	収	更	看	払	担
281	282	283	284	285	286
捜	抱	拝	拡	押	抜
287	288	289	290	291	292

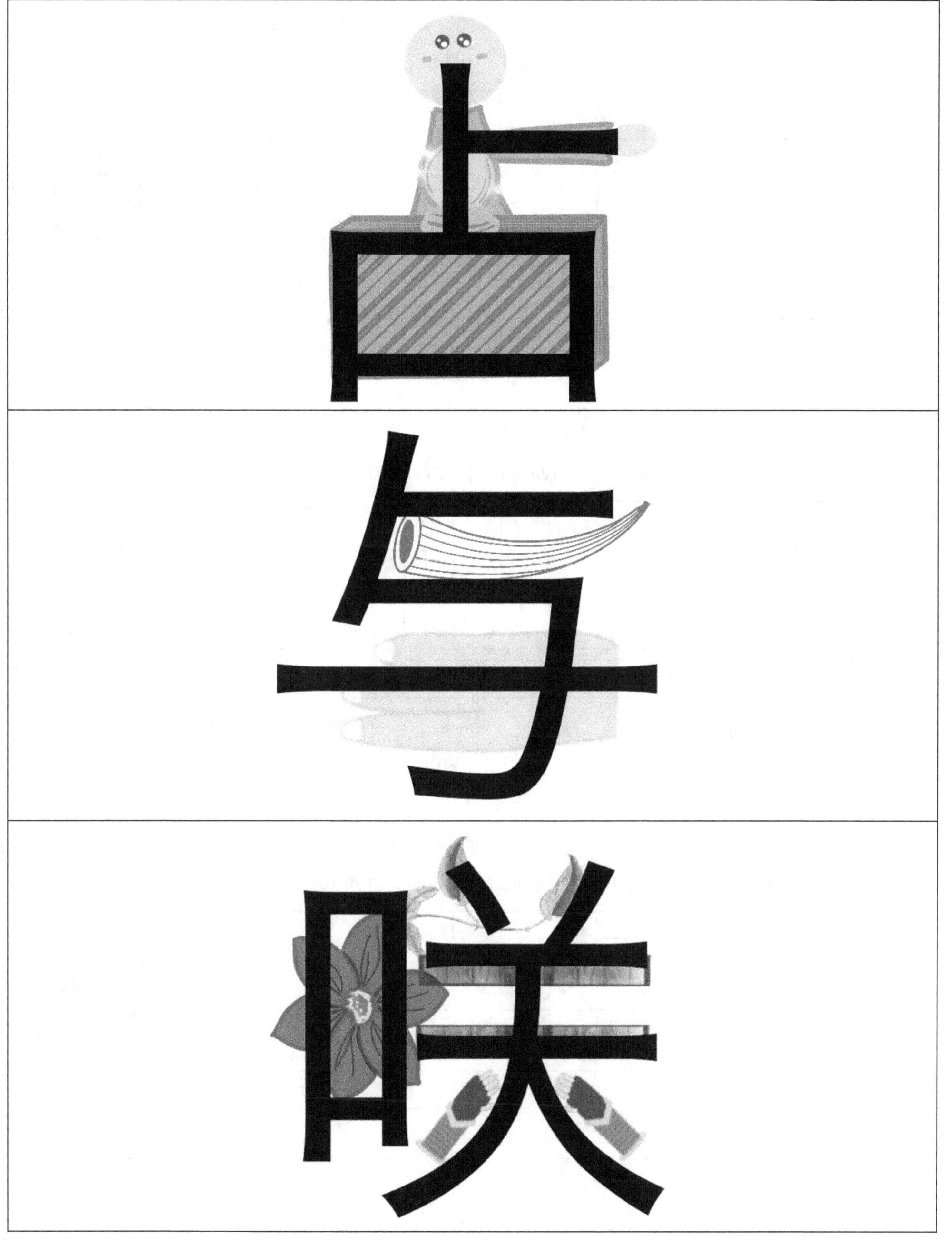

卓

与

瑛

占 FORTUNE-TELLING, FORECASTING

"This is a fortune-telling (占) stand"

Kun (うらな、し)

うらな
占 う = To forecast, to predict

し
占める = To occupy, to hold

与 BESTOW, GIVE, AWARD

"This kanji started as giving (与) ivory to others as an award"

ON (ヨ) | Kun (あた)

きゅうよ
給 与 = Allowance, grant

あた
与 える = To give (esp. to someone of lower status), to bestow

咲 BLOSSOM, BLOOM

"You can see blooming (咲) flowers all around the mouth (口) of this vase"

Kun (さ)

さ
咲く = To bloom

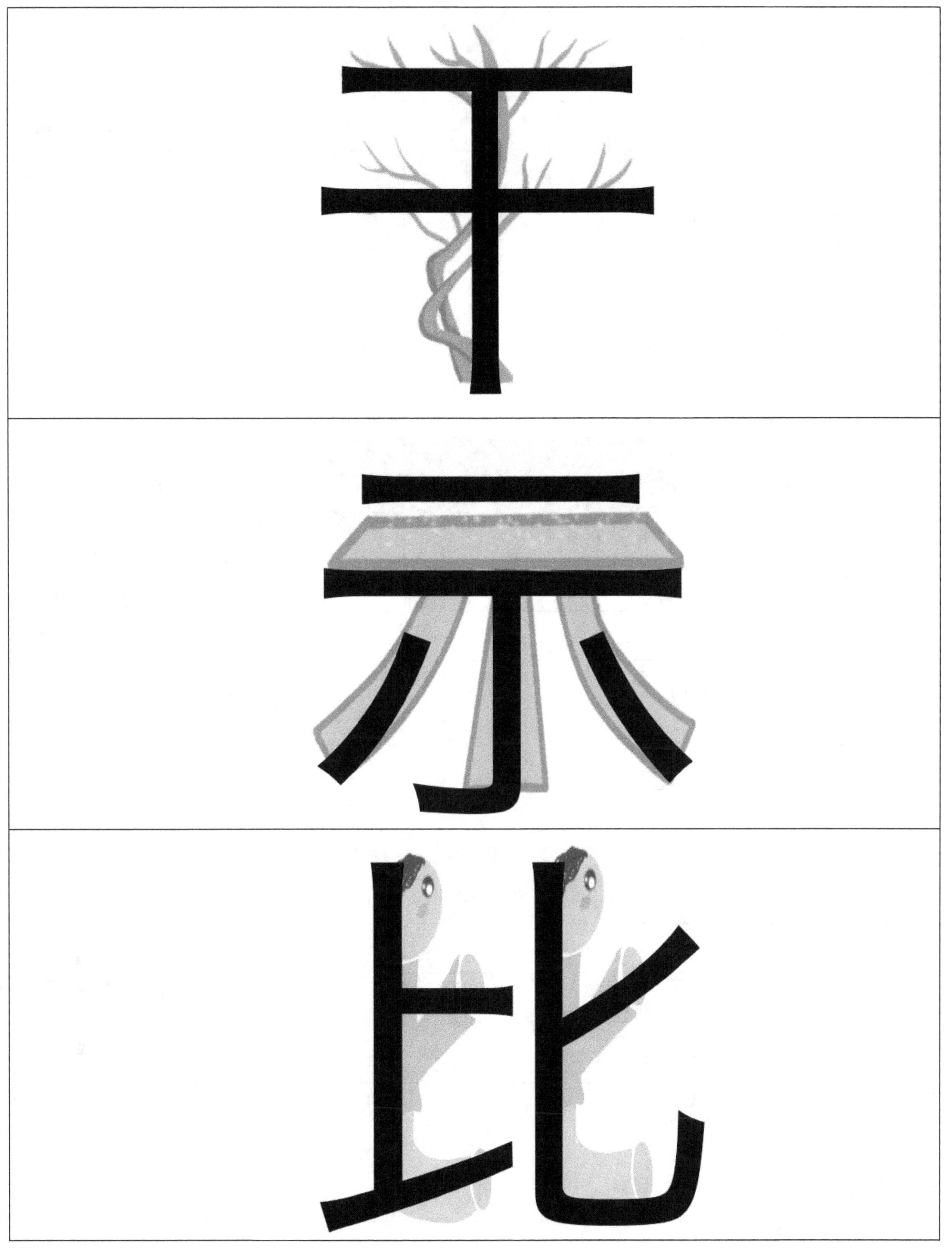

干 DRY, INTERFERE

"The branches have dried (干)"

Kun (ほ)

ほ
干す = To air, to dry

示 SHOW, INDICATE

"This kanji represents the altar where god showed (示) his message"

ON (ジ)	Kun (しめ)
けいじ 掲示 = Notice, bulletin	しめ 示す = To demonstrate

比 COMPARE, RACE, RATIO

"The two twins like to compare (比) each other"

ON (ヒ)	Kun (くら)
ひかく 比較 = Comparison ひかくてき 比較的 = Comparatively	くら 比べる = To compare

承 HEAR, LISTEN TO

"When I hear (承) my child (子) cry, I lift him with my two hands (手)"

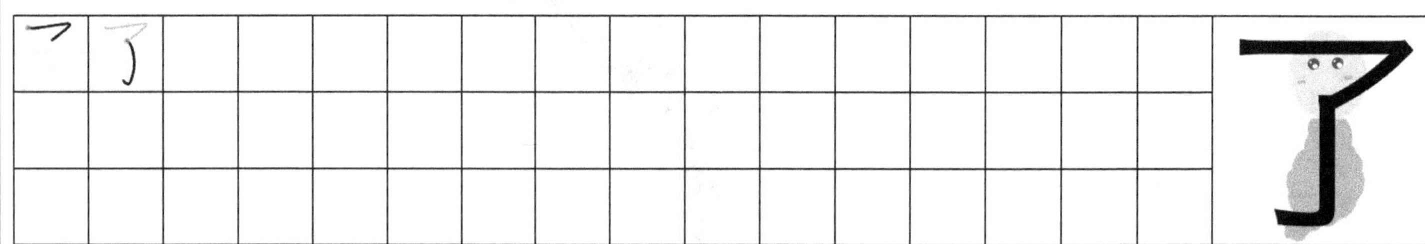

ON (ショウ)	Kun (うけたまわ)
しょうち 承 知 = Consent, acceptance しょうにん 承 認 = Recognition, approval	うけたまわ 承　る = (hum) to hear, to be told

了 COMPLETE, FINISH

"I finished (了) wrapping the baby in a blanket"

ON (リョウ)	
かんりょう 完 了 = Completion	しゅうりょう 終 了 = End, close, termination

存 EXIST, SUPPOSE, BELIEVE

"Both children (子) and sprouting seeds (才) are the meaning of existence (存)"

ON (ソン)	
せいぞん 生 存 = Existence, survival そんざい 存 在 = Existence, being	ぞん 存 じる = (hum) To know ほぞん 保 存 = Preservation, conservation

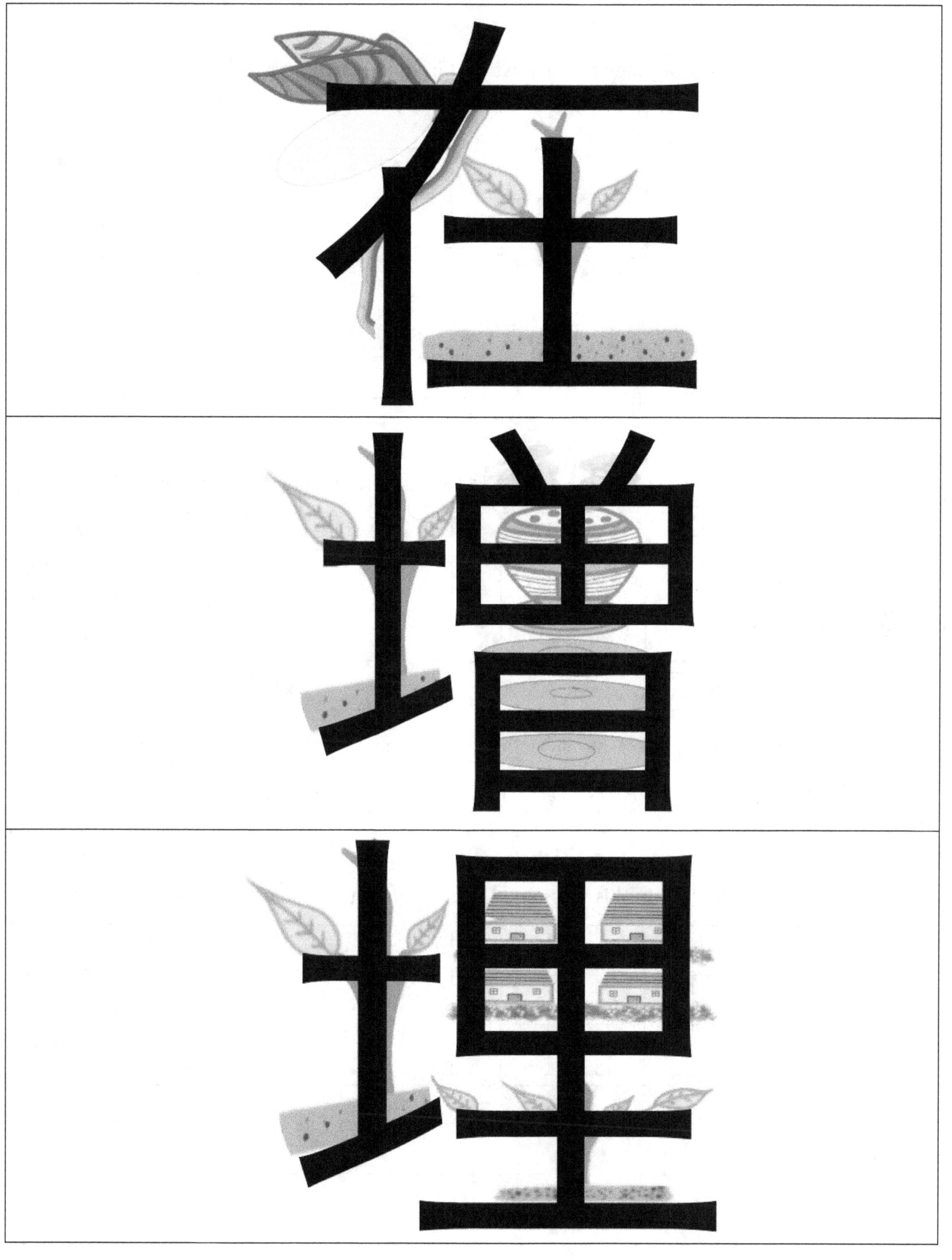

在 EXIST, OUTSKIRTS

"Sprouting seeds (才) exist (在) in nutrient rich soil (土)"

ON (ザイ)		Kun (あ)
げんざい 現 在 = Present, up to now	そんざい 存 在 = Existence, being	あ 在る = To live, to be
ざいがく 在 学 = (Enrolled) in school	たいざい 滞 在 = Stay	

増 INCREASE, ADD, GAIN

"Adding layers (曽) of good soil (土) is a way to increase (増) its nutrients"

ON (ゾウ)		Kun (ふ、 ま)	
げきぞう 激 増 = Sudden increase	ぞうげん 増 減 = Fluctuation	ふ 増える = To increase	ま 増す = To grow
ぞうか 増 加 = Increase, addition	ぞうだい 増 大 = Enlargement	ふ 増やす = To increase	

埋 BURY, BE FILLED UP

"The ground (土) in this village (里) has some much buried (埋) inside"

Kun (う)
う 埋める = To bury, to fill up

較 CONTRAST, COMPARE

"When mixing (交) car (車) components, make sure to compare (較) the compatibility"

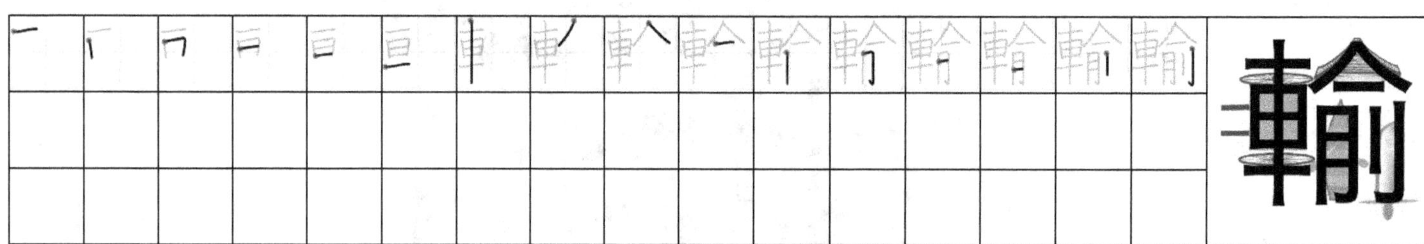

ON (カ ク)

ひかく 比 較 = Comparison	ひかくてき 比 較 的 = Relatively

輸 TRANSPORT, SEND, BE INFERIOR

"The boat (舟) is transporting (輸) articles such as knives (リ) and cars (車)"

ON (ユ)

ゆけつ 輸 血 = Blood transfusion	ゆそう 輸 送 = Transport
ゆしゅつ 輸 出 = Export	ゆにゅう 輸 入 = Import

般 CARRIER, CARRY, GENERAL

"We often carry (般) our tools (殳) in the boat (舟)"

ON (パ ン)

いっぱん 一 般 = General, liberal	ぜんぱん 全 般 = (The) whole, universal

昇
乾 乞
療

昇 RISE UP

"As soon as the sun (日) raises up (昇), I put the grains in the measuring container (升)"

Kun (のぼ)

のぼ
昇 る = To arise, to ascend

乾 DRY, DROUGHT, DESSICATE

"During sunrise (𠦝) I saw the growing plant (乙) desiccating (乾)"

ON (カン)

かんそう
乾 燥 = Dryness, aridity

かんでんち
乾 電 池 = Battery

かんぱい
乾 杯 = Toast (drink), cheers

Kun (かわ)

かわ
乾 かす = To dry (clothes, etc.), to desiccate

かわ
乾 く = To get dry

療 HEAL, CURE

"We must cure (療) his illness (疒) as his fever feels like fire (火) and is hot like the sun (日)"

ON (リョウ)

いりょう
医 療 = Medical care, medical treatment

容 CONTAIN, FORM, LOOKS

"The village (谷) forms (容) the shape of a gigantic roof (宀)"

ON (ヨウ)

ようい 容易 = Easy, simple, plain	けいようし 形容詞 = i-adjective	ないよう 内容 = Contents, matter
ようせき 容積 = Capacity, volume	けいようどうし 形容動詞 = Adjectival noun	びよう 美容 = Beauty, good figure

寝 LIE DOWN, SLEEP, REST

"Rest (寝) your hands (ヨ) on the table (爿), and feel at easy under this roof (宀)"

ON (シン) / Kun (ね)

ON (シン)	Kun (ね)		
しんだい 寝台 = Bed, couch	ねぼう 寝坊 = Sleeping in late	ねまき 寝巻 = Sleep-wear	ひるね 昼寝 = Nap (afternoon)
	ねまき 寝間着 = Sleep-wear	ね 寝る = To go to bed, sleep	

寄 DRAW NEAR, STOP IN, COLLECT

"I drew near (寄) a strange (奇) big (大) roof (宀)"

Kun (よ、より)

よ 寄せる = To come near, to gather	ちかよ 近寄る = To approach	かたよ 片寄る = To be one-sided
よ 寄る = To visit, to approach	としより 年寄 = Old people	

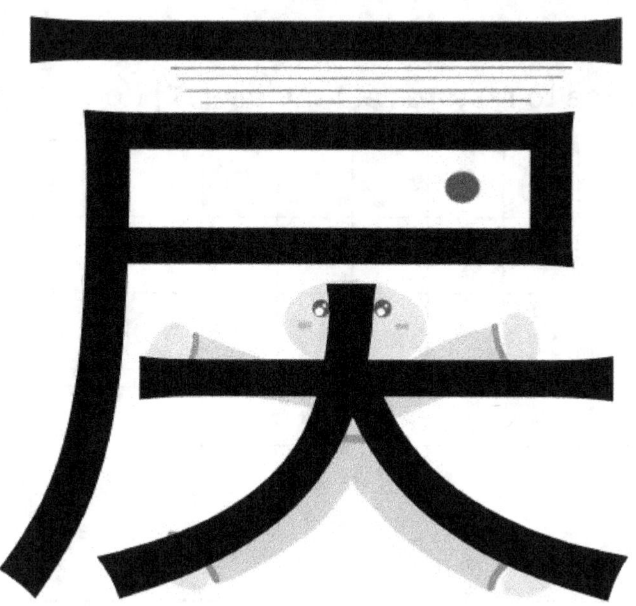

戻 RETURN, RESTORE

"Time to restore (戻) the big (大) door (戸)"

一　丁　三　尸　尸　戻　戻

Kun (もど)

はらいもど 払 戻 す = To repay もど 戻 す = To restore, to put back	もど 戻 る = To turn back, to return

突 STAB, PIERCE

"Piercing (突) this rock would only cause a big (大) hole (穴)"

丶　丷　宀　穴　空　空　突

ON (トツ)	Kun (つ)	
えんとつ 煙 突 = Chimney しょうとつ 衝 突 = Collision	つ　　あた 突 き 当 り = End (street, hallway) つ　あ 突 き 当 たる = To run into	つ 突 く = To strike つ　こ 突 っ 込 む = To plunge into

破 RIP, TEAR, BREAK

"Stone (石) climbing can tear (破) the skin (皮)"

一　丆　石　石　石　矿　矿　破　破

ON (ハ)	Kun (やぶ)	
はさん 破 産 = (Personal) Bankruptcy はへん 破 片 = Fragment	やぶ 破 く = To tear, to rip やぶ 破 る = To tear, to smash	やぶ 破 れる = To get torn

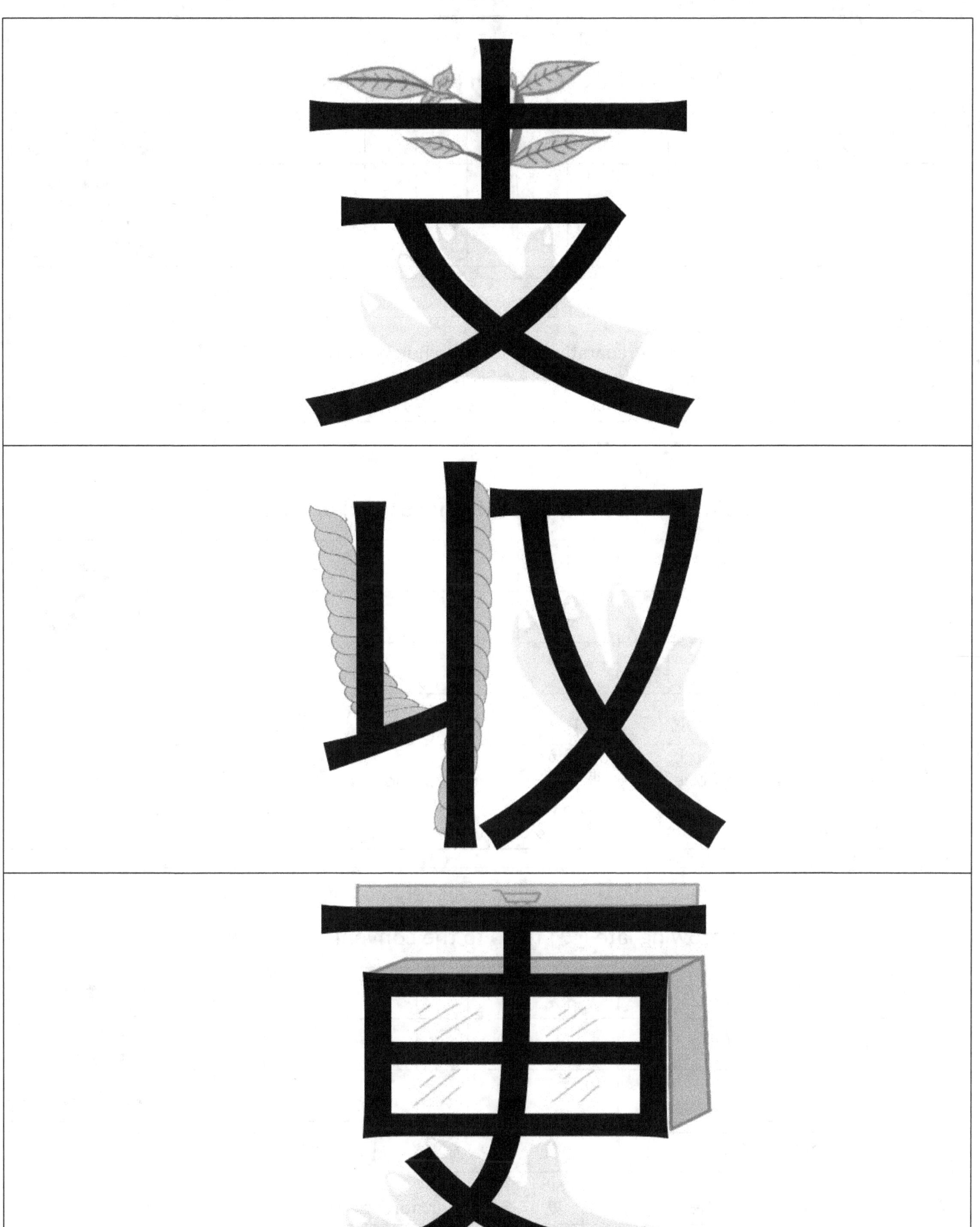

支 BRANCH, SUPPORT

"The hand (又) holds ten (十) branches (支)"

ON (シ)			Kun (ささ、つか)
しきゅう 支 給 = Allowance	したく 支 度 = Preparation	しはい 支 配 = Rule, control	ささ 支 える = To support
ししゅつ 支 出 = Expenditure	してん 支 店 = Branch store	しはら 支 払 い = Payment	さ　つか 差 し 支 え = Hindrance

収 INCOME, OBTAIN, REAP

"Obtain (収) rope (丩) to tie the hands (又) of criminals"

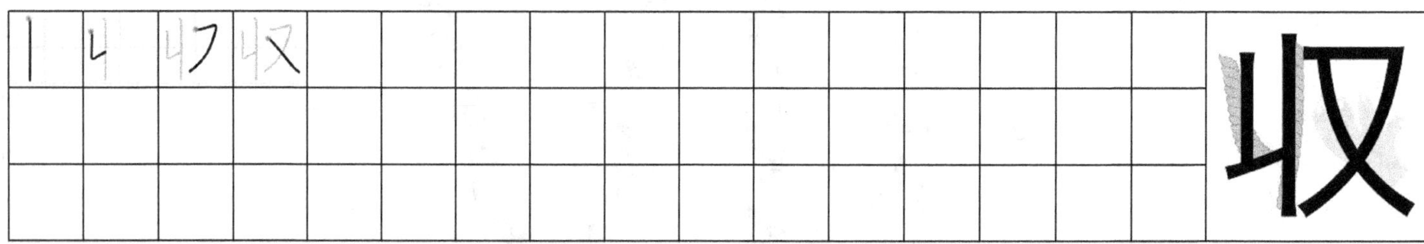

ON (シュウ)		Kun (おさ)
りょうしゅう 領 収 = Receipt (of money)	しゅうかく 収 穫 = Harvest, crop	おさ 収 める = To dedicate, to make an offering
きゅうしゅう 吸 収 = Absorption, suction	しゅうにゅう 収 入 = Income, receipts	

Note: The original meaning was arresting criminals.

更 GROW LATE, RENOVATE

"It is growing late (更) to go to the convenience store"

ON (コウ)	Kun (さら、ふ)	
へんこう 変 更 = Change, modification	さら 更 に = Furthermore, again	ふ 更 ける = To get late

Note: This kanji was originally a table and hand with a whip, giving the meaning of hitting something.

看 WATCH OVER, SEE

"To see (看) better, put a hand (手) above your eyes (目)"

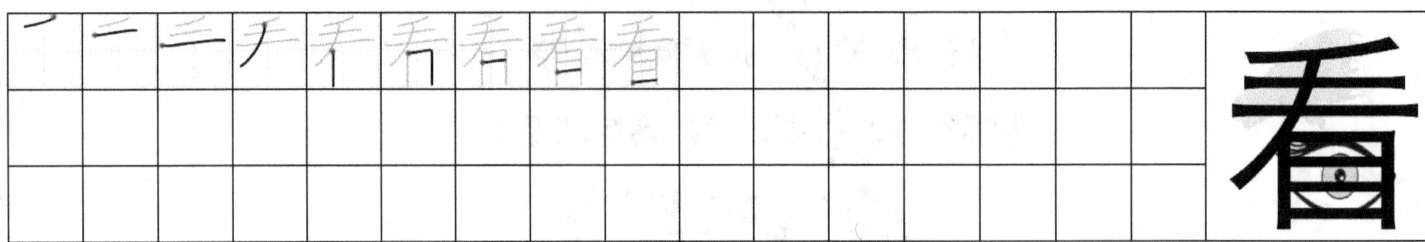

ON (カン)

かんごふ
看護婦 = (Female) nurse

かんびょう
看 病 = Nursing (a patient)

かんばん
看 板 = Sign, signboard

払 PAY, PRUNE, BANISH

"I (ム) pay (払) with the cash I have in my hand (扌)"

Kun (はら)

しはら
支 払 い = Payment

はら　こ
払 い込む = To deposit

はら
払 う = To pay, to brush

しはら
支 払 う = To pay

はらいもど
払 戻 す = To repay

よ　ぱら
酔っ 払 い = Drunkard

担 SHOULDERING, CARRY

"The job is about carrying (担) items with your hands (扌) from dawn (旦) to dusk"

ON (タン)

たんとう
担 当 = Being in charge

Kun (かつ)

かつ
担 ぐ = To shoulder, to carry on shoulder

捜
抱
拝

捜 SEARCH, LOOK FOR

"I use my hand (扌) to look for (捜) a refuge from the lighting (申) bolt"

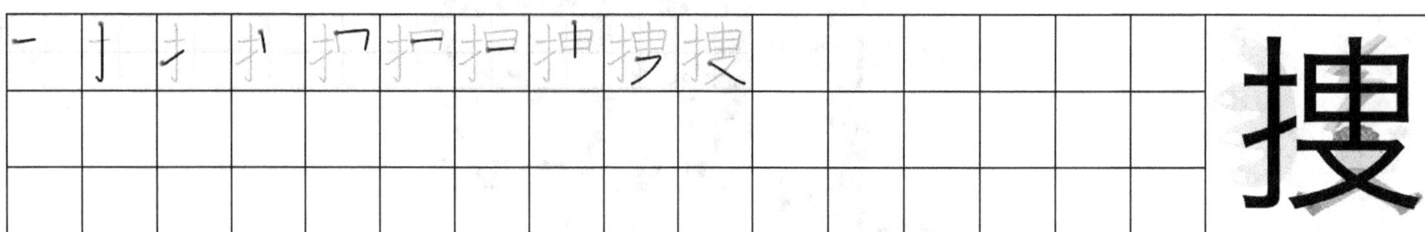

Kun (さが)

さが
捜 す = To search, to seek

抱 EMBRACE, HUG

"A hug (抱) is wrapping (包) your hands (扌) around someone"

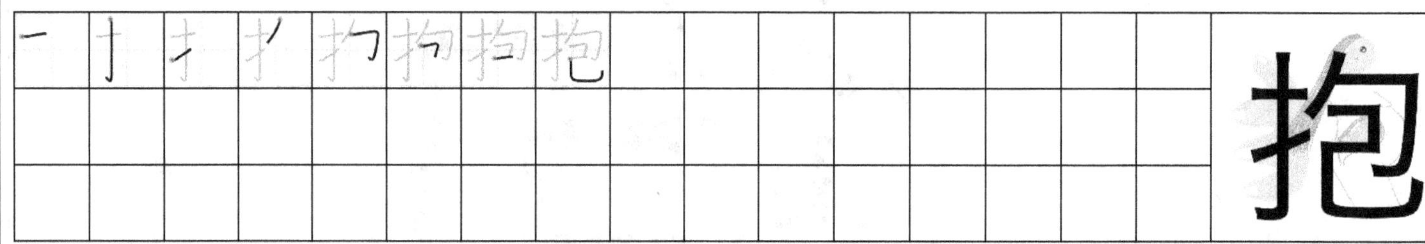

Kun (いだ、 かか、 だ)

だ
抱 く = To embrace, to hug

いだ
抱 く = To embrace

かか
抱 える = To hold, to carry under

拝 WORSHIP, ADORE

"Let's get our hands (扌) together to worship (拝) our god"

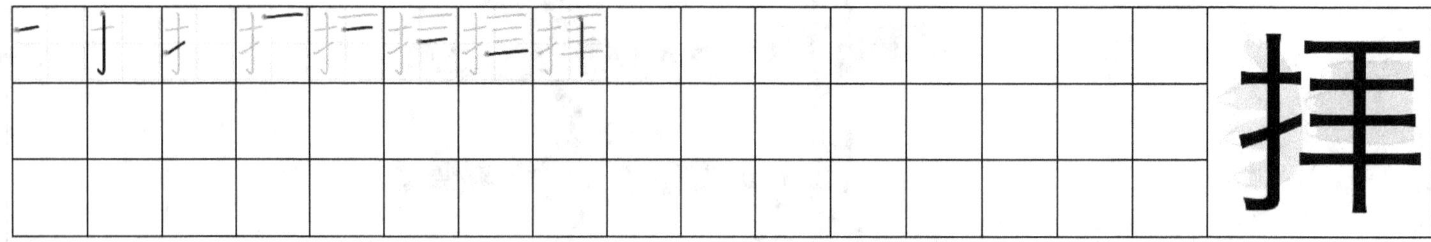

ON (ハイ)

はいけん
拝 見 = (pol) Seeing

Kun (おが)

おが
拝 む = To do reverence, to beg

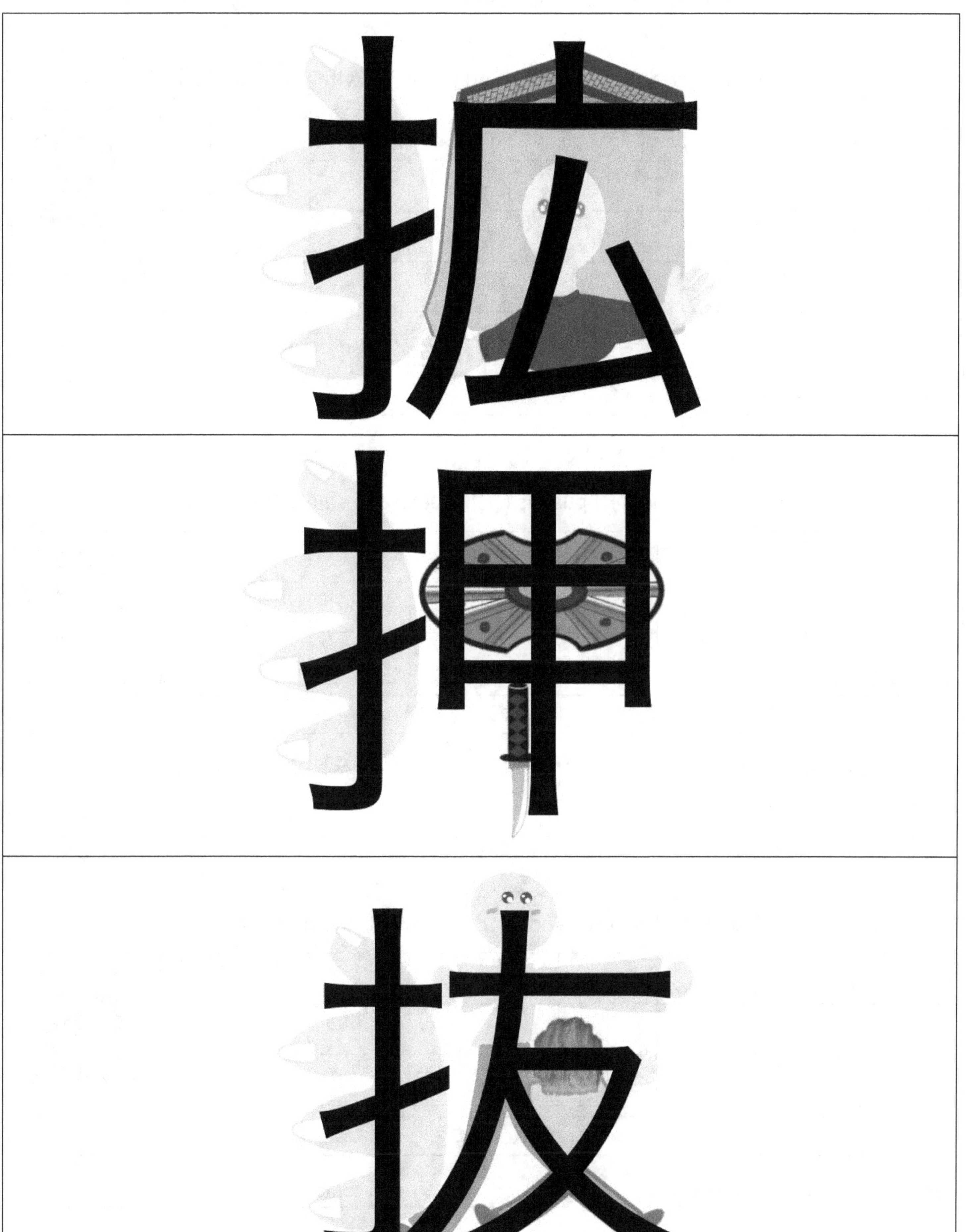

拡 BROADEN, EXTEND

"Make the tent wide (広) by extending (拡) it with your hand (扌)"

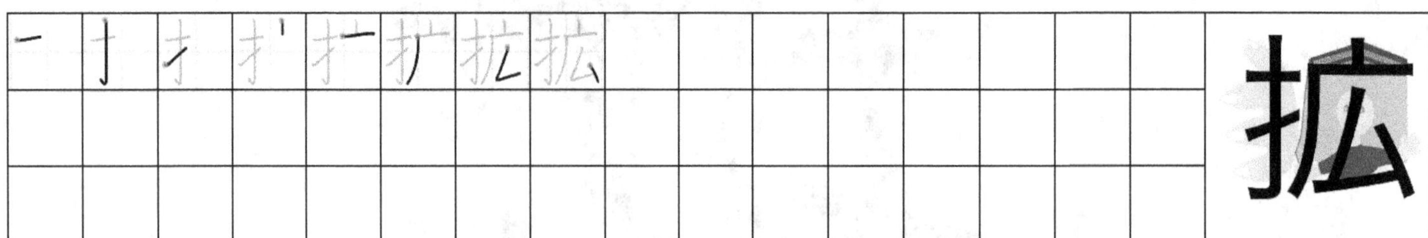

ON (カク)

かくじゅう 拡 充 = Expansion	かくちょう 拡 張 = Expansion, extension
かくだい 拡 大 = Magnification	

押 PUSH, STOP, SEAL

"The hand (扌) pushes (押) against the shield (甲)"

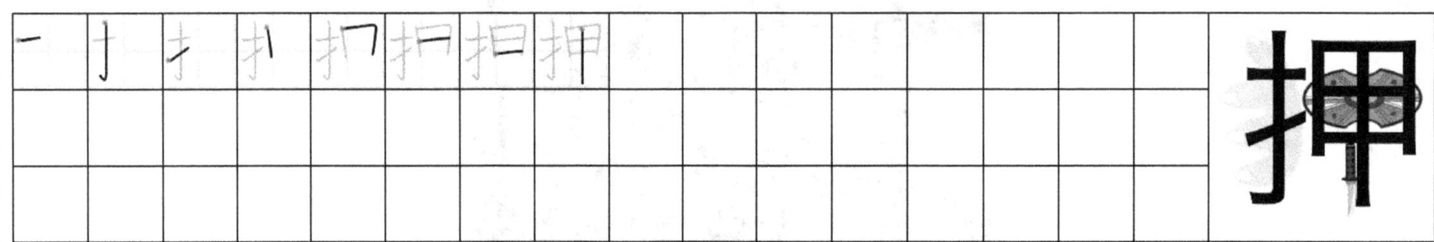

Kun (お、おさ)

お 押す = To push, to press	おい 押し入れ = Closet
おさ 押 える = To seize, to pin down	

抜 SLIP OUT, EXTRACT, PULL OUT

"I pull out (抜) my hand (扌) to comfort my friend (友)"

Kun (ぬ)

ぬ 抜く = To extract, to pull out	ぬ 抜ける = To come out

CHAPTER 14: VERBS PART II

換	損	捕	操	探	招
293	294	295	296	297	298
採	接	授	掃	掘	捨
299	300	301	302	303	304
渡	測	到	混	減	滴
305	306	307	308	309	310
沈	浮	済	溶	塗	準
311	312	313	314	315	316
泊	沸	濯	盗	凍	震
317	318	319	320	321	322
磨	座	応	慣	忘	亡
323	324	325	326	327	328

換

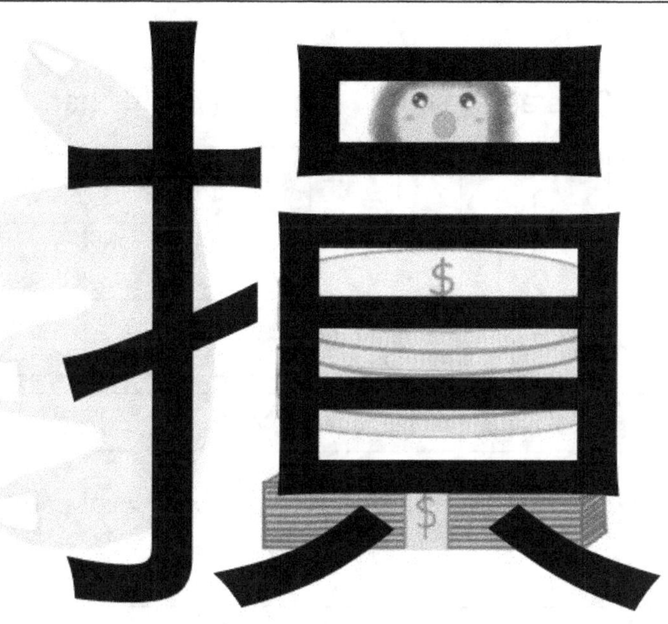

損

搞

"The big (大) person bends (⌒) and changes (換) positions with his hands (扌) four (四) times"

ON (カン)	Kun (か)	ODD (カエ)
かんき 換気 = Ventilation	のか 乗り換える = To transfer (trains)	のりかえ 乗換 = Transfer (trains)
こうかん 交換 = Exchange, interchange	か 換える = To exchange, to interchange	

損 DAMAGE, LOSS, HURT, INJURE

"The employee (員) hurts (損) his hand (扌)"

ON (ソン)	
そん 損 = Disadvantage, loss	そんとく 損得 = Loss and gain
そんがい 損害 = Damage, injury	

捕 CATCH, CAPTURE

"Catch (捕) by hand (扌) the roots of the plant (甫)"

ON (ホ)	Kun (つか、と)	
たいほ 逮捕 = Arrest, capture	つか 捕まえる = To catch, to seize	と 捕らえる = To seize, to catch
	つか 捕まる = To be caught	と 捕る = To take, to capture

操

操

招

操 MANEUVER, MANIPULATE, OPERATE

"Do not take in your hands (扌) or maneuver (操) baby birds chirping (喿)"

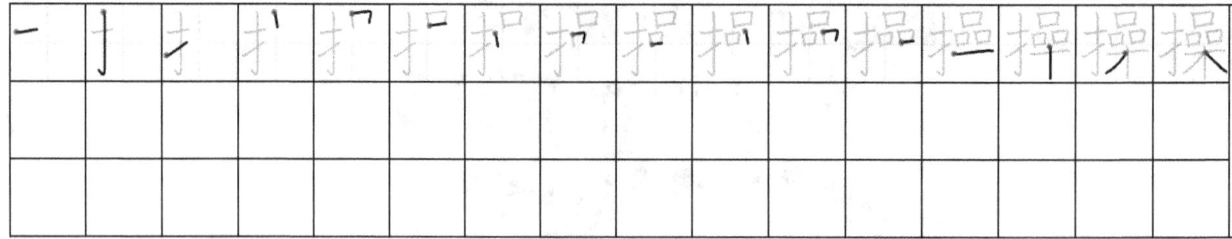

ON (ソウ)

そうさ 操 作 = Operation, management	たいそう 体 操 = Gymnastics, calisthenics

探 GROPE, SEARCH, LOOK FOR

"Use your hand (扌) to remove the trees (木) and search (探) for the cave (穴)"

Kun (さぐ、さが)

さぐ 探 る = To search, to look for	さが 探 す = To search for

招 BECKON, INVITE, SUMMON

"Just call (召) them over with your hand (扌), they will know they are invited (招)"

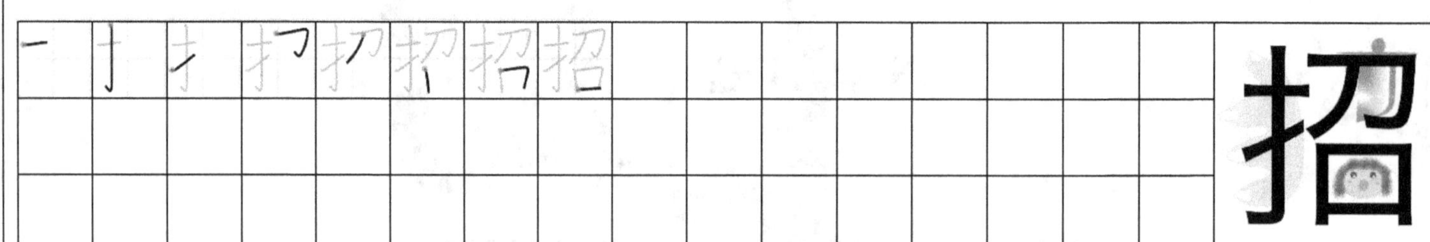

ON (ショウ)	Kun (まね)
しょうたい 招 待 = Invitation	まね 招 く = To invite

採 PICK, TAKE, FETCH

"Pick (採) with your hand (扌) anything you can get from that tree (木)"

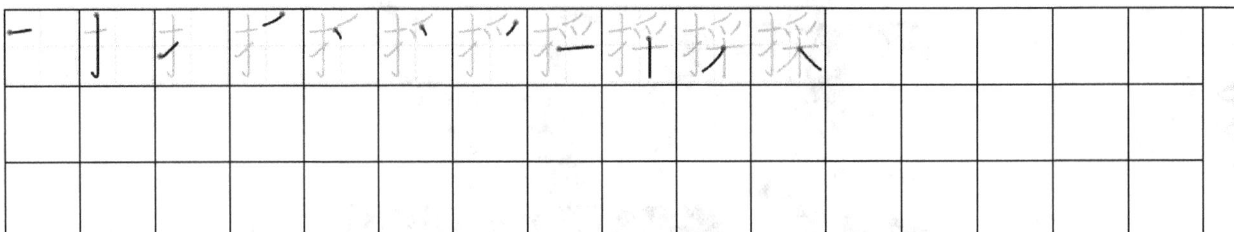

ON (サイ)	Kun (と)
さいてん 採 点 = Marking, grading	と 採る = To adopt (measure, proposal)

接 TOUCH, CONTACT, ADJOIN

"Don't touch (接) the concubine (妾) with dirty hands (扌)"

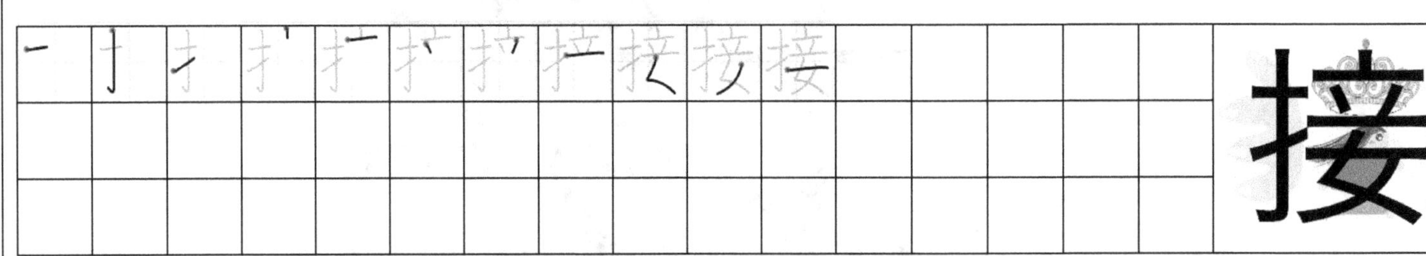

ON (セツ)			
おうせつ 応 接 = Reception	せっきん 接 近 = Getting closer	ちょくせつ 直 接 = Immediate	せっ 接 する = To touch, to come in contact with
かんせつ 間 接 = Indirection	せつぞく 接 続 = Connection	めんせつ 面 接 = Interview	

Note: Do not confuse with the kanji for "Stand" 立, the original kanji has been simplified, but the original meaning was a headdress.

授 IMPART, INSTRUCT, GRANT

"Please receive (受) the message I instruct (授) with my hands (扌)"

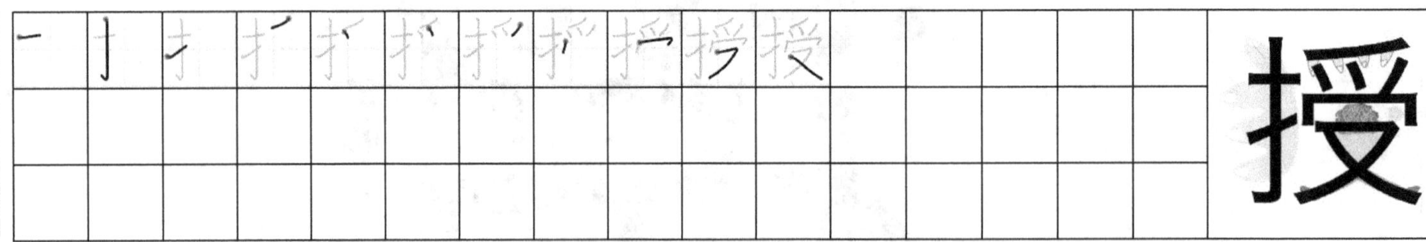

ON (ジュ)	
きょうじゅ 教 授 = Teaching, instruction	じょきょうじゅ 助 教 授 = Assistant professor
じゅぎょう 授 業 = Lesson, class work	

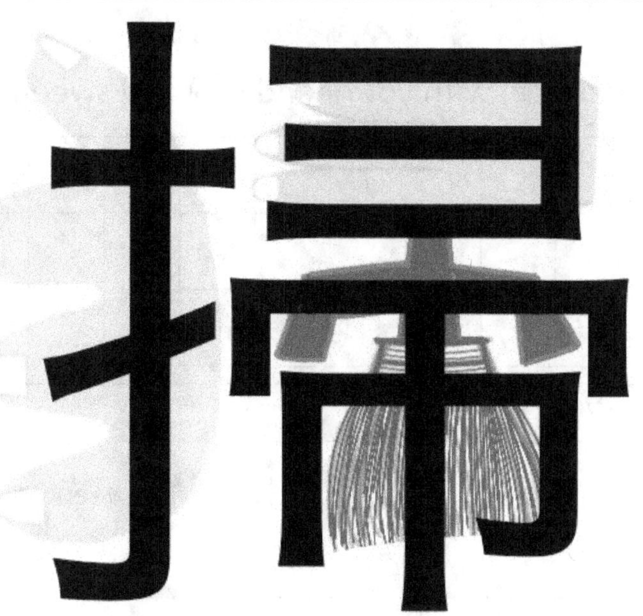

掃 SWEEP, BRUSH

"Hold the broom (帚) with your hand (扌) and sweep (掃) the floors"

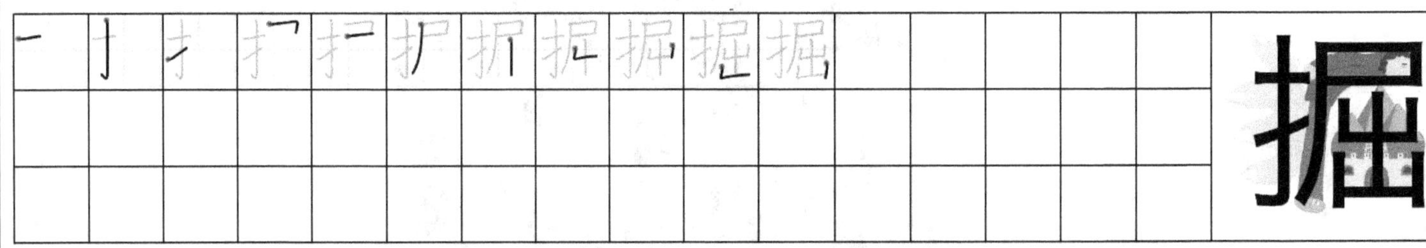

ON (ソウ)	Kun (は)
そうじ 掃 除 = Cleaning, sweeping せいそう 清 掃 = Cleaning	は 掃 く = To sweep, to brush

掘 DIG, EXCAVATE

"Dig (掘) the corpse (尸) out with your hand (扌) and get it to come out (出)"

Kun (ほ)
ほ 掘 る = To dig, to excavate

捨 THROW AWAY, DISCARD, ABANDON

"The hand (扌) waves at the abandoned (捨) guesthouse (舍)"

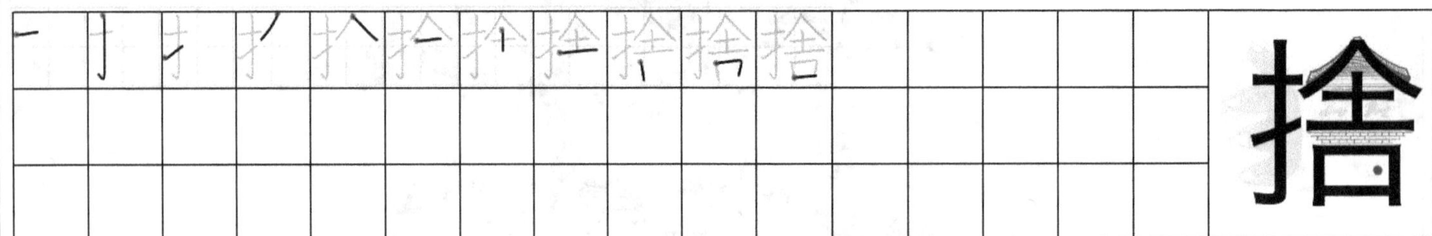

ON (シャ)	Kun (す)
ししゃごにゅう 四 捨 五 入 = Rounding up (fractions)	す 捨 てる = To throw away, to cast aside

渡 TRANSIT, CROSS, IMPORT

"For any vessel to transit (渡), the temperature degrees (度) of the water (シ) are critical"

Kun (わた)

わた
渡 す = To carry across, to hand over

測 MEASURE, PLAN, SCHEME

"There are rules (則) and standards to measure (測) water (シ) levels"

ON (ソク) | Kun (はか)

よそく
予測 = Prediction, estimation

かんそく
観 測 = Observation

そくてい
測 定 = Measurement

そくりょう
測 量 = Measurement, surveying

はか
測 る = To measure, to weigh

到 ARRIVAL, PROCEED, REACH

"The knife (リ) set arrives (至) today. Let's get the space ready before the arrival (到)"

ON (トウ)

とうちゃく
到 着 = Arrival

混

減

滴

混 MIX, BLEND, CONFUSE

"Since your descendants (昆) are as many as the waters (氵), I always confuse (混) them!"

	ON (コン)		Kun (ま)
こんざつ 混 雑 = Confusion, congestion		こんごう 混 合 = Mixing, mixture	ま 混ざる = To be mixed
こんらん 混 乱 = Disorder, chaos			ま 混ぜる = To mix

減 DWINDLE, DECREASE, REDUCE

"Close the mouth (口) of the water (氵) brook to decrease (減) the flow"

	ON (ゲン)	Kun (へ)
かげん 加 減 = Addition and subtraction, extend		へ 減らす = To abate, to decrease
ぞうげん 増 減 = Increase and decrease		へ 減る = To diminish, to abate

滴 DRIP, DROP

"A legitimate (商) plumber will find the cause of the water (氵) dripping (滴)"

ON (テキ)
すいてき 水 滴 = Drop of water

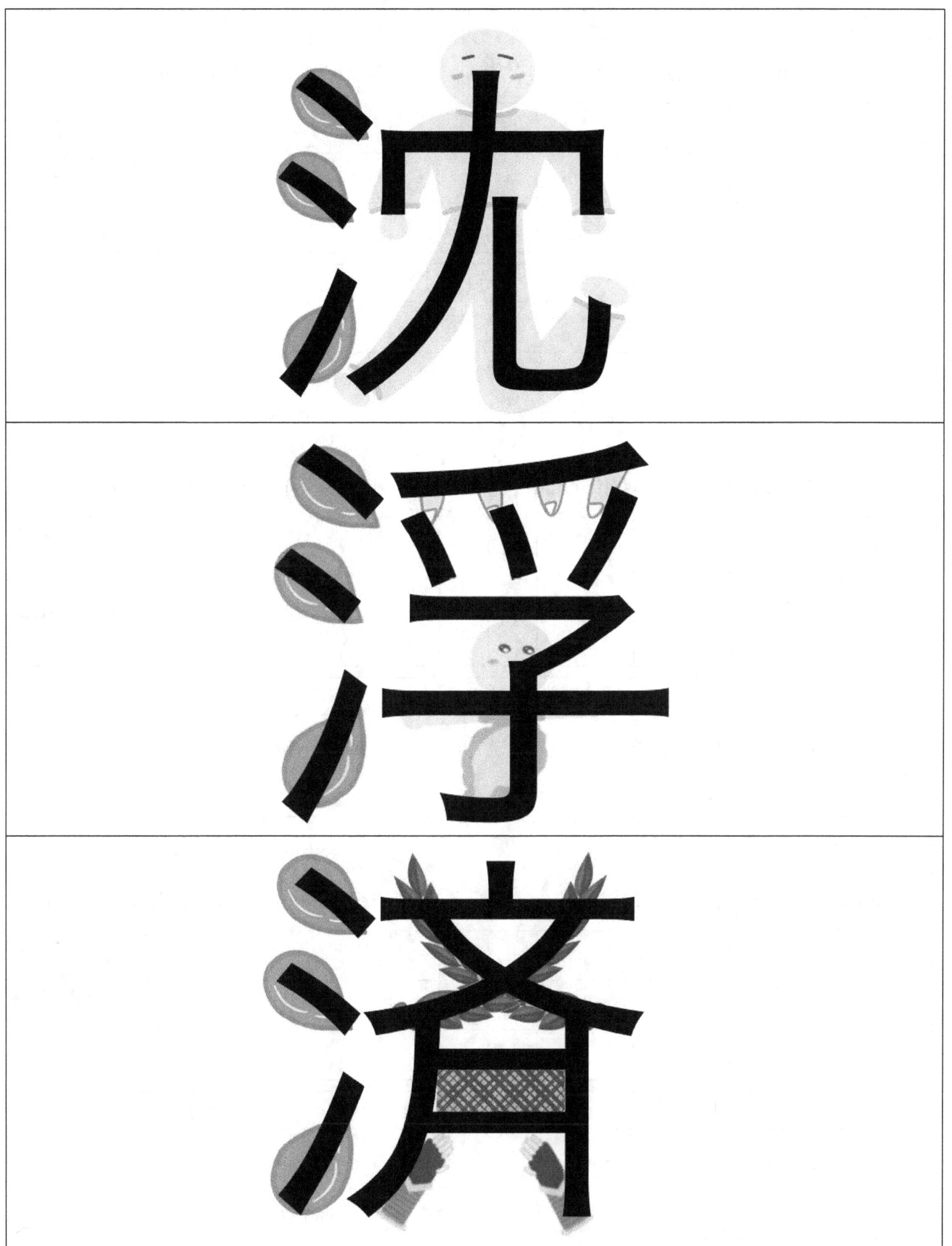

沈 SINK, BE SUBMERGED

"The person was submerged (沈) as a sacrifice to the water (氵) god"

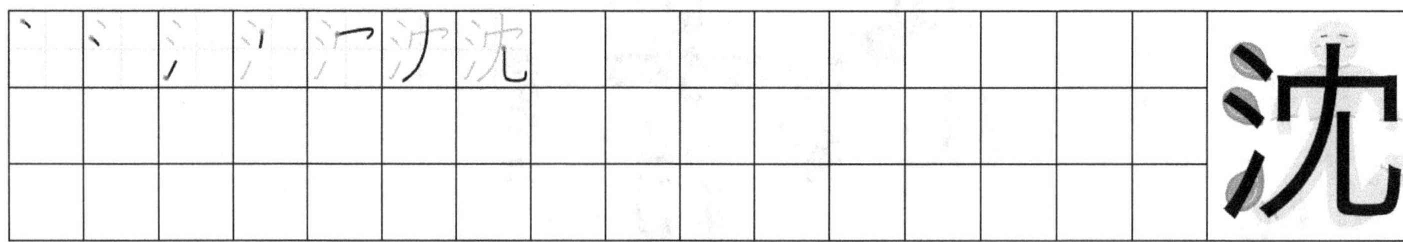

Kun (しず)

しず
沈 む = To sink

浮 FLOATING, FLOAT

"The hand (爪) holds the child, (子) while he floats (浮) in the water (氵)"

Kun (う)

う
浮かぶ = To float, to rise to surface

う
浮かべる = To float, to recall

う
浮く = To float, to become merry

済 RELIEVE, COME TO AN END

"Drinking equal (斉) amounts of water (氵) every time can help relieve (済) future pain"

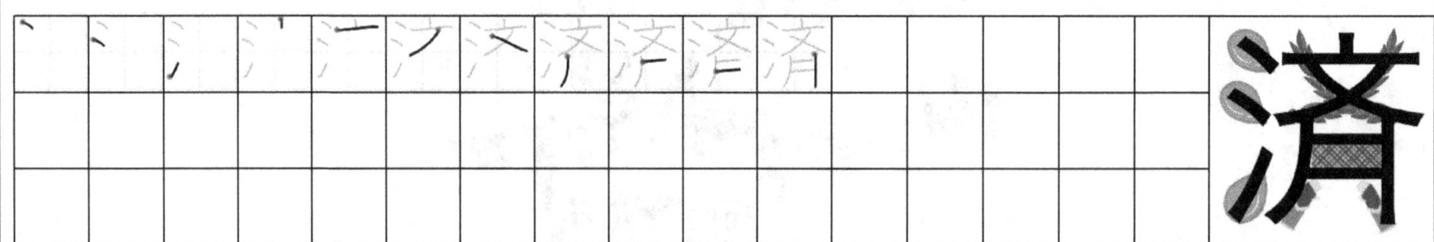

ON (ザイ)

けいざい
経 済 = Economics, business, finance

Kun (す)

す
済ませる = To finish, to get it over with

す
済む = To finish, to end

Note: This kanji was originally the name of a river.

溶

塗

準

溶 MELT, DISSOLVE

"The cup contained (容) ice that melted (溶) and now it is just water (氵)"

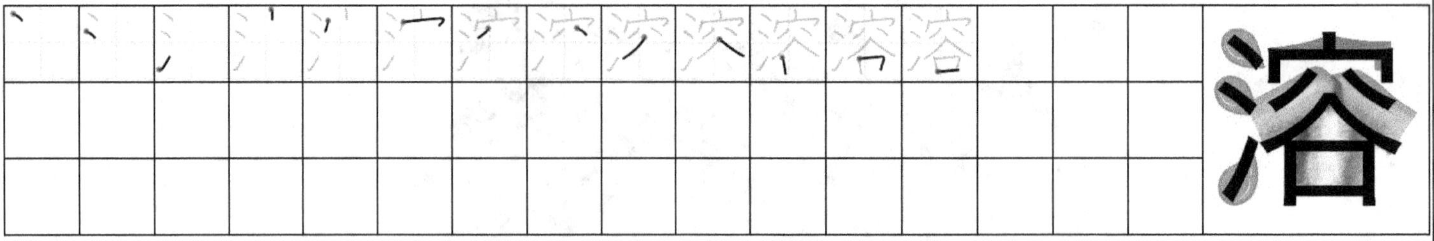

ON (ヨウ)	Kun (と)	
ようがん 溶 岩 = Lava	と 溶かす = To melt, to dissolve	と　こ 溶け込む = To melt into
	と 溶く = To dissolve (paint)	と 溶ける = To melt

塗 PAINT, PLASTER, SMEAR, COATING

"Don't paint (塗) in excess (余) as the liquid (氵) drips and falls to the ground (土)"

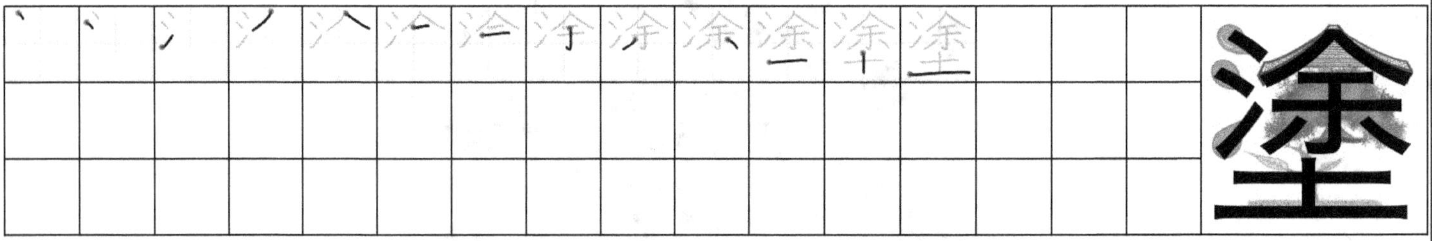

Kun (ぬ)
ぬ 塗る = To paint, to plaster

準 CORRESPOND TO, PROPORTIONATE TO

"The amount of water (氵) must correspond (準) to the number of falcons (隼) we breed"

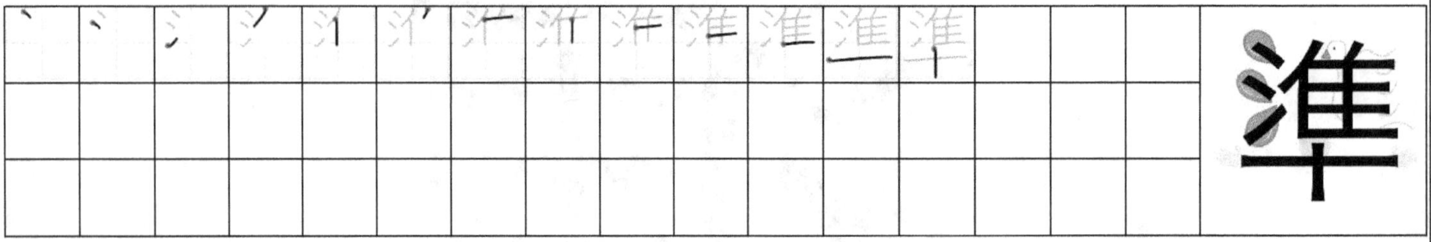

ON (ジュン)		
きじゅん 基 準 = Standard, basis	じゅんび 準 備 = Preparation, reserve	ひょうじゅん 標 準 = Standard, level
きじゅん 規 準 = Standard, basis	すいじゅん 水 準 = Water level, standard	

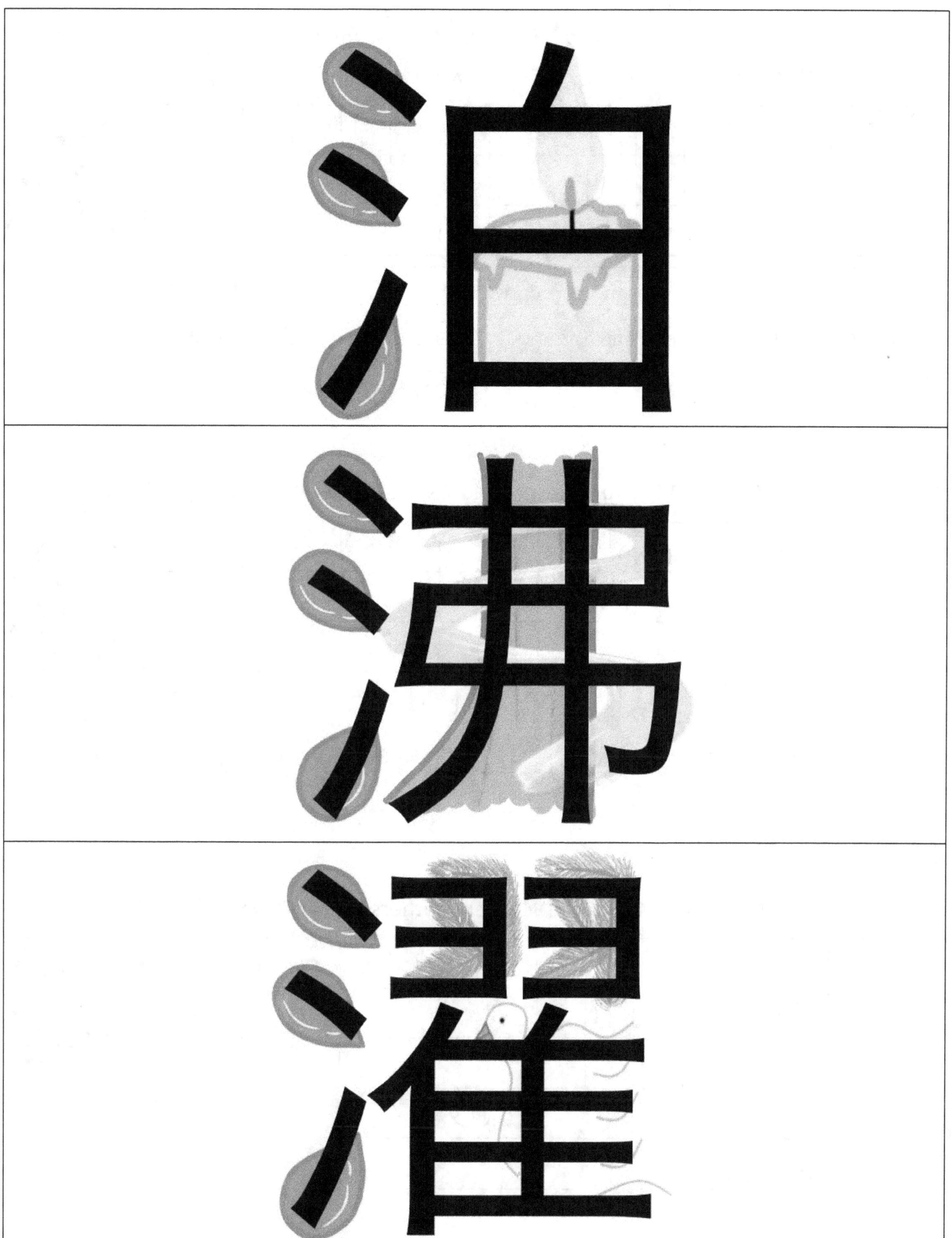

泊 OVERNIGHT STAY, PUT UP AT

"The overnight stay (泊) had warm water (氵) and white (白) candles"

	ON (ハク)		Kun (と)
しゅくはく 宿　泊　 = Lodging, accommodation		と 泊まる = To stay at (e.g. hotel) と 泊める = To lodge, to put up	

沸 BOIL, FERMENT

"Water gushing out in a spring looks like boiling (沸) water (氵)"

Kun (わ)	
わ 沸かす　= To boil, to heat	わ 沸く = To boil, to grow hot, to get excited

濯 LAUNDRY, WASH

"Little birds (隹) wash (濯) their feathers (羽) with water (氵)"

ON (タク)
せんたく 洗　濯　= Washing, laundry

盗 STEAL, ROB

"Next (次) time someone steals (盗) our bowls (皿) of food, I will go after them"

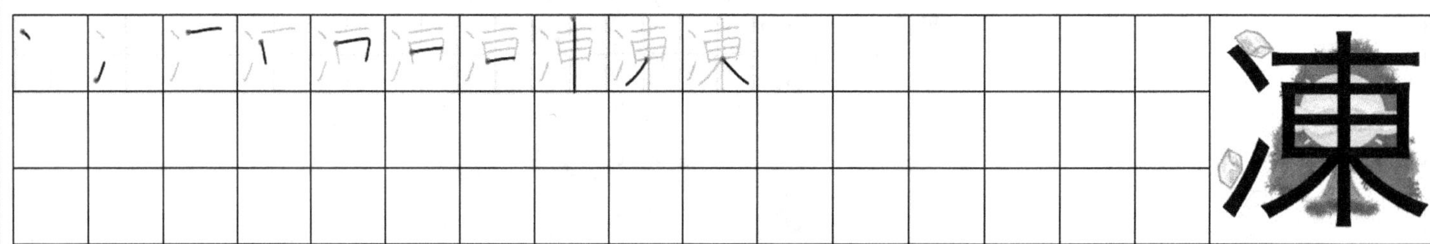

ON (トウ)	Kun (ぬす)
とうなん 盗 難 = Theft, robbery ごうとう 強 盗 = Robbery, burglary	ぬす 盗 む = To steal

凍 FROZEN, CONGEAL

"The east (東) side has frozen (凍) and there is ice (冫) all over"

ON (トウ)	Kun (こお、こご)
れいとう 冷 凍 = Freezing, cold storage	こお 凍 る = To freeze, to be frozen こご 凍 える = To freeze (of one's body)

震 QUAKE, SHAKE, TREMBLE

"The rain (雨) is so strong that even the garden forks (辰) are shaking (震)"

ON (シン)	Kun (ふる)
じしん 地 震 = Earthquake	ふる 震 える = To shiver, to shake

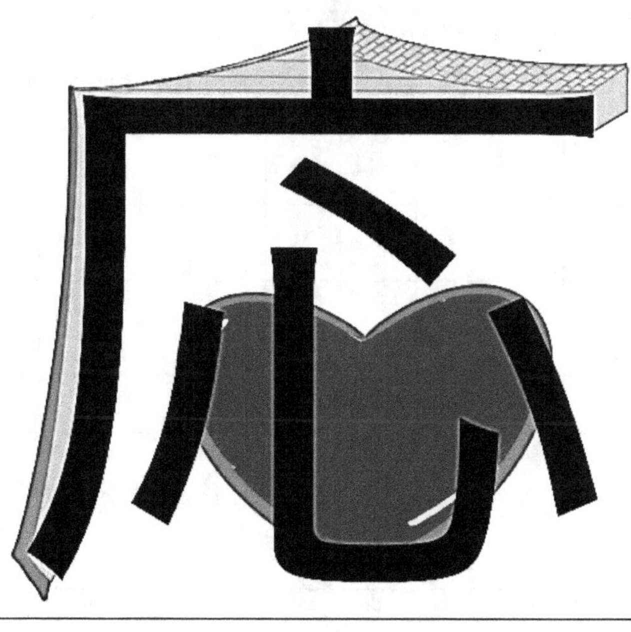

磨 GRIND, POLISH, BRUSH (TEETH)

"Use a stone (石) and linen (麻) to polish (磨)"

Kun (みが)

はみが 歯 磨 き = Toothpaste, dental brushing	みが 磨 く = To polish, to shine, to brush

座 SQUAT, SEAT, CUSHION

"There are two people (人) under the tent (广) sitting (座) on the ground (土)"

ON (ザ) / Kun (すわ)

ざしき 座 敷 = Tatami room ざせき 座 席 = Seat	ざぶとん 座 布 団 = Cushion (Japanese)	すわ 座 る = To sit

応 APPLY, REPLY, ACCEPT

"I meditate under the tent (广) to accept (応) the emotions of my heart (心)"

ON (オウ)

いちおう 一 応 = More or less おうえん 応 援 = Aid, help	おう 応 じる = To respond おう 応 ずる = To answer	おうせつ 応 接 = Reception おうたい 応 対 = Receiving	おうよう 応 用 = (practical) Application

Note: Originally a hawk which would reply to commands. Over time, it dropped the hawk and only left the heart element in the kanji.

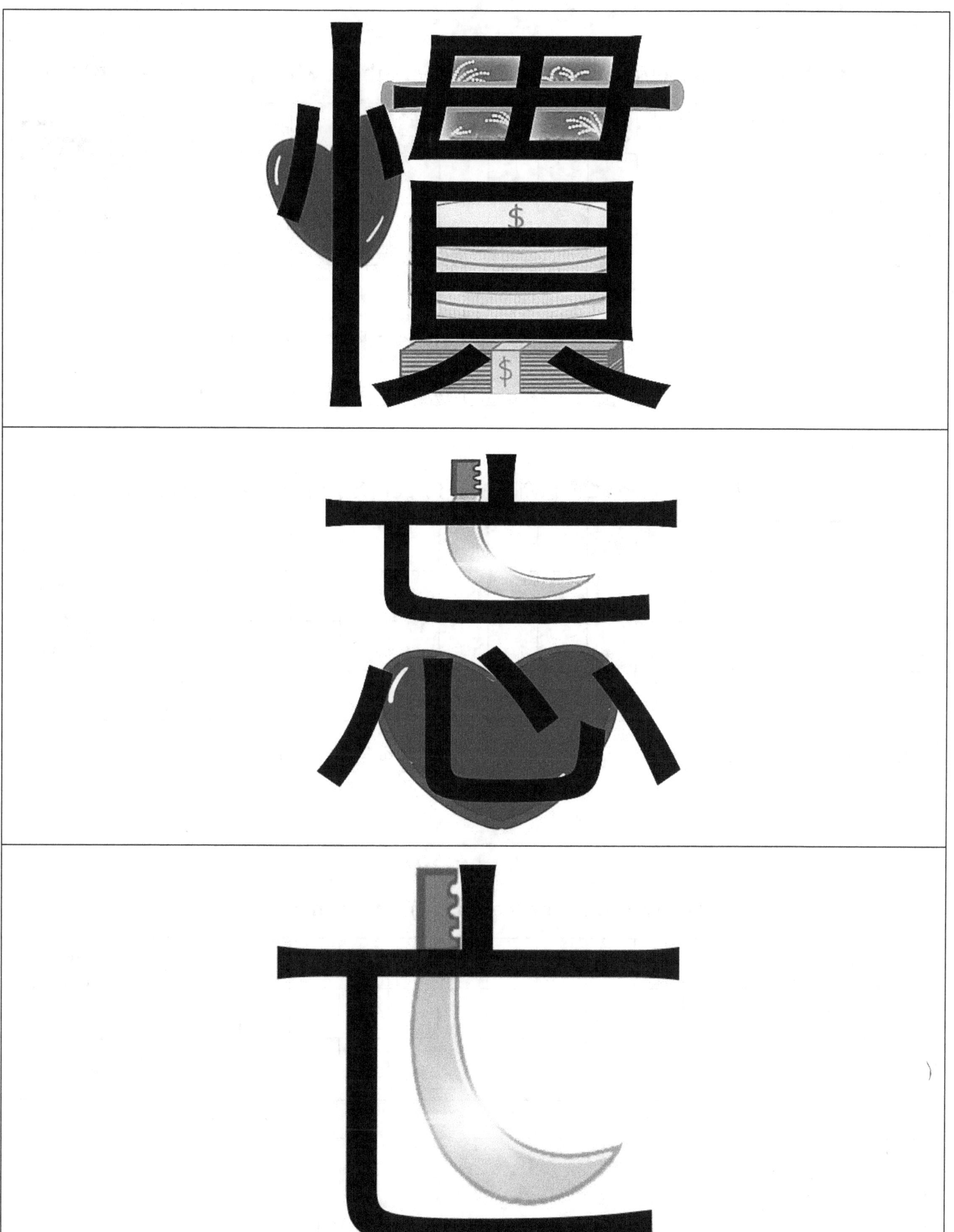

慣 ACCUSTOMED, GET USED TO

"If a situation really penetrates (貫) your heart (忄), that's when you get used (慣) to it"

ON (カン)	Kun (な)
しゅうかん 習　慣 = Custom, habit	な 慣れる = To grow accustomed to みな 見慣れる = To be familiar with

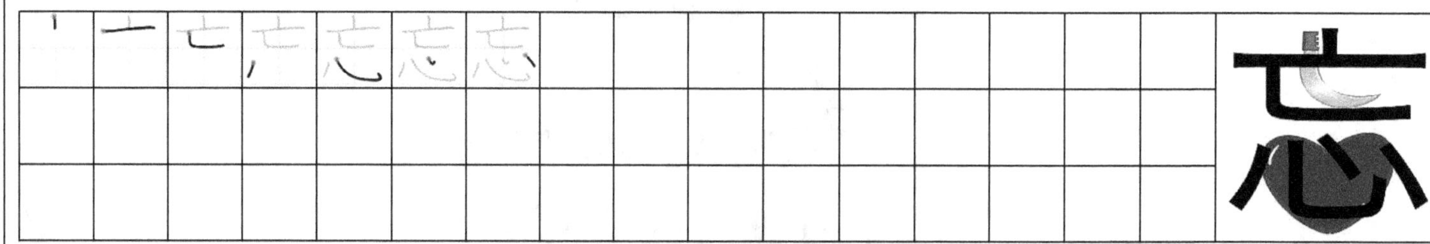

忘 FORGET

"Even after his dead (亡), I will never forget (忘) him in my heart (心)"

Kun (わす)	
わす　もの 忘れ物 = Lost article	わす 忘れる = To forget

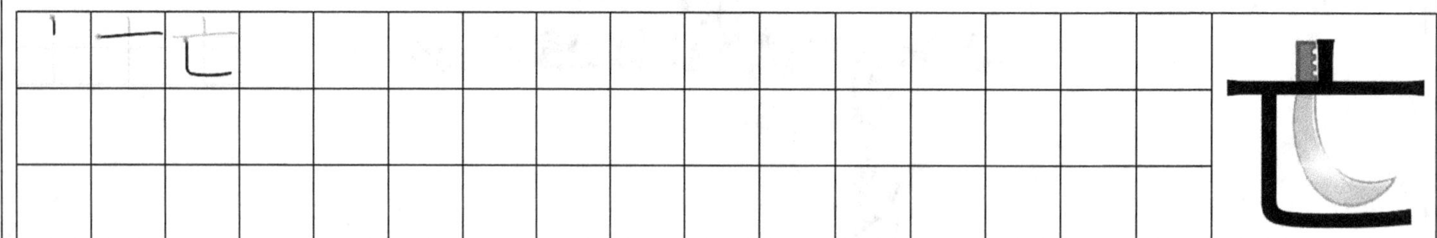

亡 DECEASED, PERISH, DYING

"He was found deceased (亡) sitting on a chair"

ON (ボウ)	Kun (な)
しぼう 死亡 = Death, mortality	な 亡くす = To lose someone (through death) な 亡くなる = To die

CHAPTER 15: VERBS PART III

設	識	認	許	誤	詰
329	330	331	332	333	334
訪	防	移	退	逃	迷
335	336	337	338	339	340
述	造	違	過	導	迎
341	342	343	344	345	346
延	超	処	倒	保	備
347	348	349	350	351	352
伸	似	伺	復	依	傾
353	354	355	356	357	358
預	頼	現	疑	張	踊
359	360	361	362	363	364

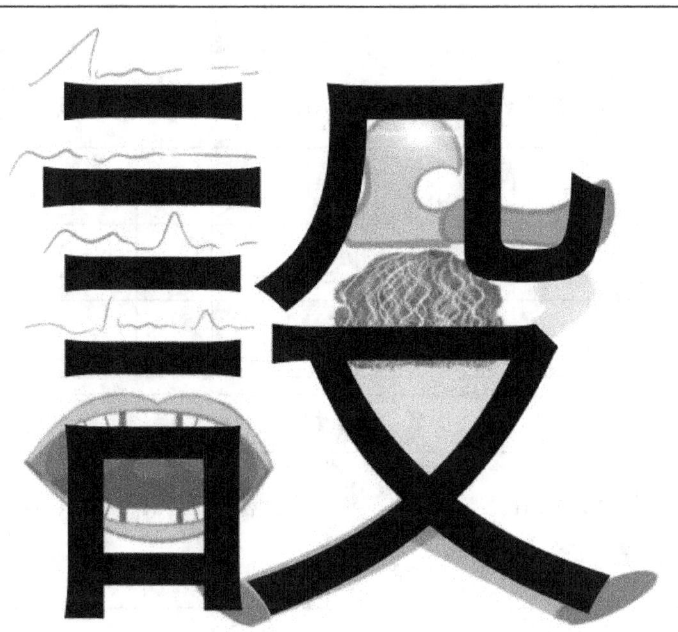

設 ESTABLISHMENT, PROVISION, PREPARE

"Say the words (言) of prayer and prepare (設) the tools (殳) to go to battle"

ON (セツ)

けんせつ
建 設 = Construction, establishment

せっけい
設 計 = Plan, design

せつび
設 備 = Equipment, device, facilities

識 DISCRIMINATING, KNOW

"Know (識) the words (言) and the sounds (音) of the enemy and get the halberds (戈) ready for battle"

ON (シキ)

いしき
意 識 = Consciousness

じょうしき
常 識 = Common sense

ちしき
知 識 = Knowledge, information

ひょうしき
標 識 = Sign, mark

認 ACKNOWLEDGE, WITNESS, DISCERN

"Learn to endure (忍) the emotional pain in your heart (心), and acknowledge (認) it"

ON (ニン) | Kun (みと)

かくにん
確 認 = Affirmation, confirmation

しょうにん
承 認 = Recognition, acknowledgement

みと
認 める = To recognize

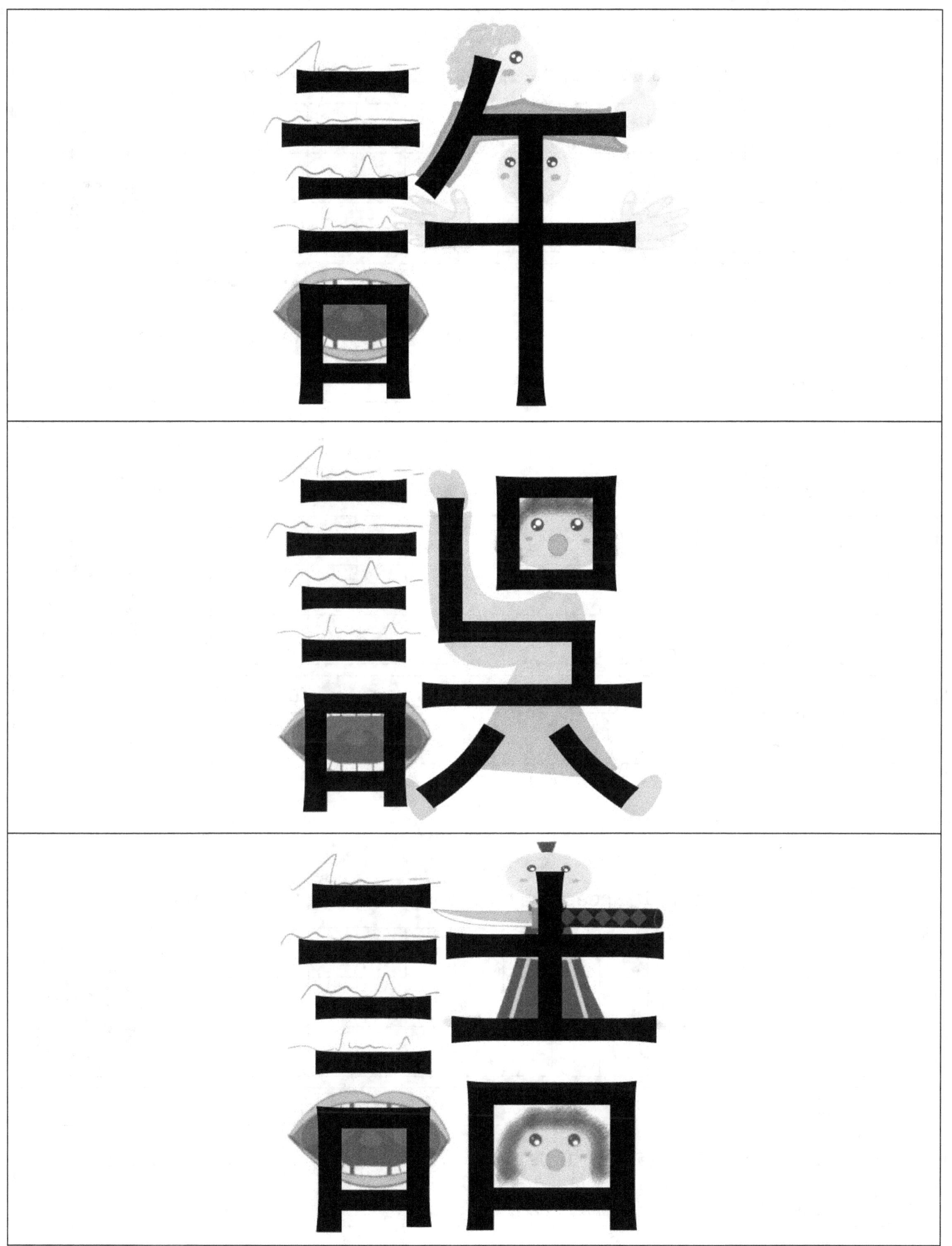

許 PERMIT, APPROVE

"I will approve (許) the speech (言) at noon (午) time"

ON (キョ)	Kun (ゆる)
きょか 許 可 = Permission, approval めんきょ 免 許 = License, permit	ゆる 許 す = To permit, to allow, to forgive

誤 MISTAKE, DO WRONG, MISLEAD

"Don't give (呉) too fast of a speech (言) or your words might be misleading (誤)"

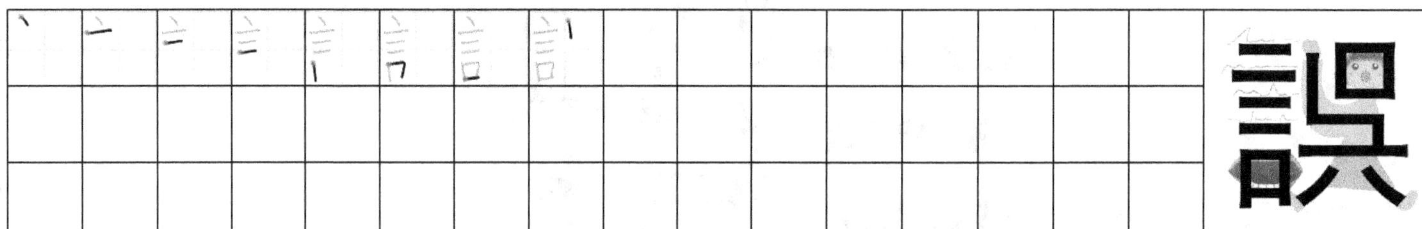

ON (ゴ)	Kun (あやま)
ごかい 誤 解 = Misunderstanding	あやま 誤 り = Error

詰 PACKED, CLOSE, REBUKE

"The samurai's (士) speech (言) was about rebuking (詰) the nation"

ODD (ヅメ)	Kun (つ)	
かんづめ 缶 詰 = Packing (in cans) びんづめ 瓶 詰 = Bottled, bottling	つ 詰 まる = To be blocked つ 詰 める = To pack, to shorten	みつ 見詰 める = To stare at, to gaze at

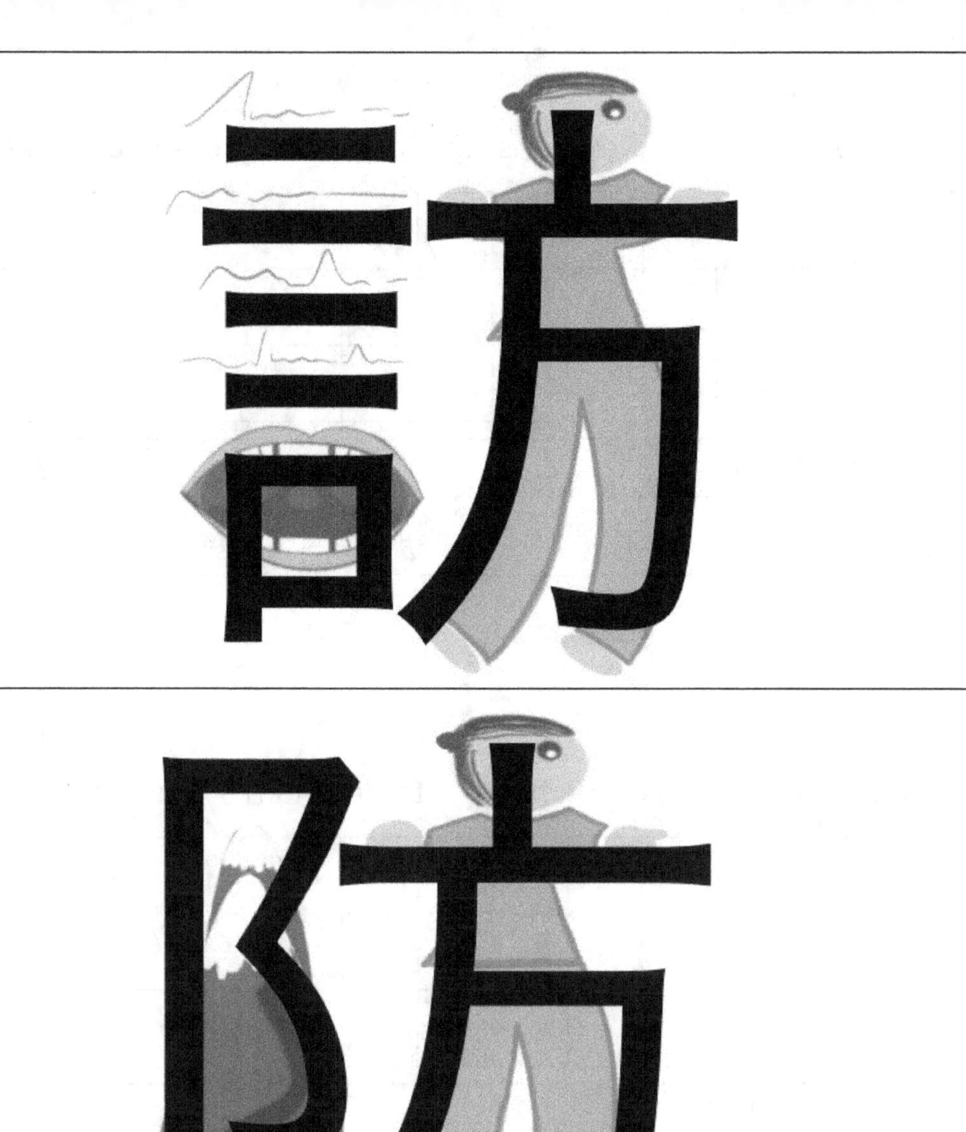

訪 VISIT, LOOK UP, OFFER SYMPATHY

"Please explain in words (言) the directions (方) to your house, so I can pay you a visit (訪)"

ON (ホウ)		Kun (たず)
ほうもん 訪 問　= Call, visit		たず 訪 ねる = To visit

防 WARD OFF, DEFEND

"Let's head in the direction (方) of the hill (阝) to defend (防) ourselves from the enemy"

ON (ボウ)		Kun (ふせ)
しょうぼう 消 防　= Fire fighting	ぼうし 防 止 = Prevention	ふせ 防 ぐ = To defend (against)
しょうぼうしょ 消 防 署　= Fire station	ぼうはん 防 犯 = Prevention of crime	

移 SHIFT, MOVE, DRIFT

"Before, it wasn't easy to shift (移) diet from the many (多) grains (禾) to eating meat"

ON (イ)	Kun (うつ)
いてん 移 転　= Moving, transfer	うつ 移 す = To change, to transfer
いどう 移 動 = Removal, migration	うつ 移 る = To move (house)

退

逃

迷

退 RETREAT, WITHDRAW, RESIGN

"Never resign (退) from the good (艮) path (辶)"

ON (タイ)		Kun (ど)
いんたい 引 退 = Retirement	たいくつ 退 屈 = Boredom	ど 退ける = To remove, to move aside
たいいん 退 院 = Leaving hospital		ど 退く = To retreat, to step aside

逃 ESCAPE, FLEE, EVADE

"Use this tortoise shell as an omen (兆) and flee (逃) through that path (辶)"

Kun (に)	
に 逃がす = To let loose, to set free	に 逃げる = To escape, to run away

迷 ASTRAY, IN DOUBT, LOST

"It is as easy to go astray (迷) on the path (辶) of life as grains of rice (米) can be scattered"

ODD (マイ)	ON (メイ)	Kun (まよ)
まいご 迷子 = Lost (stray) child	めいわく 迷 惑 = Trouble, bother	まよ 迷 う = To be puzzled
めいしん 迷 信 = Superstition		

述

造

違

述 MENTION, STATE, SPEAK

"Clearly state (述) the path (辶) where the good quality millets (朮) can be found"

ON (ジュツ)	Kun (の)
じゅつご 述 語 = Predicate	の 述べる = To state, to express

造 CREATE, MAKE, STRUCTURE

"Please inform (告) everyone that we'll create(造) a path (辶) for the cows (牛)"

ON (ゾウ)			Kun (つく)
かいぞう 改 造 = Remodeling	じんぞう 人 造 = Man-made	ぞうせん 造 船 = Shipbuilding	つく 造 る = To make
こうぞう 構 造 = Structure	せいぞう 製 造 = Manufacture		

Note: The kanji originally showed a man building a house and a boat.

違 DIFFERENCE, DIFFER

"Our paths (辶) significantly differ (違) as our feet go in opposite (韋) directions"

ON (イ)	Kun (ちが)		
そうい 相 違 = Difference	まちが 間 違える = To err	ちが 違 い = Difference	ちが 違 う = To differ (from)
いはん 違 反 = Transgression	まちが 間 違い = Mistake	ちが 違 いない = For certain	

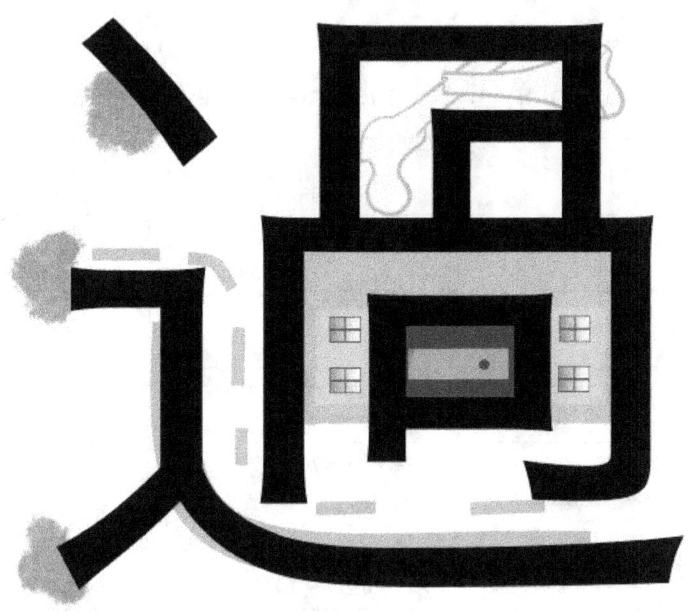

過 OVERDO, EXCEED, GO BEYOND

"Don't go beyond (過) the opening (口) at the end of the path (辶) or you will be bones (咼)"

ON (カ)			Kun (す)
かこ 過去 = The past	かじょう 過剰 = Excess	かはんすう 過半数 = Majority	す 過ぎる = To exceed, to pass by
かしつ 過失 = Error	かてい 過程 = Process	ちょうか 超過 = Excess	す 過ごす = To pass (time)

導 GUIDENCE, LEADING

"Put measures (寸) in place, and guide (導) us through the right path (道)"

ON (ドウ)
しどう 指導 = Leadership, guidance

迎 WELCOME, MEET

"Two people are meeting (迎) in this path (辶). One is standing, and the other is kneeling down (卯)"

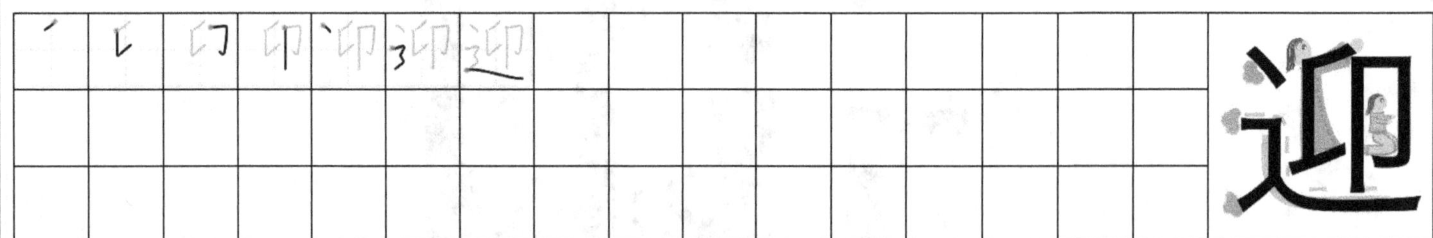

ON (ゲイ)		Kun (むか)
かんげい 歓迎 = Welcome, reception	でむか 出迎える = To meet, to greet	むか 迎える = To go out to meet
でむか 出迎え = Meeting	むか 迎え = Meeting	

延

超

处

延 STRETCHING, PROLONG

"For a correct (正) stride (乁), you must first stretch (延)"

ON (エイ)	Kun (の)
えんき 延 期　= Postponement, adjournment	の 延ばす = To lengthen
えんちょう 延　長　= Extension, elongation	の 延びる = To be prolonged

超 TRASCEND, EXCEED

"Don't exceed (超) when you call (召) me, or I'll start running (走)"

ON (チョウ)	Kun (こ)
ちょうか 超 過　= Excess, being more than	こ 超える = To exceed, to cross over
	こ 越す = To cross, to pass

処 DISPOSE, MANAGE, PLACE

"Place (処) your feet (夂) under the table (几)"

ON (ショ)
しょり 処 理 = Processing, dealing with

倒 OVERTHROW, FALL, COLLAPSE

"When that person (亻) arrived (到) home, he collapsed (倒)"

ON (ドウ)	Kun (たお)
めんどう 面 倒 = Trouble, difficulty	たお 倒 す = To throw down
めんどうくさ 面 倒 臭 い = Bothersome	たお 倒 れる = To collapse, to fall (over, down)

保 PROTECT, GUARANTEE, PRESERVE

"The person (亻) protects (保) the tree (木) and the mouths (口) that eat from it"

ON (ホ)	
ほけん 保 健 = Health preservation, hygiene	ほぞん 保 存 = Preservation, conservation
ほしょう 保 証 = Guarantee, security	

Note: This kanji originally had the element of child, which got corrupted and ended as a tree.

備 EQUIP, PROVISION

"The person (亻) is equipped (備) with arrows in a quiver (𦥑)"

ON (ビ)			Kun (そな)
じゅんび 準 備 = Preparation	せつび 設 備 = Equipment	けいび 警 備 = Security, guard	そな 備 える = To equip with
せいび 整 備 = Maintenance	よび 予 備 = Preparation		

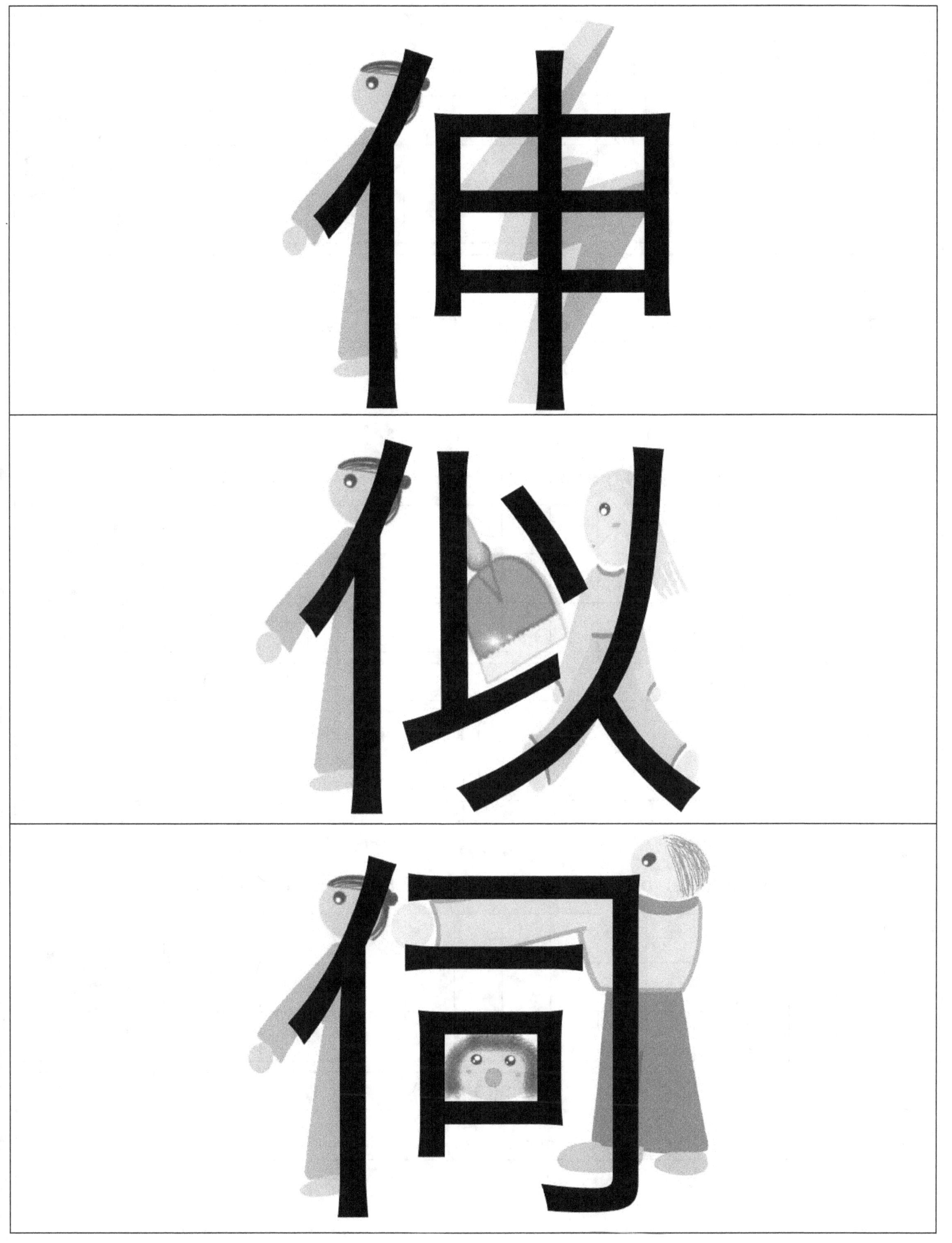

伸
似以
伺

伸 EXPAND, STRETCH

"This person (亻) stretches (伸) after each lightning (申) bolt"

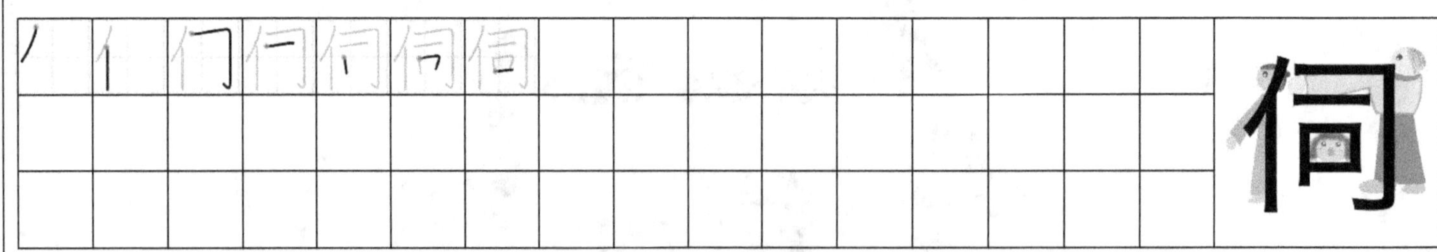

Kun (の)	
の 伸ばす = To lengthen, to stretch	の 伸びる = To stretch, to extend

似 BECOMING, RESEMBLE

"This person (亻) resembles (似) the person (人) using the hoe"

Kun (に)	ODD (ネ)
にあ 似合う = To suit, to match に 似る = To resemble, to look alike	まね 真似 = Imitating, copying まね 真似る = To mimic, to imitate

伺 PAY RESPECTS, VISIT, INQUIRE

"A polite person (亻) inquires (伺) their boss (司) respectfully"

Kun (うかが)
うかが 伺　う = To visit, to seek direction (from your superior), to inquire

復 RESTORE, RETURN TO, RESUME

"The person (人) returns (復) to sunny (日) road (彳) by foot (夂)"

ON (フク)

ふくしゅう
復 習 = Review (of learned material), revision

おうふく
往 復 = Round trip, return ticket

かいふく
回 復 = Recovery, rehabilitation

Note: The original kanji was a device that would measure grain repeatedly.

依 RELIANT, DEPEND ON

"A person (イ) depends (依) on wearing proper clothes (衣) for protection"

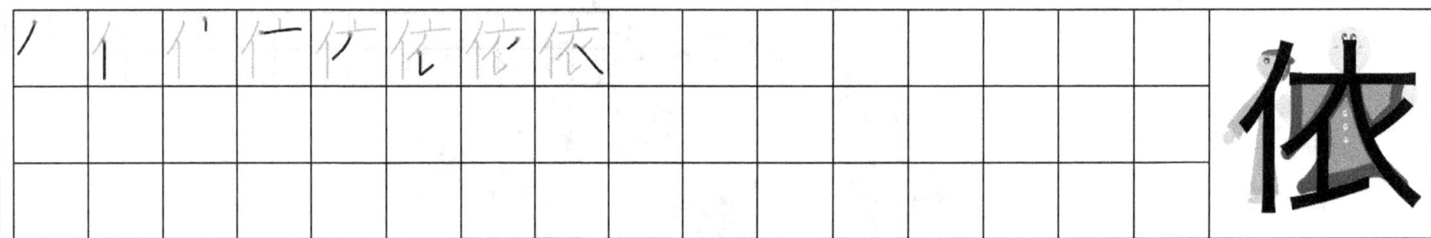

ON (イ)

いらい
依 頼 = Request, commission

傾 LEAN, INCLINE, TILT

"Tilt (傾) your head (頁) to change (化) your perspective"

ON (ケイ)

けいこう
傾 向 = Tendency, trend

Kun (かたむ)

かたむ
傾 く = To incline toward

預　項

頼　頓

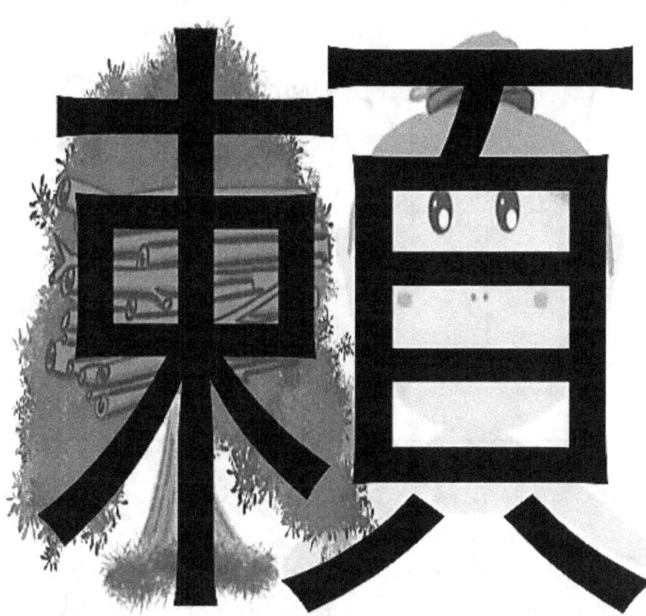

顎　現

預 DEPOSIT, CUSTODY, ENTRUST

"I (予) entrust (預) my secrets only to my head (頁)"

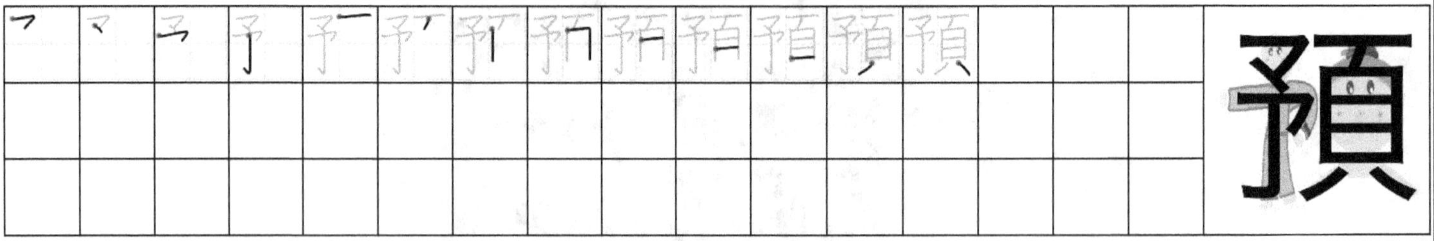

Kun (あず)

あず 預 かる = To keep in custody, to look after	あず 預 ける = To give into custody

頼 TRUST, REQUEST

"I trust (頼) my head (頁) with a bundle (束) of tasks"

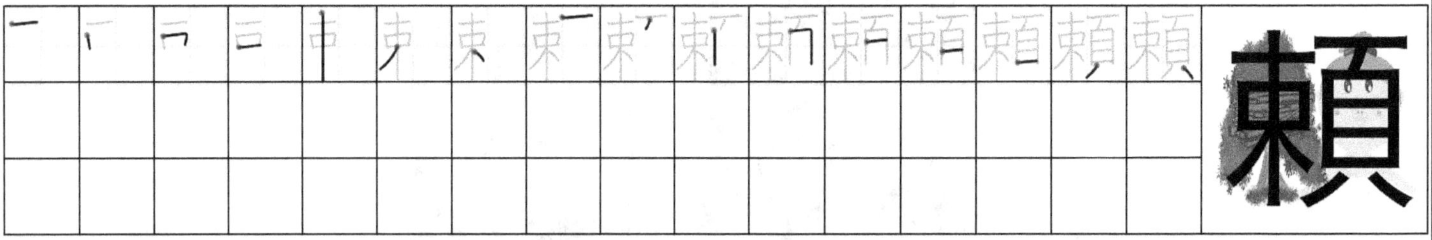

ON (ライ) — Kun (たの、たよ)

ON (ライ)	Kun (たの、たよ)	
いらい 依 頼 = Request, commission	たの 頼 む = To request, to beg	たよ 頼 る = To rely on
しんらい 信 頼 = Reliance, trust	たの 頼 もしい = Reliable, trustworthy	

Note: The original kanji had the elements of bundle, knife and money, as valuable things were carved with a knife.

現 PRESENT, EXISTING, ACTUAL

"The present (現) king (王) must watch (見) over his people"

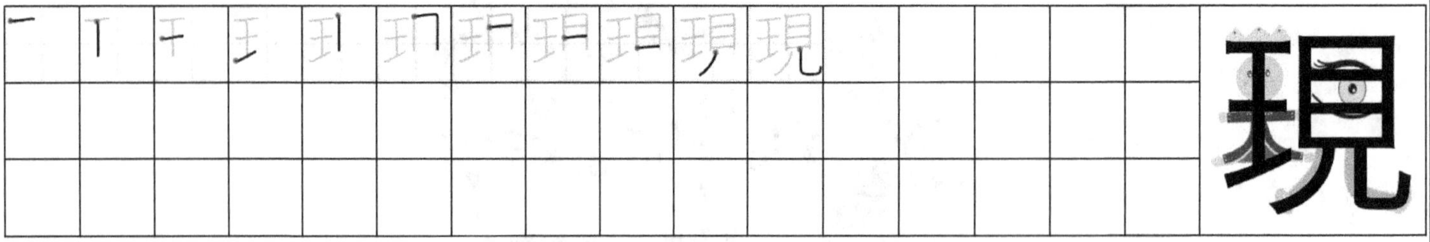

ON (ゲン) — Kun (あらわ)

ON (ゲン)			Kun (あらわ)
げんきん 現 金 = Cash	げんじつ 現 実 = Reality	げんじょう 現 状 = Present condition	あらわ 現 す = To represent
げんざい 現 在 = Present	げんだい 現 代 = Nowadays	ひょうげん 表 現 = Expression	あらわ 現 れる = To appear

疑 DOUBT, DISTRUST, BE SUSPICIOUS

"When in doubt (疑), don't just throw arrows (矢) at your decisions, but always think about what is correct (正)"

ON (ギ)		Kun (うたが)	
ぎもん 疑問 = Question, doubt		うたが 疑 う = To doubt, to distrust	

Note: The original kanji was a crossroad and a person doubting which path to take.

張 LENGTHEN, STRETCH, COUNTER FOR BOWS

"The princess with long (長) hair stretches (張) the bow (弓) to shoot the arrow"

ON (チョウ)		Kun (は)	
きんちょう 緊 張 = Tension	しゅっちょう 出 張 = Official trip	いば 威張る = To be proud	は 張る = To stick, to paste
しゅちょう 主 張 = Claim	かくちょう 拡 張 = Expansion	がんば 頑張る = To persevere	ひ ぱ 引っ張る = To pull, to draw

踊 JUMP, DANCE, LEAP

"Let the feet (足) dance (踊) while we pass through (甬) life"

Kun (おど)	
おど 踊 り = Dance	おど 踊 る = To dance

CHAPTER 16: VERBS PART IV

絶	絡	紹	経	耕	閉
365	366	367	368	369	370
構	検	築	枯	査	困
371	372	373	374	375	376
被	祈	断	荒	著	募
377	378	379	380	381	382
勤	割	越	雇	替	喫
383	384	385	386	387	388
刻	刊	刺	製	召	留
389	390	391	392	393	394
届	居	展	降	除	限
395	396	397	398	399	400

絶 DISCONTINUE, SEVER, CUT OFF, ABSTAIN

"That color (色) thread (糸) has been discontinued (絶)"

ON (ゼツ)	Kun (た)
ぜつめつ 絶 滅 = Destruction ぜったい 絶 対 = Absolute, unconditionally	た 絶えず = Constantly

絡 ENTWINE, COIL AROUND

"Each (各) thread (糸) is entwined (絡) for ease of use"

ON (ラク)
れんらく 連 絡 = Communication, connection, getting in touch

紹 INTRODUCE, INHERIT

"Let me call (召) my family and introduce (紹) them to you. We are connected like a thread (糸)"

ON (ショウ)
しょうかい 紹 介 = Introduction, presentation

経 LONGITUDE, PASS THRU

"My hand (又) passes (経) the threads (糸) thru the loom sitting on the ground (土)"

ON (ケイ)			Kun (た)
けいえい 経 営 = Administration	けいざい 経 済 = Economics	けいゆ 経 由 = Going through	た 経つ = To pass (of time)
けいけん 経 験 = Experience	けいど 経 度 = Longitude	しんけい 神 経 = Sensitivity	

Note: This kanji used to have the element of craft (工) instead of soil (土) before.

耕 PLOW, CULTIVATE

"Use the tilling tool (耒) and the water from the well (井) to plow (耕) the land"

ON (コウ)	Kun (たがや)
こうち 耕 地 = Arable land	たがや 耕 す = To plow, to cultivate

閉 CLOSED, SHUT

"The gate (門) shall remain closed (閉) while the genius (才) is thinking inside"

ON (ヘイ)	Kun (し、と)	
へいかい 閉 会 = Closure (of an event)	し 閉まる = To close, to be closed し 閉める = To close, to shut	と 閉じる = To close (e.g. book, eyes)

構 POSTURE, BUILD, PRETEND

"Connect (冓) some trees (木) with some ropes and build (構) a structure"

ON (コウ)		Kun (かま)
けっこう 結 構 = Wonderful, splendid こうせい 構 成 = Construction, formation	こうぞう 構 造 = Structure, framework	かま 構 う = To mind, to care about

検 EXAMINATION, INVESTIGATE

"The researcher (㑒) investigates (検) the wood (木)"

ON (ケン)	
けんさ 検 査 = Inspection (e.g. customs), examination (e.g. MRI)	けんとう 検 討 = Consideration, examination

築 FABRICATE, BUILD, CONSTRUCT

"Fabricate (築) round (丸) shapes with wood (木) similar to a bamboo (竹)"

ON (チク)
けんちく 建 築 = Construction, architecture (of buildings)

枯 WITHER, DRY UP

"An old (古) tree (木) withering (枯)"

Kun (か)

か
枯れる = To wither (of a plant)

査 INVESTIGATE

"Our ancestors (且) investigated (査) trees (木) for medical properties"

ON (サ)

ちょうさ
調 査 = Investigation, examination

けんさ
検 査 = Inspection (e.g. customs), examination (e.g. MRI)

じゅんさ
巡 査 = Police, officer, policeman

困 BECOME DISTRESSED, ANNOYED

"Trees (木) inside enclosures (口) become distressed (困) and don't grow anymore"

ON (コン)

こんなん
困 難 = Difficulty, distress

Kun (こま)

こま
困 る = To be troubled, to have difficulty

被

祈

断

被 INCUR, COVER, SHELTER

"Cover (被) his skin (皮) with some clothes (ネ)"

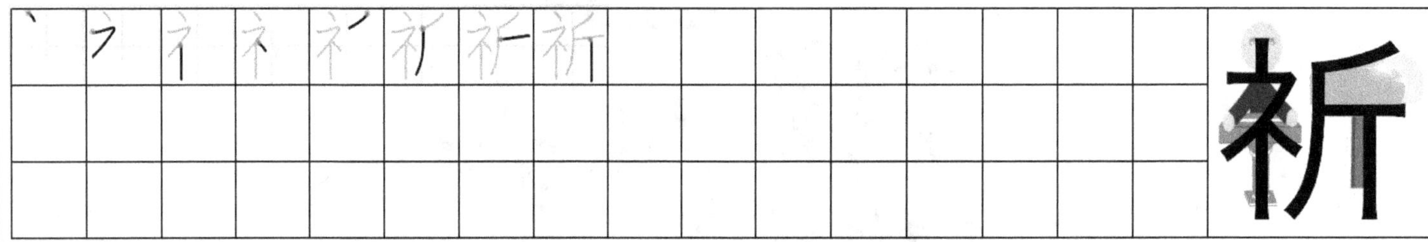

ON (ヒ)	Kun (かぶ)
ひがい 被害 = (suffering) Damage, injury	かぶ 被 せる = To cover (with something) かぶ 被 る = To put on (one's head)

祈 PRAY, WISH

"Pray (祈) for your life in the altar (ネ) and carry the axe (斤) for extra protection"

Kun (いの)
いの 祈 る = To pray, to wish

断 DECLINE, REFUSE, WARN, CUTTING

"I refuse (断) cutting the rice (米) grain with an axe (斤)"

ON (ダン)			Kun (ことわ)
だんすい 断 水 = Water outage	はんだん 判 断 = Judgement, decision	おうだん 横 断 = Crossing	ことわ 断 る = To refuse
ゆだん 油断 = Negligence	だんてい 断 定 = Conclusion, decision	しんだん 診 断 = Diagnosis	

荒

著

募

荒 LAID WASTE, ROUGH, WILD

"Humans have laid waste (荒) to plants (艹) and rivers (川) causing them to die (亡)"

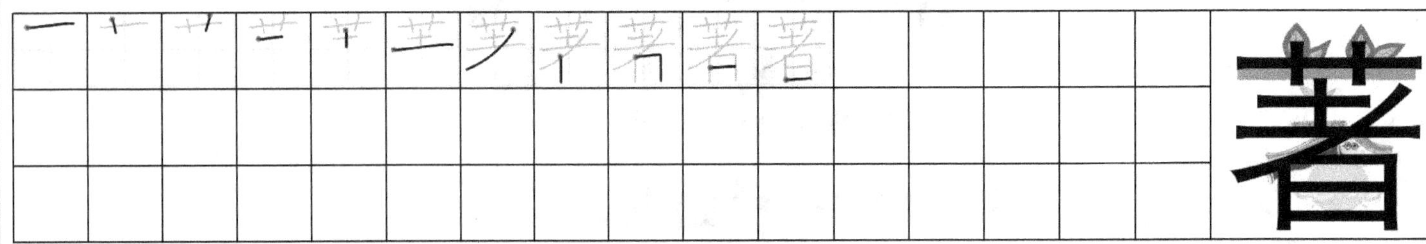

Kun (あ、あら)

あ 荒れる = To be stormy, to be rough	あら 荒 い = Rough, rude, wild

著 RENOWNED, PUBLISH, WRITE

"The person (者) writes (著) her novel with materials from plants (艹)"

ON (チョ)	Kun (あらわ)
ちょしゃ 著 者 = Author, writer	あらわ 著 す = To write, to publish

Note: Originally it was a bamboo instead of grass. Bamboo was a popular material used to make writing brushes.

募 RECRUIT, CAMPAIGN, ENLIST

"We shall recruit (募) strong (力) and vast (莫) personnel for the army"

ON (ボ)

ぼしゅう
募 集 = Recruiting, taking applications

勤 DILIGENCE, BECOME EMPLOYED

"Before, you could get employed (勤) if you were strong (力) at working with clay (堇)"

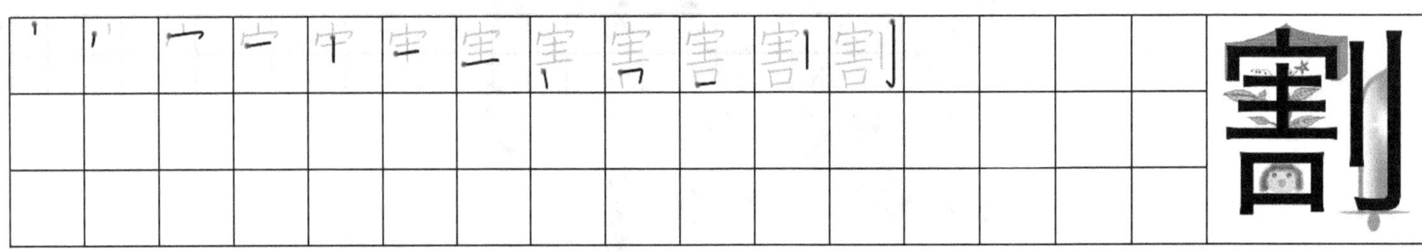

ON (キン)	Kun (つと)
しゅっきん 出 勤 = Going to work つうきん 通 勤 = Commuting to work	つと 勤 め = Service, duty

割 PROPORTION, DIVIDE, SPLIT

"The knife (リ) has split (割) the skin, causing a big injury (害)"

Kun (わり、わ)

じかんわり 時 間 割 = Schedule	わりあい 割 合 = Rate, ratio	わり 割 と = Relatively	わ 割 る = To divide
やくわり 役 割 = Part, duties	わりざん 割 算 = Division (math)	わりびき 割 引 = Discount	わ 割 れる = To break

越 SURPASS, CROSS OVER, MOVE TO

"Run (走) with your battle axe (戉) and cross over (越) the enemies' lands"

Kun (こ)

こ 越 す = To cross over (mountain)	の こ 乗 り 越 し = Riding past (one's station)	お こ 追 い 越 す = To pass (car)
ひ こ 引 っ 越 す = To change residence	ひ こ 引 っ 越 し = Changing residence	こ 越 える = To cross over

"People used to be employed (雇) to paint small birds (隹) on doors (戸) to bring good luck"

Kun (やと)

やと
雇 う = To employ, to hire

替 EXCHANGE, SPARE, SUBSTITUTE

"The husband (夫) needs a substitute (替) so he can go out and enjoy his day (日)"

ODD (ガエ、ワセ)	Kun (か)	
りょうがえ 両 替 = Money exchange	か 替える = To exchange	きが 着替える = To change one's clothes
かわせ 為 替 = Money order	きが 着替え = Changing clothes	と か 取り替える = To exchange, to swap

Note: The original kanji had two people standing and with open mouths for being tired.

喫 CONSUME, EAT, DRINK, SMOKE

"The big (大) man cuts the plants (丰) with a knife (刀), puts them in his mouth (口), and eats (喫) them"

ON (キツ)

きっさてん
喫 茶 店 = Coffee shop

きつえん
喫 煙 = Smoking

刻 ENGRAVE, CHOP, CARVING

"He is carving (刻) a boar (亥) with a knife (リ)"

	ON (コク)		Kun (きざ)
じこく 時 刻 = Time, (the hour) しんこく 深 刻 = Serious, grave		ちこく 遅 刻 = Lateness	きざ 刻 む = to carve, to engrave

刊 PUBLISH, CARVE

"Use the knife (リ) to carve (刊) the dry (干) tree""

ON (カン)
ゆうかん 夕 刊 = Evening paper

刺 THORN, PIERCE, STAB

"Thorns (束), just like pointy knives (リ), can pierce (刺) through"

ON (シ)		Kun (さ)
しげき 刺激 = Stimulus, incentive めいし 名 刺 = Business card	さ 刺さる = To stick into さしみ 刺身 = Sliced raw fish (sashimi)	さ 刺す = To pierce, to stab

製 MADE IN…, MANUFACTURE

"There are laws (制) in place to manufacture (製) clothes (衣)"

ON (セイ)

さくせい
作 製 = Manufacture, production

せいさく
製 作 = Manufacture, production

せいぞう
製 造 = Manufacture, production

せいひん
製 品 = Manufactured goods

召 SEDUCE, CALL, SUMMON

"In times of war, enemies were summoned (召), and killed with swords (刀)"

Kun (め)

め　あ
召し上がる = To eat, to drink

留 DETAIN, FASTEN, STOP

"Stop (留) everything else and focus on dividing (卯) the rice field (田) into two sections"

ON (リュウ、ル) | Kun (とど、ど)

ていりゅうじょ
停 留 所 = Bus stop

るす
留守 = Absence

りゅうがく
留 学 = Studying abroad

とど
留まる = To remain, to abide

と
留まる = To stop (moving)

と
留める = To stop, to turn off

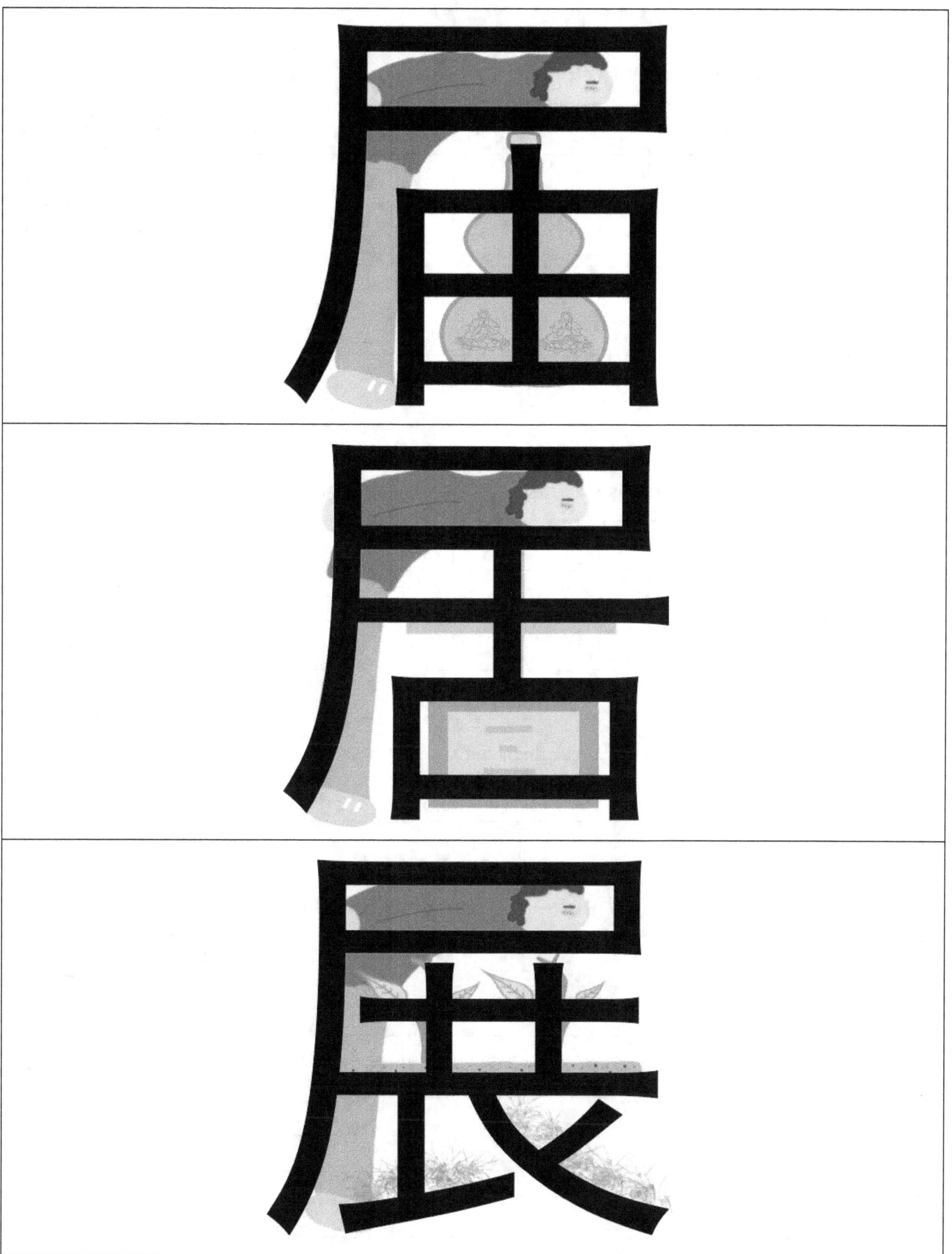

届 REACH, ARRIVE

"The corpse (尸) was found trying to reach (届) the gourd (由)"

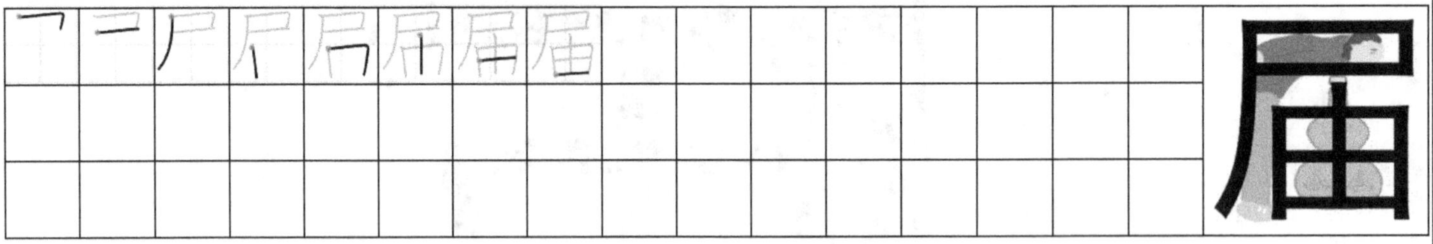

Kun (と ど)

とど 届 く = To reach	とど 届 ける = To deliver

居 RESIDE, TO BE, EXIST

"Corpses (尸) reside (居) in old (古) graves"

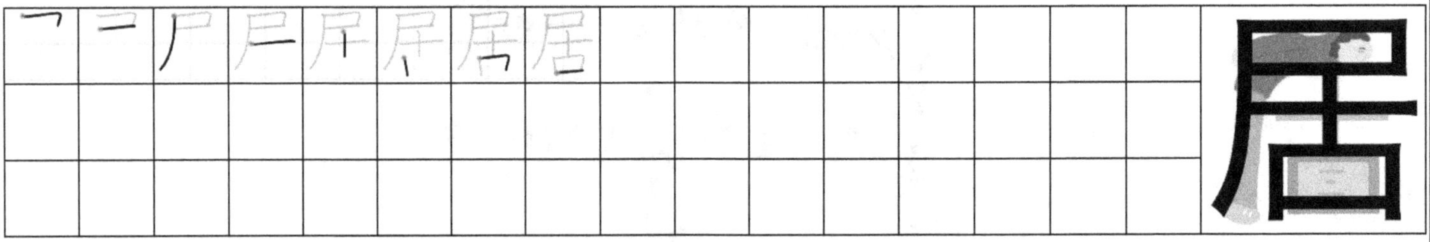

Kun (い 、 お)

い 居 る = To be, to exist お 居 る = To be, to exist	いねむ 居 眠 り = Dozing, nodding off いま 居 間 = Living room (western style)	しばい 芝 居 = Play, drama

展 UNFOLD, EXPAND

"He looked like a corpse (尸) after he expanded (展) his pottery (襄) business"

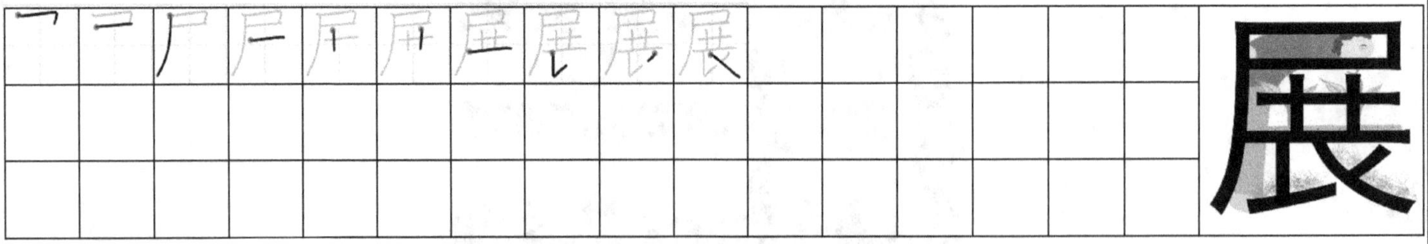

ON (テ ン)

てんかい 展 開 = Development, evolution てんらんかい 展 覧 会 = Exhibition	はってん 発 展 = Development, growth

隆

陰除

限

降 DESCEND, PRECIPITATE

"The footprints (夆) are clearly descending (降) from the hill (阝)"

ON (コウ)	Kun (お、ふ)	
いこう 以 降 = On and after かこう 下 降 = Descent, drop	お 降りる = To descend (a mountain) お 降ろす = To take down	ふ 降る = To fall (rain, snow, ash, etc)

除 EXCLUDE, REMOVE, ABOLISH

"Please remove (除) the excess (余) of dirt from the hill (阝)"

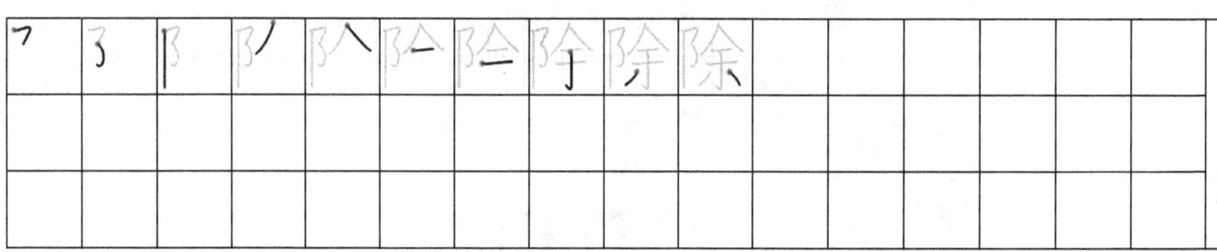

ON (ジョ、ジ)	Kun (のぞ)
さくじょ 削 除 = Elimination, deletion そうじ 掃 除 = Cleaning, sweeping	のぞ 除く = To remove, to exclude

限 LIMIT, RESTRICT

"Please limit (限) the access to the hill (阝), as it doesn't have a good (艮) path"

ON (ゲン)			Kun (かぎ)
きげん 期 限 = Term, period げんかい 限 界 = Limit, bound	げんど 限 度 = Limit せいげん 制 限 = Restriction	むげん 無 限 = Infinite	かぎ 限 り = Limit(s) かぎ 限 る = To restrict

CHAPTER 17: VERBS PART V

燥	燃	介	舞	賛	責
401	402	403	404	405	406
解	触	駐	含	否	呼
407	408	409	410	411	412
吸	叫	吹			
413	414	415			

燥 PARCH, DRY UP

"While the fire (火) was parching (燥) the forest, the birds chirped (喿) in agony"

ON (ソウ)

かんそう
乾　燥　= Dryness, aridity

燃 BURN, BLAZE, GLOW

"Fire (火) is that sort of thing (然) that can burn (燃) anything"

Kun (も)

も 燃やす = To burn	も 燃える = To burn, to get fired up

介 JAMMED IN, MEDIATE

"Two people (亻), with their backs to each other, are jammed in (介) under a roof"

ON (カイ)

しょうかい 紹　介　= Introduction	やっかい 厄　介　= Trouble, burden

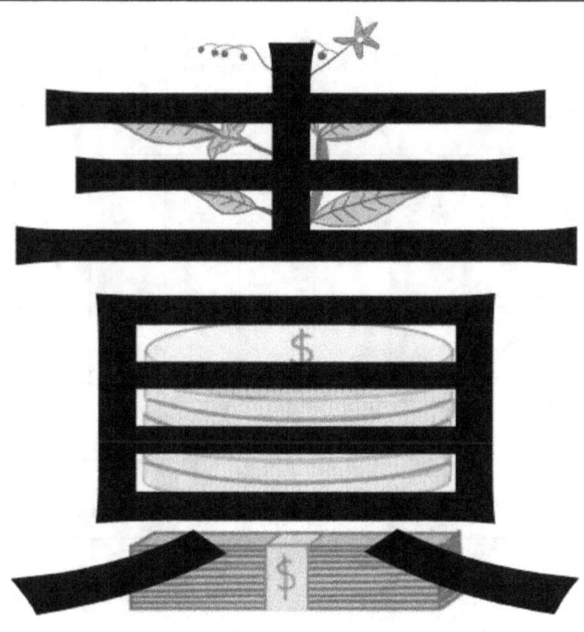

舞 DANCE, CIRCLE, WHEEL

"Use both feet (舛) to dance (舞)"

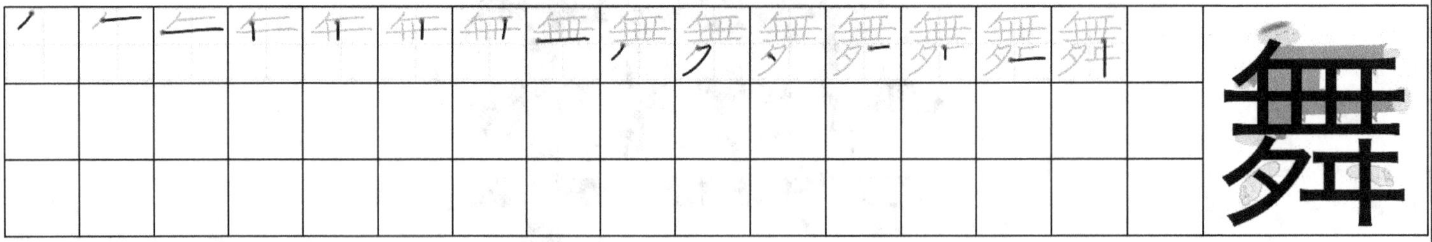

ON (ブ)	Kun (ま)	
ぶたい 舞台 = Stage (theater)	ふるま 振舞う = To behave, to entertain みま 見舞い = Visiting ill people	みま 見舞う = To ask after (health)

賛 APPROVE, PRAISE, ASSIST

"In the old days, husbands (夫) had to approve (賛) any money (貝) decisions"

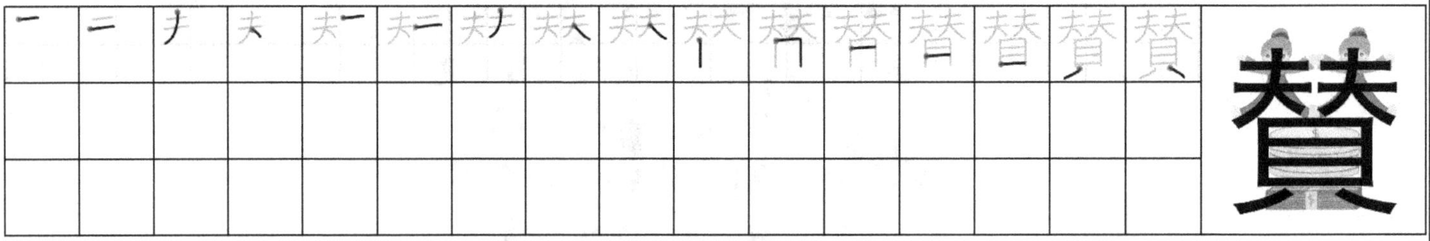

ON (サン)
さんせい 賛成 = Approval

責 BLAME, CONDEMN

"I blame (責) myself for only spending money (貝) on plants (龶)"

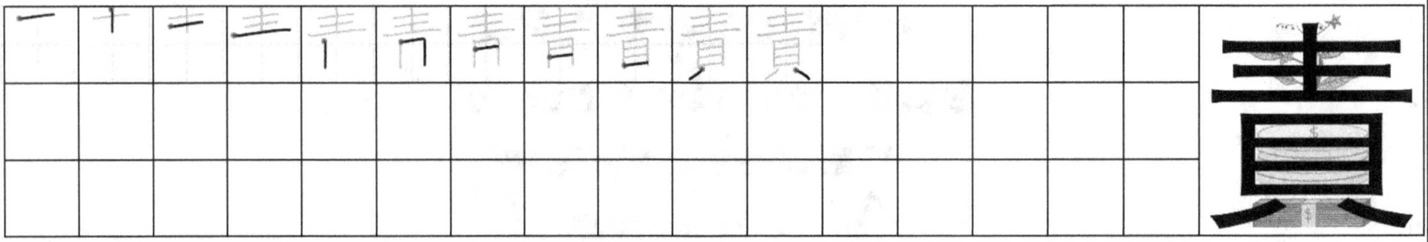

ON (セキ)	Kun (せ)
せきにん 責任 = Duty, responsibility	せ 責める = To condemn, to blame

解 UNRAVEL, EXPLANATION, SOLVE, UNTIE

"The sword (刀) unties (解) the horn (角) from the cow (牛)"

ON (カイ)			Kun (と)
かいけつ 解 決 = Settlement	かいせつ 解 説 = Explanation	かいほう 解 放 = Release	と 解く = To unfasten
かいさん 解 散 = Breakup (meeting)	ごかい 誤 解 = Misunderstanding	けんかい 見 解 = Opinion	と 解ける = To be solved

触 TOUCH, CONTACT, FEEL

"The insect (虫) touches (触) the horns (角)"

Kun (さわ、ふ)	
さわ 触 る = To touch, to feel	ふ 触れる = To touch, to feel

駐 STOP-OVER, RESIDE IN

"The master (主) decides to stop-over (駐) after riding his horse (馬) for some time"

ON (チュウ)	
ちゅうしゃ 駐 車 = Parking (e.g. car)	ちゅうしゃじょう 駐 車 場 = Parking lot

含 CONTAIN, INCLUDE, HOLD IN THE MOUTH

"Right now (今), I could hold in my mouth (含) tons of food!"

Kun (ふく)

ふく 含 む = To hold in the mouth	ふく 含 める = To include, to instruct

否 NO, NEGATE, DECLINE

"You can say "no" (不) with your mouth (口) or just decline (否) with your head"

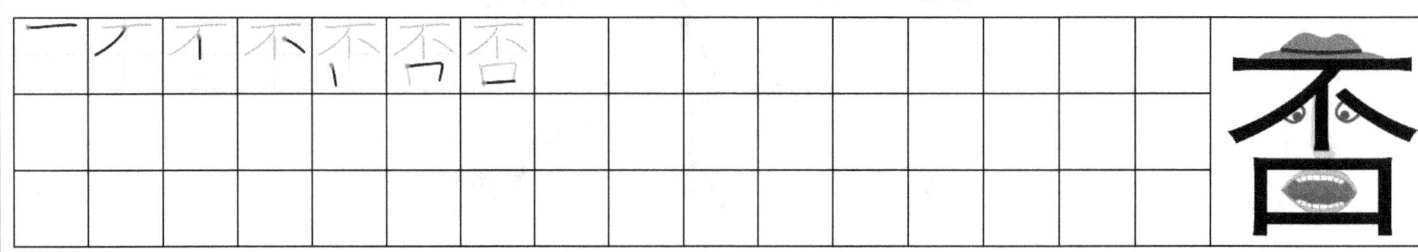

ON (ヒ) | **Kun (いや)**

ひてい 否 定 = Negation, denial	いや 否 = No, nay

呼 CALL, INVITE

"The baby opens his mouth (口) to call (呼) his mom"

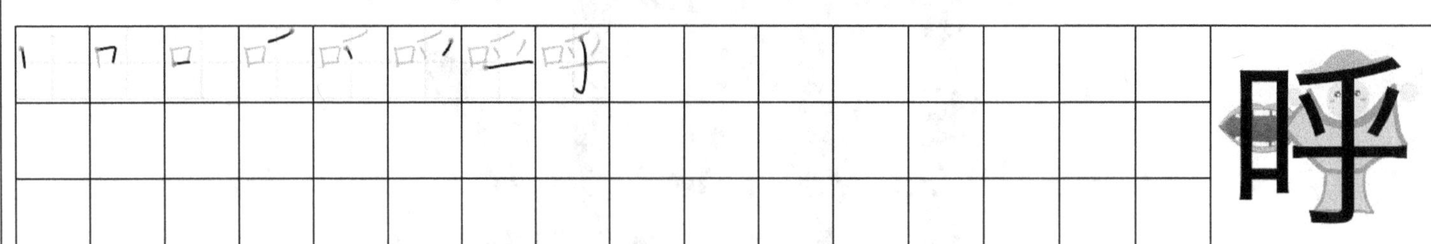

ON (コ) | **Kun (よ)**

こきゅう 呼 吸 = Breathing, respiration	よ 呼びかける = To call out to よ　だ 呼び出す = To summon	よ 呼ぶ = To call out

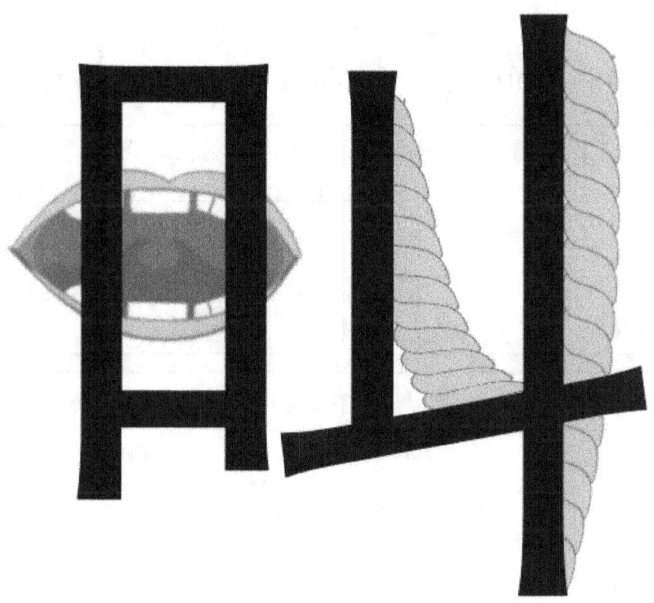

吸 SUCK, INHALE

"Inhale (吸) through your mouth (口) and reach (及) all the potential of your lungs"

ON (キュウ)	Kun (す)
きゅうしゅう 吸　収　= Absorption, suction こきゅう 呼　吸　= Breath, respiration	す 吸う = To smoke

叫 SHOUT, EXCLAIM

""He shouts (叫) with his mouth (口) while trying to undo the entangled ropes (丩)"

Kun (さけ)
さけ 叫 ぶ = To shout

吹 BLOW, BREATHE

"He lacks (欠) enough strength in his mouth (口) to blow (吹)"

Kun (ふ)	
ふ 吹く　= To blow, to breathe out	ふぶき 吹雪 = Snow storm, blizzard

This book covers the 415 Kanji found in the Japanese Language Proficiency Test N2 and the main idea is to cover as much material as possible related to each Kanji.

If you wish to join me in this journey of learning Japanese, check out my social media! There you can ask questions and join our conversations!

@JLPTKanjiMnemonics

Also, if you have any suggestions or improvements for this book, feel free to e-mail me at:

jlptkanjimnemonics@gmail.com

ありがとうございます！

INDEX